AUTHORITY REVISITED

NOMOS

XXIX

NOMOS

Harvard University Press

The Liberal Arts Press

Atherton Press

Aldine-Atherton Press

Lieber-Atherton Press

New York University Press

NOMOS XXIX

Yearbook of the American Society for Political and Legal Philosophy

AUTHORITY REVISITED

Edited by

J. Roland Pennock, *Swarthmore College*

and

John W. Chapman, *University of Pittsburgh*

New York and London: New York University Press · 1987

Authority Revisited: Nomos XXIX
edited by J. Roland Pennock and John W. Chapman
Copyright © 1987 by New York University
Manufactured in the United States of America

Library of Congress Cataloging-in-Publication Data

Authority revisited.

  (Nomos ; 29)
  Includes bibliographies and index.
  1. Authority. 2. Political science. 3. Law—
Philosophy. I. Pennock, J. Roland (James Roland),
1906–   II. Chapman, John William, 1923–
III. Series.
JA75.A97 1987   320.2   86-21071
  ISBN 0-8147-6601-3

CONTENTS

PART II: CONTEXTS: CONSTITUTIONAL, ADMINISTRATIVE, AND NONGOVERNMENTAL

CONTRIBUTORS

TERENCE BALL
Political Science, University of Minnesota

MICHAEL D. BAYLES
Philosophy, Center for Applied Philosophy, University of Florida

WILLIAM E. CONNOLLY
Political Science, The Johns Hopkins University

MICHAEL DAVIS
Philosophy, University of Illinois at Chicago

TIMOTHY FULLER
Political Science, The Colorado College

MARTIN P. GOLDING
Philosophy and Law, Duke University

RUSSELL HARDIN
Political Science and Philosophy, University of Chicago

KATHLEEN B. JONES
Political Philosophy and Feminist Theory, San Diego State University

STEVEN LUKES
Politics and Sociology, Balliol College, Oxford

MICHAEL J. PERRY
Law, Northwestern University

JOSEPH RAZ
Philosophy, Balliol College, Oxford

NANCY L. ROSENBLUM
Political Science, Brown University

AUSTIN SARAT
Political Science, Amherst College

FREDERICK SCHAUER
Law, University of Michigan

KIM LANE SCHEPPELE
Political Science and Sociology, University of Michigan

KAROL EDWARD SOŁTAN
Political Science, University of Maryland

MARK TUSHNET
Law, Georgetown University

PREFACE

When The American Society for Political and Legal Philosophy voted for "Authority Revisited" as the topic for its 29th annual meeting, it did not imply that we had run out of new topics! Clearly what it did mean is that a lot of water had flowed over the dam since the first meeting of the Society in 1957. Not only is "authority" at least as relevant to the state of the world as it was then, but the condition of political and legal philosophy has also changed, and advanced.

It is interesting that the article on authority in the *Encyclopedia of the Social Sciences* (1938), written by Roberto Michels, defined it as "the capacity, innate or acquired, for exercising ascendancy over a group," adding that "it is a manifestation of power and implies obedience on the part of those subject to it. One of the principal means of exercising authority is dispensation of rewards and punishments." The emphasis is on power, backed up by force.

Thirty years later, Robert L. Peabody, in the *International Encyclopedia of the Social Sciences,* is far more cautious, noting that social scientists are in wide disagreement as to how the concept should be used. He specifically takes issue with Michels, and he cites the differences between the definitions offered by Lasswell and Kaplan on the one hand and Carl Friedrich on the other as indicative of the range of views on the subject. Peabody remarks by way of conclusion that "The ambiguity of everyday language, the mixture of fact and value implicit in the term, the omnipresence of the phenomenon in all cultures, and the multiple approaches to the study of authority . . . have [all] contributed to the confusion often accompanying the use of the concept." Whether our volume does anything to alleviate this confusion, which still exists, is for the reader to judge. One thing, however, is clear from the frequent appearance of the words "ambiguity" and "perspectives" and similar cautionary flags: our authors are keenly aware of the complexity of the concept under consideration.

This volume grows out of our 1984 meetings, held in Washington in conjunction with the convention of the American Political Science Association in August of that year. Roughly half of its chapters come from the meeting, the others having been subsequently solicited by the editors. Withal we lay no claim to a comprehensive treatment of the subject. In particular we regret the lack of cultural comparisons of the nature and consequences of authority. In this connection, we direct the reader's attention to Lucian Pye's *Asian Power and Politics: The Cultural Dimensions of Authority* (Harvard University Press: 1985), in which he lays out the "paternalistic dependency" that arose in the East and contrasts it with Western experience. We are deeply in the debt, once again, of John Locke for having so firmly and conclusively divorced political from paternal authority.

Briefly but warmly we wish to express our thanks to those who have helped us along the way. First of all, the Society once more expresses gratitude to the Ritter Foundation for financial assistance, especially useful for enabling us to bring scholars from abroad to contribute to our deliberations, and to the Exxon Foundation for the ongoing work of the Society. To George Kateb we owe our thanks for arranging the program on authority for the 1984 meetings. Eleanor Greitzer, Assistant to the Editors, as always, has contributed incalculably to the ease and effectiveness of our task. Despina Gimbel, Managing Editor of the New York University Press, has been understanding as well as efficient in taking us from the original manuscript to the published product.

J.R.P.
J.W.C.

INTRODUCTION

J. ROLAND PENNOCK

John Adams noted that democracies generally commit suicide. No government can survive for long without authority, as Ferdinand Marcos could testify. And authority, many believe, is threatened in modern society. True, not all advance the same reasons for this danger. They all, for one reason or another, see and foresee a growing lack of consensus. For some, as for Mark Tushnet in this volume, the threat is a sharpening sense of class distinction. For Samuel Huntington, the problem stems from an overemphasis on egalitarianism.[1] For others, like Hannah Arendt, political consensus has rested upon the "holy trinity" of religion, authority, and tradition; and, her argument continued, the loss or weakening of any one of these pillars rendered the others insecure. In her view, Luther, by his attack on the Church, destroyed the power of religion, and Hobbes wrecked tradition.[2]

Few today would claim that authority is not in question almost everywhere, yet doomsayers have reason to take pause. It is worthy of remark that no one in this volume takes as dark a view as did Arendt in her essay "What was Authority?" where she declared that "It is my contention . . . that authority has vanished from the modern world."[3] The same may be said of Michel Crozier, who opined that the situation in Europe was so dangerous that it was likely that the Communist Party would take over by default, being the only remaining institution possessing authority.[4] One does not have to wear rose-tinted glasses to say that the political authority of the regimes of Western Europe is today at least as strong as it was in 1958 or 1975.

In other respects it is worth drawing some comparisons and contrasts between the present volume and *NOMOS I*. Where similar points are made, it is almost always true that today's

1

authors press the analysis further than did their predecessors—
a comforting finding. Hendel speaks of "the complicity of the
wills of all men [as] essential to establishing rightful public authority." Joseph Raz's discussion of consensus agrees but goes
much beyond this point. Friedrich's argument that "authority
rests upon the ability to issue communications which are capable of reasoned elaboration" has been the starting point for many
discussions since then.[5] Here Mark Tushnet contends that this
idea "no longer has any real intellectual force."[6] George E.G.
Catlin, in the earlier volume, contended that "authority is power
exercised in accordance with convention."[7] Finally, Talcott Par-
son's essay in the first *NOMOS* saw authority from a different
perspective than any of those just discussed. He saw it as "the
complex of institutionalized rights to control the actions of
members of the society with reference to their bearing on the
attainment of collective goals."[8] This idea is elaborated on by
Richard Flathman as he is discussed by Timothy Fuller.

To be sure, the two volumes exhibit contrasts as well as similarities and continuations. One has already been mentioned in
the case of Friedrich and Tushnet. Another relates to the attention given to legal matters. For some reason that first volume
of the series had very little to say about strictly legal matters.
Jerome Hall contributed a chapter titled "Authority and the
Law" and Adamson Hoebel did a short piece called "Authority
in Primitive Societies." That was the sum of it. This volume, on
the other hand, contains a substantial section on the authority
of the text in American Constitutional law, reflecting the current interest in, and controversy about, the proper role of courts,
and especially of the Supreme Court, in dealing with constitutional issues.

We have grouped the chapters, or essays, various though they
are in many respects, under two headings, the first more general in nature and the second more specific. Part I leads off, as
did our meetings, with William Connolly's discussion "Modern
Authority and Ambiguity." Most students of the subject recognize the necessity of authority, yet also see its dangers. Some
rely on self-interest for compliance, some on consent or trust,
while others hold that society must find a new *telos* before effective authority can be maintained. Connolly himself admits to
some fears that faith in the future of "the civilization of pro-

ductivity" may be waning, raising serious problems for the authority of existing regimes.

In tune with Connolly's emphasis on ambiguity, Frederick Schauer elaborates on the virtues as well as the unavoidability of a proper vagueness and of the authority that vagueness creates. "Only by appreciating the control we have over indeterminacy can we begin to understand fully the mechanisms of authority," he concludes. (37)

Terence Ball follows with a consideration of two ideal types of the concept of authority. The "emotivist" model equates authority with what gets itself obeyed, blurring the distinction between the legitimate and the illegitimate. The other, which he dubs "epistemocratic," also blurs an important distinction, this time between the proper (restricted) role of the expert and his/her exercise of political power in technocratic fashion. Ideas, he argues, do have consequences.

Steven Lukes presents us with a wide variety of perspectives on authority. Using them as a frame of reference, he considers the analyses of Weber, Friedman, and Flathman, all "relativized" accounts. Finding difficulties with all of them, he turns to a theory that seeks to avoid these problems by offering "a straightforwardly rationalist 'critical justificatory' theory believed to be independent of any prior 'relativized' account." He believes that Joseph Raz's account is an improvement on its predecessors, yet doubts that it solves all the problems, even agreeing with Flathman's conclusion that to start with a nonrelativized notion is a dubious enterprise.

Next comes Joseph Raz himself—not however the source to which Lukes refers, but a piece written for this volume without, so far as I know, having seen Lukes's contribution. His topic is the role of consent in authority. For him, consent comes at the end of the line; it concludes the spectrum of processes that lead to the formation of trust in one's government. It is this element of trust, as contrasted with that concept of individual autonomy, that entails deciding every issue on the merits of each case.

As I have already remarked, Mark Tushnet, commenting on Lukes, takes issue with Friedrich's concept of authority. He is thinking especially of the authority of judicial decisions, whose authority, he holds, depends not a whit upon the reasoning set forth in the court opinions. What is required is consensus, and it is dissolving as losers come "to see themselves as outsiders in the general stream of things." (100)

Nancy L. Rosenblum, in a paper entitled "Studying Authority: Keeping Pluralism in Mind," heartily concurs with Connolly's designation of authority as "ambiguous." She defends a notion of "pluralistic" authority, which she calls "romantic" because she associates it with "individuality and with desires for self-development and self-expression." (104) Pluralistic authority, she maintains, as well as autonomy and community, is necessary for self-development, for personality.

"Authority and the Individual in Civil Association: Oakeshott, Flathman, Yves Simon." The title of Timothy Fuller's paper doesn't tell it all but it is at least a good introduction. He brackets Flathman, a liberal, with two conservatives whose conservatisms represent interesting similarities but a final contrast. Unlike most students of authority, at least as they are represented here, Flathman gives a large role to rights, sometimes almost subordinating authority to them. Flirting with anarchism, Flathman ends up with a "resolute irresolution" that, Fuller declares, is characteristic of contemporary liberalism.

Kathleen B. Jones, in her essay "On Authority: Or, Why Women Are Not Entitled to Speak," seeks to broaden the concept of authority. The orthodox concept, she believes, has tended to exclude women from its exercise and, in doing so, has excluded the important element of compassion. Like other contributors she properly finds ambiguity in the concept and feels that traditional usage rejects the compassionate element precisely to avoid ambiguity. This she believes is a mistake.

Next comes the essay by Kim Lane Scheppele and Karol Edward Soltan, entitled "The Authority of Alternatives." It introduces the most radical concept of authority herein discussed. It is their contention that the will of a person "in authority" has nothing directly to do with the matter. Rather it is a question of what it is in a person—a text, an explanation, a justification, or whatever—that attracts persons to make a particular choice. Most of their essay deals with positive authority, but the concluding section relates positive to normative authority, a much more limiting concept.

Part I concludes with Russell Hardin's contribution, which is radical in a quite different way from that of Scheppele and Soltan. It is provocatively titled "Does Might Make Right?" Unlike some provocative titles, this one is not a buildup for a letdown: might *does* make right—sometimes and in a way. He starts with an easy case: if force is used to get people to use a certain rule of the road, like driving on the right, surely the law that sustains it has authority. But this is only the beginning. Are utilitarianism and distributive justice incompatible? Not necessarily. Step by step, he arrives at an obligation to obey the law, but the authority of the law must rest on its service to us, even though it may serve us differentially.

Part II turns to authority in specific contexts. The first three chapters relate to the authority of the Constitutional text. Here Michael J. Perry leads off with "Authority of Text, Tradition, and Reason." He favors a nonoriginalist interpretation of the Constitution, but one for which the text, as well as tradition and community, are authoritative. What is this text? "As I conceive it, the constitutional text is a symbol of the aspirations of the political tradition (which is not to say that that's all it is), and, as such, it constrains in the way and to the extent that aspirations of the tradition constrain." (232) The Court must search the living tradition for political-moral knowledge, a task for which it is singularly fitted because of its relatively disinterested position.

Austin Sarat takes issue with Perry's position on the ground that he does not get sufficiently beyond originalism, which Sarat argues, is triply defective.

Martin P. Golding compares and contrasts Perry with Karl Llewellyn. Both oppose originalism, but Llewellyn, a child of the Great Depression, sought a theory that was descriptive only, whereas Perry, an offspring of the Great Rights Explosion, seeks norms, and envisages going beyond the values of the text. Golding raises numerous questions about this theory. For instance, with respect to Perry's emphasis upon the "living tradition," he asks how we can tell when a tradition is "living" and when it is in disarray or moribund.

Turning from the courts to administration, Michael D. Bayles carries on with, and beyond, Friedrich's *potentiality* of reasoned elaboration. He argues that administrators must give actual expression to sound reasons for their actions. They gain authority only by achieving a reputation for having acted in the past for sound reasons. Thus the traditional hierarchical model for administration is not a model for its justification. The latter must come from the bottom up. So likewise, he suggests, with the justification of a whole regime; a regime will lack authority if it is arbitrary in its dealing with the people.

Finally, we come to the consideration of authority in a nongovernmental context. Michael Davis asks why a professional code should have moral authority other than ordinary morality. He takes as an example the ABA's Model Code of Professional Responsibility. Does it have inherent authority? In brief, he argues that a code, such as this one, is essential to the solution of the coordination problem. Lawyers' work is relevantly different from that of businessmen in that the lawyer cannot assume a series of continuing relations with the same people. The opportunity for the development of a conventional code, one that does not need to be written or to have special enforcement machinery, does not exist for lawyers practicing in modern society, as it does for businessmen.

These are but hints of what our authors have to say. For the meat of it, I turn you over to them.

NOTES

1. Michel Crozier, Samuel P. Huntington and Joji Watanuki, *The Crisis of Democracy* (New York: New York University Press, 1975), p. 115.
2. *Authority, NOMOS I,* ed. Carl J. Friedrich (Cambridge: Harvard University Press, 1958), p. 105.
3. Ibid., p. 81.
4. *The Crisis of Democracy*, p. 47.
5. *Authority*, p. 29.
6. Mark Tushnet, "Comment on Lukes," this volume, p. 98.
7. *Authority*, p. 129. This statement invites comparison with Russell Hardin's discussion of the role of convention and the role of force in the establishment of convention. See "Does Might Make Right?" this volume, chapter 11.
8. *Authority*, p. 210.

PART I

CONCEPTS, PERSPECTIVES, AND JUSTIFICATIONS

1

MODERN AUTHORITY AND AMBIGUITY

WILLIAM E. CONNOLLY

"As long as there have been men and they lived, they have all felt this tragic ambiguity of their condition, but as long as there have been philosophers and they have thought, most of them have tried to mask it."
—Simone de Beauvoir, *The Ethics of Ambiguity*

THE ISSUE OF AUTHORITY

Authority is an indispensable and dangerous practice. Its dual character, present in every society, is particularly salient in modern societies, for the conventionalization of social life renders it more susceptible to imperatives of authoritative coordination and those subject to that coordination more resistant to its claims. Modern authority, at its best, is more respectful of individual dignity than previous forms. But any theory appreciative of this achievement must also attend to the burdens and dangers accompanying it.

Much of modern discourse about authority attempts to avoid its danger by defining one of its determining elements away. One constellation of theorists pretends that the dilemmas can be avoided by replacing (or at least supplanting) authority with coordination through incentive systems, making it in the private interests of persons and institutions to act in the public interest. But these theories conveniently ignore the authoritative background essential to the operation of such systems and they also obscure the manipulative and coercive character of governance through incentive systems. Another constellation acknowledges the necessity of authority, but construes it to rest upon the consent of citizens who promise to abide by laws and rules established and enforced by proper procedures. Consent is in fact necessary to the modern practice of authority, but consent, when it is offered, applies not only to procedures for decision but to a larger set of understandings, ends and purposes that help to constitute a way of life. Moreover, modern consent theories are too often articulated at a level too abstract to ascertain to what degree consent is spawned by coercive institutional pressures or offered within an institutional setting that enables it to be free. Consent theories are either too abstract to illuminate the modern practice of authority or they are thrown into the morass of issues occasioned by its dual character.

Another constellation of theorists would concur with these points, but interpret them to mean that modernity and authority must remain allergic to each other until the belief in a social *telos* is restored to modern societies. Authority, from this point of view, is necessarily in decline because the basic ontological understandings of modernity are incompatible with its operation. There are imporant truths hidden in this latter formulation, but its basic premise and its stark conclusion are unfounded. *Telos*, in any strong sense of the word, cannot be restored to modernity, but the practice of modern authority is possible without a restoration.

I wish to argue, first, that while the preconditions for traditional authority have receded there is ontological space in modernity for a mode of authority appropriate to it; second, that this mode of authority is indispensable to a good way of life; third, that the most common substitutes offered to replace the practice of authority (i.e., interest manipulation and consensual morality) are, as full-blown *substitutes*, mad dreams that can become living nightmares; fourth, that the mode of authority appropriate to modernity involves an appreciation of its ambiguous character; and fifth, that an appreciation of ambiguity must be installed in the institutional matrix of society if authority is to assume its appropriate place in modern life. I will not defend all of these claims with equal fervor, though each is part of the conception of authority I seek to explore.

MODERN AND PRE-MODERN AUTHORITY

Authority, according to Hannah Arendt in the first *NOMOS* volume, which was devoted to this topic, can no longer be sustained in modern life because its ontological basis has disappeared. An external standard to which authorities can appeal has been lost. She wrote, "Historically we know of a variety of sources to which authoritative rulers could appeal in order to justify their power; it could be the law of nature, or the commands of God, or the Platonic ideas or ancient customs, or a great event in the past . . . In all these cases legitimacy derives from something outside the range of human deeds. . . ."[1]

If we consider one of the periods when the ontological preconditions for the operation of Arendtian authority were secure we might also delineate more clearly some of the distinctive characteristics of modern authority. The late Middle Ages combined several of the sources "outside the range of human deeds" in its theory and practice of authority.

Central to this world was God the Creator, the Designer and the Sovereign whose will was discernible to humans, though darkly and imperfectly, in the things, events, words, deeds, and living beings that constituted the world. The natural world was alive with God's purpose; it contained a majestic harmony, a *telos,* which humans could glimpse if they exerted themselves in the right ways, and these glimpses gave support and guidance in governing their lives. Authority, then, permeated this world. It could be found in sacred texts—a feature of the medieval quest for knowledge that encouraged it to look to the past to understand the correct order of things in the present. It was also located in spectacular events and in the fabric of those established customs and traditions touched by a divine hand.

Authorities, in this setting, appealed to some privileged access to the purposiveness of the world. Through careful study of ancient texts or by living in communion with God or by being specially ordained by God they could interpret authoritatively signs available to them and they could then act with authority.

To feel the pull of authority in these circumstances is to seek to emulate conduct embodied in an exemplary individual or text. That is, perhaps, what Hannah Arendt meant when she said that "if authority is to be defined at all it must be in contradistinction to both coercive power and persuasion through arguments."

The relation between a standard outside the scope of human deeds and human understanding of its implication for those deeds did remain problematic. Understanding of *telos* constantly faded into mystery and ambiguity because of the inherent limitations of the earthly commentators. But the signs were there to be read and they did provide a standard of appeal for authority beyond human deeds themselves.

A teleological ontology seems to presuppose a transcendental designer. Thus it is not surprising that the retreat of God from the mundane world, the withdrawal of *telos* from the world, and the decline of traditional authority moved together. We can understand why Hannah Arendt insists that religion, tradition, and authority engender one another, and moreover why the weakening of one element in this trio inevitably weakens the others.[2]

One way to characterize the shift from medieval to modern life at the ontological level is to say that subjectivity, previously finding perfect expression in God and imperfectly manifested in words, things, events, and living beings, now withdraws from its other spheres and migrates to the human self. The element of subjectivity (will and intelligent purpose) becomes concentrated in the self. And the world in which human subjects act is transformed by this migration. Nature, drained of *telos*, becomes either a set of unruly forces that must be subjected to human control or a deposit of objects to be understood through humanly constructed categories and used for human purposes; words no longer manifest divine meanings to be glimpsed by humans but are understood to be human constructions; knowledge shifts its locus from commentary on ancient texts to a grounding in human perception, experimentation, and logic. A whole new setting is thus provided for the definition and justification of authority and it becomes questionable whether the ground of authority can any longer "derive from something outside the range of human deeds." Several features of this new setting deserve elaboration.

1. If subjectivity has become identified with the self, the self is thereby set up to be the standard of authority outside the scope of human deeds. The quest to justify authority in modernity is the quest to ground it in the rational consent of agents who agree (or promise) to obey rules and officials installed according to proper procedures. Consent theories face several difficulties—they pose the question of what characteristics of the self and what circumstances constitute consent, whether consent to a set of procedures can suffice to ground authority unless it is also linked to consent to a shared set of ends, and whether the new world possesses the resources to establish common ends worthy of consent. Two questions assume special importance. First, is the modern understanding of the self as an agent morally compatible with the exercise of authority at all? Second, is it possible to treat the subject as a transcendental standard against which a variety of historically lived understandings of the self can be measured or is it necessary to see the subject as a specific product of modernity that cannot provide an independent ground for modern authority? Though the difficulties are severe, the relation among agency, consent, and authority must always be close in modernity; for without the element of consent the moral presumption of agents to accept authority can find no footing.

2. After the withdrawal of purpose from the world, after the corollary accentuation of human will and agency, social customs take on a new coloration. They become conventions that are, directly or indirectly, the product of individual and collective will. They are therefore understood to be revisable through willful action and to be hateful forms of constraint and imposition when they do not correspond to the will of those living by them. When the conventionalization of social life is joined to the modern need to coordinate and organize so many aspects of life the potential scope of authority broadens impressively. The disappearance of *telos* intensifies and extends imperatives of authoritative coordination by making each custom appear as a willful convention that could be otherwise, and it also weakens traditional supports for authoritative coordination. The tendency for those subjected to the will of authorities to experience that will as authoritarian is rooted in this interplay among the accentuation of will, conventionalization, and the intensified imperatives of social coordination.

3. The ontological background of traditional authority gives special place to the past in appraising performance in the present. This privilege is rooted, for example, in the epistemic status of sacred documents and in the significance accorded to founding acts in defining the propriety of current customs. The practice of traditional authority is inevitably linked to faith in the authenticity of those primordial moments; the authoritative character of those moments in turn is bound up with faith in the benign, if mysterious, intentions of a God who implanted signs of His will in the world. Faith does not disappear in the modern practice of authority; its basis and location merely shift. Modern conceptions of the world assume a more futuristic orientation whereby theories, experiments, and tests improve over time. And, similarly, modern projects are designed to realize an anticipated future more than to maintain or restore a pure condition located in the past. Thus the faith necessary to the operation of authority now becomes faith that obedience to a set of procedures, norms, and authorities today will help to foster the sort of world we want for ourselves or progeny tomorrow. Suspension of the wish to act on one's own wishes, interests, or judgments involves faith that the authoritative standards governing conduct today will tend in the long run to realize the ends that justify them. If the secularization of authority means that faith is translated into trust, it also installs the future as the connecting link between trust and authority. Modern authority is future-oriented and any understanding of its operation must contain an interpretation of the extent to which faith in the future our institutions are designed to build is justified.

4. If faith continues to be essential to modern authority, mystery does not disappear from its vicinity either. Rather, it migrates from the relation between human deeds and cosmic purpose to the inner psychology of those over whom authority is exercised. The appearance of the self as subject, with its associated theory of consent, is haunted by the corollary appearance of theories of the unconscious and personal identification. These theories, murky and indefinite in character, seek to explain why the pull of authority is sometimes stronger than rational considerations on its behalf or why resentment against authority often seems to outstrip the onerous character of its demands or why people sometimes pretend to accept authority when they are in fact subjected to coercive pressures. For in-

stance, though the relation of bidder to complier in any established relation of obedience typically embodies a mixture of authority, power, manipulation, and incentives, parties tend, when
obedience is steady and secure, to inflate the importance of authority in the relationship.[3] The bidder, seeking to appear legitimate, can preserve that appearance by inflating the role of
authority in sustaining obedience and deflating that of power;
and the recipient, seeking to appear as a free agent acting on
principle and not easily susceptible to coercion, is similarly encouraged to inflate the importance of the first element. Indirect
signs enable one to interpret the degree to which such inflation
occurs—for example, when there is strict adherance to the letter of the law accompanied by creative efforts to evade its spirit,
or when overt endorsement of the law is undermined by covert
attempts to evade, elude, or subvert the application of the rules
to oneself. The erosion of modern authority is much more likely
to assume these latter forms than to find expression in the explicit repudiation of authority itself. If the ontology of modernity makes consent essential to the practice of authority, then
these same circumstances also locate much of the mystery and
danger of authority in the muddy waters of unconscious drives
and personal identification. The enlightened, rational character
of obedience through consent also locates irrational dimensions
of authority in the depth psychology of the consenting adult.

5. A world drained of immanent purpose is one in which
important human achievements are likely to be ambiguous. If
we are not designed to fit into a world itself designed to house
us, then the designs *we* construct are likely to encounter resistance and opposition within the self and from the world. Any
successful social construction is likely to require the exclusion,
denial, or repudiation of that which does not fit within its frame.
For example, the treatment of the self as a free, responsible
subject also spawns delinquency, irresponsibility, perversity, and
amorality as ways of being that fall below the threshold of responsible agency.[4] It is not that previous less subject-centered
forms of life lacked vice, but that modern life constitutes oth-
erness through the various ways in which it fails to live up to
the standards of self as subject. The very constitution of subjectivity as a standard of selfhood encourages the formation and
containment of that which deviates from the standard.

Similarly, if it is true, as it seems to be, that no way of life can sustain authority unless its members share a conception of the good life, it also seems true that any specific conception of the good life must exclude or denigrate elements that might otherwise be worthy of endorsement. They are excluded because they do not fit into the particular frame of good institutionally supported in that society. It is not just a fact, for instance, that extended kinship ties, along with the sociality and special supports they provide, do not flourish within a market economy. That fact is an index of the ambiguous character of any complex human achievement; it is possible, in a world no longer interpreted through teleological categories, to acknowledge that every complex social achievement contains unavoidable losses and that every established regularity tends to subjugate irregularities lodged within it.

When we understand nature to be an unruly set of forces not designed to coalesce with our needs and when we understand the embodied self to contain elements that do not fit neatly into the social selves we design, we become suspicious of any social construct that appears to be fully harmonious or complete. The space for "deconstruction" and "genealogy" in modern life lies in the understanding that since there is no ontological basis for the expectation of fully harmonious unities, each such apparent unity can be deconstructed—can be shown to contain anomalous, irregular, disparate elements that have had this unity imposed upon them. A theory of authority, indeed a theory of ethics or politics, that acknowledges this feature of modernity will also appreciate the ambiguous character of achievements it prizes the most.

We can crystallize the import of these five characteristics by saying that today consensual authority is fragile, while alternative modes of social discipline possess self-regenerating capacities. Thus, the accentuation of will and convention, the expanded need for social coordination, the orientation of the present to the future, the psychologization of authority, and the ambiguity of human achievements coalesce in some circumstances to render modern authority fragile. The finely woven interdependence of modern life makes it relatively easy for disturbances at one point in the system to disrupt essential social transactions, converting what would have been a local disturbance in a previous age into a new trial of modern authority.

The motive to disrupt the smooth operation of the system may flow from disaffection from the future it promises for oneself or one's children or resentment against arbitrary treatment by authorities or the sense that onerous conventions could be changed if only there were a public will to do so. The 1968 revolt in France, the Polish Solidarity movement, terrorist activities, Teamster strikes and the Tylenol poisoning episodes in the United States provide dramatic instances of the fragility of authority, while tax evasion, illegal aliens, public corruption, illicit drug dealing, and child abuse provide more insidious examples of the same phenomenon.

But some of the same elements that render authority fragile generate authoritarian modes of social control. Whenever a disruption is highly successful in unsettling established transactions, our very interdependency—the very lack of self-sufficiency in modern life—generates public consent (and sometimes urgent demands) to restore the smooth operation of the order by coercive means. Both the fragility of authority and the regenerative capacity of disciplinary control are grounded in the consent of the governed broadly construed.

This duality is built right into the structure of contemporary life. It is, one might say, one of the ways contrivances of social control (that is, the mix of authority, coercion, manipulation, and incentives which regulate conduct in particular practices) maintain the appearance of authority when a more robust consent to its operation is not forthcoming.[5]

The account given so far of the circumstances of modern authority has some affinities to Alasdair MacIntyre's *After Virtue*.[6] In modern life, MacIntyre says, where Aristotelian teleology has been "repudiated," virtue and authority tend to disappear. They are replaced by authoritarian, bureaucratic control and periodic eruptions of nihilistic violence. But MacIntyre's formulation is more stark than the one I endorse and his remedy is at odds with the one I wish to pursue. He contends that authority and virtue can be rescued only by restoring belief in teleology, and he thinks this is possible (if unlikely now to be adopted), once we correct defective understandings of self, morality, and society bequeathed to us by the Enlightenment.

Without developing the case in detail I contend that strong teleological doctrines were not lost or repudiated; they rather came unravelled by the very attempts in the late medieval and early modern eras to perfect them. They exhausted and devalued themselves in the effort, for instance, to square the idea of an omnipotent creator with a world that limited God's creative will by expressing a rational design. Medieval nominalism sacrificed *telos* to save God; the God saved became too distant from the world to maintain the supportive relation among religion, authority and tradition identified by Arendt.[7] It is possible, after the self-destruction of strong teleological doctrines, to defend a much weaker version of the idea, in which *telos,* while drained from the cosmos, nature, and even to a significant degree from human bodies, is located in human projects. But the material deployed to realize those projects, because *it* can no longer be assumed to tend toward a natural harmony, also generates resistance and recalcitrance to their realization. A weakened teleology, when its implications are traced out, cannot sustain the traditional theory of virtue and authority MacIntyre advocates. It rather suggests an ethic of ambiguity. Any attempt to restore traditional authority and virtue in these circumstances eventually degenerates into an authoritarian effort to impose a unified image of the good on those who resist it.

Indeed, I suspect that the recent surge of interest in the Straussian distinction between the esoteric version of a doctrine and its exoteric presentation is rooted in the growing fear among theorists that authority and virtue, necessary to the operation of a good society, cannot be grounded without a strong teleology while the ontological basis for such a doctrine cannot now be established. Under these circumstances the exoteric formulation insists that the ground for the desired theory is solid while the esoteric presentation acknowledges it to be very shaky indeed. The pretense of solidity, it is thought, must be sustained to ward off the nihilism that would result if the masses felt these rumblings beneath their feet.

Some theorists maintain the split between an esoteric doctrine reserved for a few prepared to receive it and an exoteric version offered to those unable to live with the truth; other theorists may contain the split within themselves, censoring internally thoughts and doubts that might prove dangerous if pressed very far. But wherever the split between the enunciated and the secret doctrine is located it contains antidemocratic and authoritarian implications: the dangers each courts are more ominous than the ones from which we are to be protected. That at least is the operating assumption guiding this discussion of authority.

AUTHORITY AND AMBIGUITY

What does it mean to acknowledge the ambiguous character of social achievements in the very practice of authority? Why is it a good thing to do? And what implications does it carry for the form of public life?

Consider first the case for affirming authority in modern life. It resides in the fact that every mode of social life selects from a broad range of possible ways of living together a smaller set that can be maintained within one social form. Order, then, implies limits and modern orders additionally require extensive coordination of institutions and individuals to ensure that each meshes to a reasonable degree with the operation of the others. Authority, rightly instituted, is a mode of coordination that treats individuals with the respect due them without requiring each to possess an impossibly high degree of knowledge about every sector of social life or an unreasonably high level of civic virtue. It is an appropriate mode of coordination in societies where social knowledge is specialized, interests are diverse, and the requirements of common action are relatively high.

In circumstances where the ends served by the existing institutional structure are experienced as authoritative by participants, a preliminary condition is established for authority as one favored mode of social coordination.[8] But such an authoritative background, though essential to authority, does not suffice. Authority requires authorities who, because of the positions they hold and their mode of selection, interpret the specific meaning and import of that background in concrete settings. The open texture of the authoritative background, the need to decide between alternative interpretations of that background in specific settings to settle upon an authoritative rule, law or policy, and the presumptive agreement by citizens to obey properly designated officials following prescribed procedures when social coordination is required coalesce to create the circumstances for authority, and for the exercise of authority by authorities. In these circumstances there is a presumption in favor of obedience to authority even where many of those called upon to comply disagree with the decision or when it reflects beliefs from which they dissent. Authority is exercised over their specific actions rather than their specific beliefs (though its exercise still requires a background of generally shared beliefs).

When I voluntarily obey a traffic officer, a university dean, a union leader or a judge exercising authority over me, I do so not merely because I agree with the necessity or wisdom of the verdict nor because I fear reprisal for refusing to comply, nor because I want other people to make my decisions for me, but because I agree that the life we share in common requires commonalities of action in a variety of settings, that in some of those settings such commonalities are best achieved through authoritative coordination, and that this latter coordination, given the gap between particular imperatives of coordination and the porous texture of the common background of shared standards, requires authorities occupying particular positions to announce decisions, verdicts, and directives in their areas of competence. And this presumption in favor of the exercise of authority is supported by a background faith that over the long run its common acceptance will maintain and advance those social purposes and ends we prize the most. When that faith disappears the operation of authority unravels; it gives way to disorder or to the other modes of social control or, more likely, to both together.

These considerations support a presumption in favor of the exercise of authority. But the ambiguous character of the authoritative background from which authority derives and the constant danger of its abuse support the case for an appreciation of ambiguity in the operation of authority. If there is no harmonious unity toward which individuals and societies tend, no state which, once reached, brings to unified fruition all of the ends and virtues worthy of our admiration, if we are accidents thrown into a world not designed to establish full harmony between nature and culture or between the public good and the good of the individual or within the self, we must expect that every operative set of authoritative norms contains arbitrary elements within it. These elements are not (or not necessarily) arbitrary in the sense that the preferred way of life could still be maintained if they were shucked off. (They would then be eliminable evils.) They are arbitrary in the sense that while indispensable to this way of life there are other forms of living, admirable in their own way, in which this specific set would not be necessary. To see this is to see, first, that every good way of life imposes arbitrary limits, exclusions, losses, burdens, and sacrifices on its members to sustain itself and, second, that these burdens are likely to be distributed asymmetrically across lines of gender, class, generation or region.

To honor equality (an admirable thing) is also to demean excellence in certain ways; to institutionalize individualism is to sacrifice the solace and benefits of community; to exercise freedom is to experience the closure that accompanies choice among incompatible and often irreversible projects; to secure stable identities through gender demarcation is to exclude the hermaphrodite from such an identity and to suppress that in others which does not fit neatly into its frame; to prize the rule of law is to invite the extension of litigiousness into new corners of social life; to institutionalize respect for the responsible agent is to sow institutional disrespect for those unqualified or unwilling to exercise responsibility; to give primacy to mathematicization in the social construction of knowledge is to denigrate individuals whose thought escapes that mold and to depreciate ways of knowing which do not fit into its frame. And lest the point be misread, to reverse these priorities would be to install another set of losses and impositions.

Any authoritative set of norms and standards is, at its best, an ambiguous achievement; it excludes and denigrates that which does not fit into its confines. Since social achievement is not possible without this shadow of ambiguity the question becomes: which achievements are worthy of our endorsement once the ambiguity within them is recognized? A second question also becomes pertinent: Why is it that ideals which compete for hegemony today are typically articulated in ways that occlude the ambiguity residing within them?

It would perhaps be banal to iterate these points were they not closely associated with another. Nietzsche, who launched the most relentless assault on transcendental and teleological doctrines, also identified a powerful human urge to suppress disharmonies within its most cherished achievements. "German philosophy," Nietzsche says in *Will to Power,* pointing dramatically to its culmination in Kant and Hegel, "is the most fundamental form of romanticism and homesickness there has ever been." And, again, speaking of an urge found in every self, a longing which threatens to become an imperious demand, "one longs for that place in which alone one can be at home."[9] When a child is homesick it cannot say no to the longing that overwhelms it; it demands elimination of the feeling of emptiness by returning to its home. The adult urge to find a home, to pretend that the best order to be realized in this world or another can resolve alienation, has fueled a series of ontologies in Western history that pretend to fulfill it. But we can now see through these pretenses and confront the urge propelling them. In doing so we support the case for authority while avoiding its worst dangers.

An established practice of authority is most dangerous when it expresses the urge to treat society as a home because its exercise then functions to repress, exclude, and deny that which is discordant with the harmony pursued.

The institutionalization of an ambiguous orientation to authority concedes a necessary role to authority while exposing dangers in the urge to integrate so much of the common life into its orbit. The most ominous danger confronting modern authority is that our experience of its fragility, in conjunction with the anxiety that experience evokes, will impel too many to concede too much to it, to suppress awareness of the dangers and injustices that accompany its successful exercise.

The institutionalization of ambiguity thus emerges as a strategy to confront and blunt homesickness within us. But how is ambiguity institutionalized? Some tribal societies contain rituals and myths that affirm the authority of the order available to them while acknowledging arbitrary elements in the forms through which they live. Thus the trickster myth, apparently finding expression in several tribal societies, evokes experience of disunities in the self and the world that cannot and should not find full expression in the common life. The Trickster, a protean self whose multiple centers of action conflict with one another, acknowledges a struggle others tend to suppress. Once when the Trickster was skinning a buffalo with his right arm:

his left arm grabbed the buffalo. "Give that back to me, it is mine! Stop that or I will use my knife on you." So spoke the right arm. "I will cut you to pieces, that is what I will do to you," continued the right arm. . . . Again and again this was repeated. In this manner did Trickster make both his arms quarrel. That quarrel soon turned into a vicious fight and the left arm was badly cut up. "Oh, oh! Why did I do this? Why have I done this? I have made myself suffer!" The left arm was indeed bleeding profusely.[10]

The repetition of scenes like this in *The Trickster* evokes the idea that the organization of the self necessary to the good life shared with others is also destructive of elements in the self that do not fit into this organization. "The principle of ambivalence is incorporated into the myths and rituals of primitive peoples to an extraordinary degree . . . And this laughing at oneself means accepting the ambivalence of the human condition, for which civilization gives us very little instruction or structured opportunity."[11]

There are other examples. The Lele, for instance, have a tightly demarcated set of categories for organizing the world around them. But they also confront limits in this organization by relating in a special way to things and animals that do not fit neatly into the categorical structure. They confront the dirt created by their own order through rituals of worship of pollution, acknowledging, though indirectly and obliquely, that the form they need to impose upon the world does not correspond to the world in all its complexity.[12] Perhaps the most pertinent rites for our purposes are seasonal festivals of reversal in some tribal societies where those normally in command are now commanded, those who command sexual favors face demands upon themselves, those who are served do the serving, and, in general, that which is regularly subordinated to maintain the limits of the order now escapes subordination. These rites through their temporary character affirm the authoritative character of established norms, but through the mechanism of reversal they also provide a glimpse into the violence and sacrifices normally required to maintain it. When this ambiguity is ritually acknowledged the normal way of life may be lived a little more loosely; more space may be sought for discrepancy and creativity within it. Through these rites "each may thereby learn to play his own routine roles afresh, surely with renewed understanding, possibly with greater grace, perhaps with reciprocating love." [13]

These rites embody an appreciation of ambiguity, but they do so in a world morally and ontologically distant from modernity. The teleological conception of the cosmos within which the rituals are situated probably makes it easier to affirm ambiguities in the constructions of tribal life; for they can be interpreted as pointing obliquely to a higher order which is mysterious to humans but coherent and intelligible in itself. The modern appreciation of ambiguity cannot so easily rest upon this act of faith, and the resistance to its expression may thereby be more severe.

Modern ambiguity must find expression within a medium appropriate to its own structure of life. Politics provides the appropriate vehicle. Modern politics, when the preconditions are right and it functions at its best, simultaneously operates to unsettle dimensions of the common life that have assumed a fixed character and to achieve a temporary settlement in areas where a common decision is needed but the resources of knowledge or administrative procedure are insufficient to resolve the issue. Modern politics, again at its best, is the institutionalization of ambiguity; it keeps alive that which might otherwise be killed by the weight of authority or necessity; it helps that which is subordinate to find its own voice and perhaps, to expand the space in which it can be for itself rather than only for the order. If authority tends to concede too much to the yearning for harmony, politics encourages us to confront the urge itself.

Politics and authority stand in a relation of interdependence and opposition to one another. And this ambiguity, too, must be kept alive. For without authority politics degenerates into violence or coercion, but with authority politics provides an indispensable corrective to its intensification and overextension. The forces in modernity that tend to displace politics, to convert it into administration or authoritative command or economic rationality or terrorism, subvert this appreciation of ambiguity. Indeed, some of the same dimensions of contemporary life that render authority fragile squeeze the space within which politics can be the medium for the expression of ambiguity. This is particularly true when we consider the relation between modern authority and faith in the future available to modernity.

If faith in the future—in the future established institutions are designed to foster—is jeopardized, and if the established institutional structure is not easily or readily susceptible to redesign, the stage is set for the erosion of authority and ambiguity together. Something like that is happening in modern societies.

It is difficult to identify all the elements involved in this contemporary devaluation of the future available to our civilization. Certainly the capacity to launch nuclear holocaust is involved. Another source resides in the gap between the promises that legitimize the political economy of growth and the disciplines it must impose today to generate growth. Modern democracies depend upon constant economic growth to draw all citizens into the good life they support and to temper the scale and intensity of social conflict. The institutions of work, investment, and consumption and the dependence of the state on tax dividends generated by the privately incorporated economy combine today to convert economic growth from an end into a systemic imperative. And the imperative is now pursued under unfavorable conditions of realization. Implicit doubts about the ability to sustain this pursuit into the future and resentment against the disciplines imposed to fulfill the imperative encourage a variety of constituencies to evade and subvert the roles assigned to them. This proliferation of evasions in turn encourages state and private bureaucracies to devise more reliable means to maintain a closer connection between role assignment and performance.[14] This dialectic tends to subvert authority and politics together.

Academic policy analyses defined around the problematics of "reindustrialization," "rationalization," "incentive systems," and "zero-sum economics" all concede, though obliquely, that the disciplines required for the continued pursuit of growth must now be imposed on many who resist them. They implicitly acknowledge that faith in the future available to the civilization of productivity is waning and that authority and virtue must increasingly be supplanted by finely grained methods of social control.

When confidence in the future recedes, authority gives way to other modes of social control and these disciplines in turn accentuate impulses to resist and elude them. But, under these circumstances, each evasion, because of its destructive effects on systemic imperatives, eventually becomes the occasion for developing new instruments of discipline. Order is maintained, but authority, ambiguity, and politics tend to be squeezed. For the latter requires a relatively high degree of confidence in the future established institutions are designed to bring and a reasonable degree of slack between the dominant ends supported by the system and the modes of conduct open to those who live in it.

The ontology of modern life is hospitable enough to authority and ambiguity, but the future that contemporary institutions are designed to build may be rather inhospitable to both.

NOTES

1. Hannah Arendt, "What Was Authority?" in *NOMOS I, Authority*, ed. Carl J. Friedrich (Cambridge: Harvard University Press, 1958), p. 82.
2. Arendt, *ibid.*, p. 86.
3. I explore the relation between authority and various forms of power in my book *The Terms of Political Discourse*, 2nd ed. (Princeton: Princeton University Press, 1983). The relation between "in authority" and "an authority," which is presupposed in this essay, is also defended there. Richard Sennett's *Authority* (New York: Knopf, 1980) includes a thoughtful discussion of the psychological dimension of authority. The fear that the formal and justificatory side of authority may be swamped if its psychological dimension is emphasized is understandable, but the fear does not justify the tendency to ignore this dimension altogether.
4. The most provocative treatment of this thesis is to be found in Michel Foucault, *Madness and Civilization* (New York: Random House, 1965), *Discipline and Punish* (New York: Pantheon, 1977), and *The History of Sexuality* (New York: Random House, 1980).
5. Unconscious contrivances of social control are considered in Connolly, "Discipline, Politics and Ambiguity," *Political Theory* (August 1983): 325–341. Unconscious contrivances operate when an available evasion makes it advisable for the evader to maintain a low

profile in other respects. Thus the illegal alien, to protect him or herself from the authorities, is placed in "a weak position to complain about wages or working conditions, to establish roots in the broader community, to organize collectively, or to participate in the political life of the society. Illegality . . . subjects the alien to a self-imposed discipline and silence designed to shield him from the eye of the public authorities." Examples can be multiplied. Unconscious contrivances of control tend to flourish when the imperative of social coordination remains salient and legitimate authority is weak.

6. Alasdair MacIntyre, *After Virtue* (South Bend: University of Notre Dame Press, 1981).

7. The best account of how the self-devaluation of teleological theories emerged through the history of attempts to perfect the relation between God the Creator and the expressive character of the world is to be found in Hans Blumenberg, *The Legitimacy of the Modern Age* (Cambridge: MIT Press, 1983). His account reveals a series of severe defects in those theories that claim that we have unnecessarily repudiated or forgotten this legacy. It also, in my judgment, underestimates the difficulties and dilemmas internal to modernity itself.

8. The connections and disconnections between the authoritative background and the exercise of authority are explored thoughtfully in Richard Flathman, *The Practice of Authority* (Chicago: University of Chicago Press, 1980).

9. Friedrich Nietzsche, *Will to Power*, trans. Walter Kaufman and R.J. Hollingdale (New York: Vintage Books, 1967), p. 225.

10. Paul Radin, *The Trickster: A Study in American Mythology* (New York: Schocken Books, 1972), p. 8.

11. Stanley Diamond, "Introduction" to Paul Radin, *The Trickster*.

12. Mary Douglas, *Purity and Danger* (London: Routledge and Kegan Paul, 1966).

13. Victor Turner, *The Ritual Process* (Ithaca: Cornell University Press, 1969), pp. 187–188.

14. The case for this interpretation is made in my book *Appearance and Reality in Politics* (Cambridge: Cambridge University Press, 1983), chapters 4, 5, and 6 and my "Progress, Growth and Pessimism in America," *democracy* (Fall 1983): 22–31.

2

AUTHORITY AND INDETERMINACY

FREDERICK SCHAUER

THE QUEST FOR COHERENCE

We live in an age of theory-builders. A currently pervasive philosophical mode seeks to reconcile much or all of the world and our existence within it, producing theories purporting to minimize the importance or eliminate the existence of the inconsistencies apparent in political and moral life. For much of contemporary moral, social, political, and legal philosophy, "coherence" is both the goal and the standard of evaluation

Some coherence theories are unitary, in the sense of using one pervasive and relatively simple principle to generate or to explain most more particular political or moral judgments.[1] Here we see a series of generated specifications that are at least consistent with each other, and may even relate to each other in some stronger sense of coherence. Other coherence theories abjure the elegant simplicity of unitary theories, relying instead on a larger array of more specific principles, each directed toward but a part of our social and moral existence, but still fitting with each other like the parts of a jigsaw puzzle, with no inconsistencies, and with the exclusions of each part constituting the inclusions of another.[2] And then there are mixed coherence theories, employing a series of specific principles, but employing as well principles of ordering that exclude the possibility of inconsistencies between the specific principles, and thus in the process relate the specific principles to each other so that they create a larger whole.[3]

Coherence theories, even as normative ideals, are possibly just wrong. The nature of our social, political, and moral existence may be such that intuitionism, in the Rawlsian sense of that word, may gain in accuracy what it loses in beauty, in simplicity, or in elegance. But confronting this hoary question of moral philosophy is not my agenda here. It may very well be that intuitionism is problematic as ideal theory, and it may be that the proper task of moral and political philosophy is to explore the ways in which, aspirationally, the tensions of our moral and political existence might be minimized. But even if this is so, such exercises of ideal theory, if taken to be just that, need not be inconsistent with the view that in our non-ideal world human beings are fallible, and human institutions have limits. Thus it may be futile, or indeed harmful, to attempt to design a master plan fitting together all of the pieces of our existing social, political, and moral world. In the world in which we live, our attempts to confront the moral and factual complexity will inevitably be Janus-faced, simultaneously producing advantages and disadvantages, costs and benefits, rights and wrongs. Moreover, these attempts underscore what is even a substantial indeterminacy with respect to what counts as an advantage or a disadvantage, what counts as a cost or benefit, and what counts as a right or a wrong.

We are thus faced with living in and dealing with a complex society significantly characterized by a profound lack of teleological unity. In the face of this indeterminacy of goal, a number of responses are possible, but I want to focus here on one response that is particularly related to the organizing theme of this volume—authority. The response to moral indeterminacy in the modern world that attracts my attention is the relationship between authority and the indeterminacy of ends and means, and the consequent possibility, somewhat paradoxically, that the intentional *creation* of indeterminacy is an important way of dealing with the complexity of modern society. Thus for me the question is not limited to how we should *accept* the indeterminacy of the authoritative background of the world in which we live,[4] but includes and indeed focuses on the *creation* of indeterminacy as perhaps the most useful tool we have in adapting to modernity.

The Notion of Open Texture

It is unfortunately common among many contemporary writers about law and about politics to use the term "open texture," but to use it as a synonym for "vagueness." Thus we see, for example, frequent references to the Constitution of the United States as open-textured because it contains such vague terms as "freedom of speech," "due process of law," "cruel and unusual punishment," and "equal protection of the laws." Undoubtedly these and other phrases are vague, but to describe them as open-textured risks losing the distinct and crucially important point first described by the philosopher Friedrich Waismann when he used the German word *porosität* and then translated it into English as "open texture."[5] Open texture to Waismann was not vagueness, but rather *potential* vagueness, and an ineliminable potential vagueness at that. The metaphor of open texture was Waismann's way of showing that no term, no matter how seemingly specific, precise, or carefully and completely defined, could not become vague—indeterminate—in the face of a changing world, in the face of our imperfect knowledge of an uncertain future, and in the face of our inevitably uncertain views about how we would confront the future. Put more simply, we cannot determine with certainty now that which we cannot even imagine. J.L. Austin captured the point well with his example of the exploding goldfinch.[6] We might think that the term "goldfinch" was quite precise and definitionally bounded in all directions. Something is either a goldfinch or it is not, depending on the possession *vel non* of certain well-established characteristics. It looks as if there are no close cases, nothing analogous to trying to determine whether a thinly thatched man was "bald," or whether an amphibious automobile was a "boat." But imagine that we were to encounter a bird that we first thought was clearly a goldfinch, possessing all of the characteristics, positive and negative, hitherto taken to be sufficient properly to apply the specific term "goldfinch"—except that the bird then exploded before our eyes. In this event, Austin observes that "we don't know what to say." All of a sudden our existing linguistic apparatus has failed us, and we have no appropriate response. Our previously determinate term had just, as applied in this case, become vague.

Waismann's point, and Austin's as well, was that *all* language was in exactly this way *potentially* vague, and it is this potential but not currently identifiable vagueness that represents the phenomenon of open texture. Austin used a precise term like "goldfinch" to illustrate the point because open texture is not a function of terms that we can currently identify as being indeterminate in a particular way. Rather, as long as the future may surprise us, any term, no matter how seemingly specific, may yet become vague. Vagueness, therefore, once identified, is in theory eliminable, because by identifying the vagueness we have identified the way to provide the requisite specification. For example, we could eliminate the existing vagueness in the term "bald" by specifying the exact number of hairs necessary for a person to be considered as not being bald. We might not, for numerous reasons, wish to do this, but the means are theoretically at our disposal. And if we did this, we would have eliminated the existing vagueness, but we would not have eliminated the potential vagueness, the open texture. What if, for example, someone was discovered who was three hairs short of being not-bald, but who had four blades of grass growing out of his head. Would this person be bald? Again, we do not know what to say, and this is therefore all we can say. Thus open texture is that potential vagueness that is ineliminable, and we cannot eliminate it precisely because at a given point in time we cannot identify it.

Once we understand the concept of open texture, we have learned something about vagueness as well. Because just as open texture is to be defined as potential vagueness and contrasted with existing and identifiable vagueness, so too does thinking about open texture lead us to appreciate the risks of attempting to eliminate vagueness. For if it is the case that open texture is never eliminable, attempts to eliminate from our linguistic apparatus all actual and potential vagueness are at the very least futile. But futility is not all. It may be that attempting to eliminate vagueness has risks as well, risks that are especially apparent when we leave abstract thinking about language and look more specifically at the language of the law.

OPEN TEXTURE AND THE LANGUAGE OF LAW

As I have tried to show, taking open texture as a synonym for vagueness obscures the distinction between the two, and thus also obscures the ultimate futility of searching for precision in all definitional directions. This futile search may have risks, and we see them in examining the language of law. As H.L.A. Hart has most prominently explained, Waismann's insights about open texture are especially relevant to thinking about the law.[7]

Open texture may occur in the law in two ways. Specific terms used in the law are themselves open-textured in exactly the way they are in language, and thus law is at least as open-textured as its component language. Moreover, when these terms are combined into legal norms designed to address certain forms of conduct, a seemingly specific norm that is currently determinate with respect to its intended or apparent applications may become vague when new forms of behavior, or new events in the world, create indeterminacies not imagined and possibly not imaginable when the norm was first drafted. If, in an attempt to eliminate currently perceived indeterminacies, we attempt to make our laws too specific, the exploding goldfinches of the world will create difficulties when an unforeseen world clashes with laws whose specificity leaves no room for change. In law, of course, we refer to these events not as exploding goldfinches, but as *loopholes*—the particular form of legal pathology that is the product of excess specificity and an excess craving for certainty intersecting with a changing world, with limited human foresight, and with the likelihood that societies will, over time, change their views of how they wish to manage in and with the world.

So what do we do in law to accommodate to and deal with the problem of open texture? As we frequently do with language (think of "bald," "nice," "dark," "important," and, of course, that old jurisprudential chestnut, "vehicle") we *intentionally* create vagueness—indeterminacy—to increase our flexibility for the future. In doing so we of course reduce the certainty and predictability of the law. People can adapt their behavior much more easily to that section of the Internal Revenue Code that requires them to file their returns by April 15 than corporations can adapt their behavior to the Sherman Act's prohibition of "every contract, combination . . . or conspiracy in restraint of trade or commerce," or than public officials can adapt their behavior to the constitutional requirement that they not deny anyone "equal protection of the laws."[8] But although we reduce predictability and its consequent repose by employing vague legal language, we gain in exchange the ability of the law-applying authority to tailor more easily the law to the complexities and movement of the world. Think, for example, of why we talk about loopholes in the Internal Revenue Code, but why by contrast it seems so odd to refer to a "loophole" in something so vague as the First Amendment, or the due process or equal protection clauses of the Fourteenth Amendment. And consider as well Willard Quine's observation (adapted from I.A. Richards) that "a painter with a limited palette can achieve more precise representations by thinning and combining his colors than a mosaic worker can achieve with his limited variety of tiles, and the skillful superimposing of vaguenesses has similar advantages over the fitting together of precise technical terms."[9] Almost paradoxically, therefore, a crucial tool for dealing with an uncertain and rapidly changing world whose size and complexity further limits our knowledge of it is at times to create more indeterminacy and more uncertainty, but here an intentional rather than an inevitable indeterminacy.

When we employ intentional indeterminacy in the law, we in the process increase the authority of law-applying and law-interpreting individuals or institutions, paradigmatically judges and courts, but perhaps more importantly and more frequently regulatory agencies, legislatures, and the cop on the beat. Each of these agents has authority of two different types. One is the authority to apply the legal norm to the objects of that norm, as when a police officer exercises authority pursuant to the 55 miles per hour speed limit to apprehend a driver traveling at 63 miles per hour. The second type of authority is the authority to decide which objects are in fact covered by a legal norm, as when a judge decides that driving at 87 miles per hour violates a norm formulated in terms of a prohibition on "reckless driving." Although there is no rigid line between these two types of authority, it is important to recognize the way that application of the clear and clarifying of the cloudy are substantially different activities. Both are exercises of authority, but the second one is particularly relevant here. An increase in the indeterminacy of the relevant norm, an increase that may be a product of desiring to achieve flexibility in the face of a quickly moving complex world, invariably increases authority in the second sense.[10] As we increase the indeterminacy of the governing norm, we increase the law-*making* authority of those whose function is ostensibly limited to law-applying. As a result, we can increase the extent of our adaptability to future uncertainty by increasing the vagueness of those linguistic normative constraints on authority that are part of what we commonly call "law."

The relationship between the vagueness of a legal norm and the consequent authority of those who interpret it has a double aspect. Initially, we can say that vagueness creates authority,[11] in the sense that increasing the vagueness of the relevant norm increases the interpretative authority of judges or other interpreting officials. As a result, the intentional deployment of vagueness is a way of increasing the authority of some class of officials or other interpreters. Perhaps more significantly, however, the authority thus created is necessarily an authority exercised without what would otherwise be the constraints of the linguistically articulated norm. If law means anything at all, it at least includes the idea that certain norms will make certain options less available than they would have been absent the norm, and that on occasion decisionmakers will find that the decision they would make absent the norm is at odds with the decision suggested by the norm. The pull of the norm may not be absolute, and is perhaps better analogized to a presumption, but it is still the case that norm-constrained decisionmaking will occasionally lead in a different direction than decisionmaking that permits the decisionmaker to take into account the full range of facts, and the full richness of various considerations, that relate to the immediate decision. By increasing the size of the linguistic interstices within which decisionmakers exercise authority in the second sense described above, we free those decisionmakers from the shackles that have been placed on them by the past. As a result, we make it more possible for decisionmakers to adapt their decisions to those changing facts about the world, and changing values within the world, that could not have been anticipated at the time the norm was formulated. We see, therefore, that indeterminacy is an important way to give decisionmakers authority of a certain type, the authority to adapt their decisions to a changing world as it is then perceived by them, to adapt their decisions to the exploding goldfinches of the world at the time that the goldfinch explodes. The lesson of open texture is that there will always be situations in which the rules of the past, linguistic or otherwise, just will not work. By weakening the linguistic precision of legal rules, we weaken the pull of the past, and in that way increase the authority of decisionmakers to deal with the future when and only when we get there.

OPEN TEXTURE IN A POLITICAL WORLD

All of the foregoing applies not only to law. It is equally relevant, albeit in a more ephemeral way, to those aspects of society's authoritative background not commonly referred to as "law." Professor William E. Connolly, for example,[12] argues that the tensions and complexities of modern politics are possibly a way of dealing with the indeterminacy of society's authoritative background. He maintains that we use modern politics to create that authority which in turn provides the specification, when needed, of an indeterminate authoritative background. In doing so, we accept as well the bindingness on us of even those specifications with which we disagree, for without such acceptance social coordination would be impossible.

Professor Connolly's perspective seems to suggest an analogy with a lifeboat, where authority is given to one so that all may live.[13] Yet in a lifeboat the goal—living—is shared by all, but essential to understanding modernity is understanding the ways in which most modern societies have little shared sense of a single goal. In Connolly's view authority in the form of modern politics is a way of dealing with this fact. Authority, however, is capable of dealing with spatial and temporal diffuseness of goal only if the mechanisms for creating authority are made intentionally indeterminate, only if the authoritative background itself contains sufficient flexibility to accommodate imperfect knowledge, diffuseness of goal, and an uncertain future. By making the authoritative background indeterminate, we increase the authority of those *in* authority, accepting greater power over us in exchange for increased adaptability.

Examples of this intentional indeterminacy of authoritative background abound in American political life. For example, we accept and at times encourage an electoral process in which decisions and campaigns are based less on specific programs and more on some amorphous sense of political qualifications. There are of course numerous not necessarily mutually exclusive ways to interpret this phenomenon. But at least one interpretation is that an increasingly uncertain future makes it decreasingly wise to rely on what a political official will do about some issue that we now perceive as a measure of how that official will manage the future. It may be, therefore, that by abjuring issue politics we make the mandates of our political officials less determinate, thus increasing their authority when the unforeseen becomes reality.

Similarly, much of political life, here and elsewhere, places enormous importance on the use of a number of broad and vague expressions that are more symbolic than substantive. Examples that come immediately to mind include "liberty," "freedom," "justice," "equality," "land of opportunity," and "fiscal responsibility." Certainly the United States has no monopoly on political sloganeering, nor does the present when compared to the past. Nevertheless it is useful to think about the phenomenon, even if it is universal and timeless. For it is only a contingent fact that a speaker using this style of discourse is not immediately asked or required to provide specification for these vague and emotive words. To the extent that this language is tolerated or even encouraged as the dominant mode of discourse in political life, once again we can be said to have fostered an intentional rather than inevitable indeterminacy as a way of increasing the authority of our leaders to decide themselves how they will deal with the future when it arises.

As a final example, consider the indeterminacy of many of our most important symbolic documents, including those having legal force in the strictest sense, such as the Constitution, and those without legal force but which are very much a part of what we are all about, such as the Mayflower Compact, the Declaration of Independence, the Gettysburg Address, and Franklin Roosevelt's Four Freedoms. When these documents are compared to texts such as the Koran and the Talmud, it becomes apparent that we are quite willing to accept a great deal of textual indeterminacy, and implicitly accept the interpretive freedom and consequent authority that is created by that indeterminacy.

There are, of course, many examples other than these of the

ways in which important parts of the authoritative background of this country are intentionally indeterminate. But I do not want to provide an exhaustive list here, and I do not purport to be a sociologist of the American political experience. Rather, I want only to emphasize that nothing in the nature of the world—even the modern world—requires an authoritative background of such extreme indeterminacy. We cannot of course eliminate all indeterminacy in the formulation of all of those social and political institutions that together can be said to constitute our authoritative background, or our social text. But that indeterminacy is not completely eliminable does not mean that it is not variable and therefore reducible. At the very least, it must be conceded that we exist in a society that has much more indeterminacy in its authoritative structures than is minimally necessary. We conduct political and social discourse in a language that could be much more precise, and we create and describe our political and social institutions in forms soaked with indeterminacy. In doing so, we have increased the authority of those whose mandate over us takes place in the very gaps left by this indeterminacy. We could consequently constrain the authority of these authorities by decreasing the size of these gaps, but in doing so we would decrease our flexibility, and in doing so decrease our ability to manage an increasing social complexity, and an increasingly uncertain future.

The question of authority and indeterminacy is therefore the question not only of how much indeterminacy we have, but of how much indeterminacy to create. For we ought to recognize the control we have not just of authority, but of indeterminacy as well. Once we acknowledge that we have control over the specificity of our institutions, we can begin to use specificity as a tool. The use of specificity and indeterminacy, in varying degrees and in different places, is a way both of creating and controlling authority. Only by appreciating the control we have over indeterminacy can we begin to understand fully the mechanisms of authority.

NOTES

1. I am thinking, for example, of Ronald Dworkin's use of "equal concern and respect." Ronald Dworkin, "Liberalism," in Stuart Hampshire, ed., *Public and Private Morality* (Cambridge: Cambridge University Press, 1978), p. 113.

2. See, for example, Charles Fried, *Right and Wrong* (Cambridge: Harvard University Press, 1978).

3. The archetype is of course John Rawls, *A Theory of Justice* (Cambridge: Harvard University Press, 1971).

4. In this regard, compare my perspective with that of Professor William E. Connolly in this volume.

5. Friedrich Waismann, "Verifiability," in A. Flew, ed., *Essays on Logic and Language*, First Series (Oxford: Basil Blackwell, 1951), p. 117. For useful exposition, see Mats Furberg, *Saying and Meaning* (Oxford: Basil Blackwell, 1963); Avishai Margalit, "Open Texture," in Avishai Margalit, ed., *Meaning and Use* (Boston: D. Reidel, 1979), p. 141.

6. J.L. Austin, "Other Minds," in *Philosophical Papers*, 3rd ed. (Oxford: Oxford University Press, 1979), p. 88.

7. H.L.A. Hart, *The Concept of Law* (Oxford: Clarendon Press, 1961), especially chapter 7. See also G.P. Baker, "Defeasability and Meaning," in P.M.S. Hacker and J. Raz, eds., *Law, Morality, and Society: Essays in Honour of H.L.A. Hart* (Oxford: Clarendon Press, 1977), p. 26.

8. I recognize, of course, that case law interpretation may make vague language considerably less so in application, just as it may make specific language considerably more so in application. But the general point remains, and is fully applicable to vague or precise guidance from the cases themselves.

9. Willard Van Orman Quine, *Word and Object* (Cambridge: MIT Press, 1960), p. 127.

10. Increases in authority in the second sense bring with them, of course, increases of authority in the first sense. But the opposite is not true. Increasing the range of objects to which a norm may be applied does not necessarily increase the opportunities for interpreting or clarifying the norm. The general size of a circle is not logically related to the sharpness of the line that delineates it.

11. See Gidon Gottlieb, *The Logic of Choice* (London: Allen & Unwin, 1968); Charles Curtis, "A Better Theory of Legal Interpretation," *Vanderbilt Law Review*, 3 (1950): 407.

12. Connolly, op. cit.

13. For a theory of law that starts from the lifeboat perspective, and indeed uses this analogy, see Philip Soper, *A Theory of Law* (Cambridge: Harvard University Press, 1984).

3

AUTHORITY AND CONCEPTUAL CHANGE

TERENCE BALL

Even more than most of the concepts constitutive of moral discourse and political practice—justice, freedom, equality, power—authority appears to be peculiarly problematic. Just why this should be so is a persistent topic of debate among modern political philosophers. In attempting to shed some new light on an old topic I plan to proceed as follows. I shall begin by suggesting that the problematic character of "authority" is less a matter for armchair analysis than for historical inquiry. This would show just how that concept came to be understood in different ways as it was embedded in successive conceptual schemes. One of the few political thinkers to have attempted something like this is Hannah Arendt, whose understanding of what "authority" (really) is, or was, is rather narrowly tied to one historically specific experience. A more adequate conceptual history would show how "authority" has been repeatedly reconstructed by being relocated in different conceptual schemes or theories.

My main focus will be upon two relatively recent attempts to reconstruct authority. These I shall, for the sake of simplicity and analytical clarity, present as ideal types. The first is the emotivist view that an authoritative law, policy, or command is any one that people feel, for whatever reason, that they ought to obey. The second, "epistemocratic" understanding of authority is tied to claims of technical expertise or specialized knowledge. These two understandings of authority are advanced and defended by some modern social scientists—the first by several behaviorally oriented political scientists, and the second by the prophets of the coming of a knowledge-based "post-industrial" society. I shall conclude with some critical reflections upon these newly emergent understandings of authority.

AUTHORITY RECONSTRUCTIVE

Why, a commentator asked several years ago, is authority such a problem?[1] A partial and provisional answer might look like this. Human societies are communicatively constituted. The concepts that make possible particular kinds of communication—and therefore particular kinds of communities, be they religious, moral, political, or even scientific—are characteristically embedded in conceptual schemes, frameworks or theories from which they derive their place and function in a community's discursive constitution and reconstitution. When a scheme is overthrown, outgrown, or otherwise discredited, the concepts constituting it lose their meaning, or retain only a simulacrum of their original meaning. Such, arguably, is the case in much of modern Western society with "virtue," and more certainly with once-respectable scientific concepts like "aether" and "phlogiston." The same might also be said of "authority." Authority—or any other concept, for that matter—becomes problematic and therefore philosophically interesting when its value as one of the common coins of communication is called into question.

To render authority intelligible and meaningful, we might take any one of three tacks. The first is historical, reconstructing the framework in which these concepts were originally used. The second is to expose contradictions and incoherencies inhering in contemporary concepts and the practices they constitute.[2] The third tack consists of trying to revive and rehabilitate contested concepts by redefining and relocating them in a more modern, more familiar, and therefore presumably more intelligible framework.[3]

The first and second tacks were taken, and the third criticized, by Hannah Arendt in her contribution to the first volume of the *NOMOS* series. Her essay, entitled "What Was Authority?" was a sensitive reconstruction of an earlier Romano-religious framework in which authority, or *auctoritas*, was not at all peculiar or deserving of philosophical attention. For my purposes, three features of Arendt's analysis are especially noteworthy. The first is that although she did not employ the now-fashionable notion of a conceptual scheme, she did nevertheless stress the importance of recalling the framework in which the concept of authority originally functioned. Secondly, she showed that concepts—in this case "authority"—have histories and are, in Kierkegaard's phrase, incapable of withstanding the ravages of time.[4] Some concepts, indeed, must be spoken of in the past tense. Thus she asked, What *was* authority? And, more startlingly still, she maintained that "authority has disappeared from the modern world."[5] Thirdly, Arendt tellingly criticized several modern attempts to rehabilitate and modernize the concept of authority by functionalizing or operationalizing it.

By the "functionalizing" of authority Arendt referred to the tendency—once especially evident among some social scientists—to regard authority as essentially equivalent to power, violence, coercion, intimidation, or whatever else might make people obey. Although arguably exaggerated in several respects, Arendt's portrait of the functionally oriented social scientist nevertheless contains, like any caricature, an important grain of truth. "Their concern is only with functions, and whatever fulfills the same function can, according to this view, be called the same." Hence "if violence fulfills the same function as authority—namely, makes people obey—then violence is authority." "It is," she adds, "as though I had the right to call the heel of my shoe a hammer because I, like most women, use it to drive nails into the wall."[6]

Arendt's own view, "based on the conviction of the importance of making distinctions,"[7] stands in stark contrast to the social scientist's search for functional equivalence, and in some respects resembles the "ordinary language" philosopher's penchant for discerning minute distinctions between ostensible synonyms. The main danger in conflating or equating different concepts and in failing to draw fine distinctions is not abstractly philosophical but concretely political. Political communities are communicatively constituted. To the degree that different concepts are muddled, their meanings conflated, and distinctions

obliterated or ignored, the political-cum-communicative constitution of that community is endangered. We will, she warns,

> have ceased to live in a common world where the words
> we have in common possess an unquestionable meaning-
> fulness, so that, short of being condemned to live verbally
> in an altogether meaningless world, we grant each other
> the right to retreat into our own worlds of meaning, and
> demand only that each of us remain consistent within his
> own private terminology.[8]

A community whose members are incapable of distinguishing between violence and authority will see nothing wrong in
attempting to use the former to fulfill the function of the latter.
The result will be "that we shall use violence and pretend to
have restored authority. . . ."[9] Nor is this a purely academic
matter. For the language of the social scientist—the policy scientist, planner, expert, or manager—is increasingly dominant
in what passes for political discourse, debate, and discussion. In
a kind of conceptual counterpart of Gresham's law, debased
language drives out the more valuable currencies of communication. Only by conflating authority and violence can policy
makers speak of near-genocidal campaigns as "pacification programs" and the like.

Arendt is hardly alone in decrying the contemporary deformation of authority. Hans-Georg Gadamer maintains that the
Enlightenment's "prejudice against prejudice" *(Vorurteil)* and
"tradition" results in "the denigration of authority." The result
is that "within the Enlightenment the very *concept* of authority
becomes deformed. On the basis of its concept of reason and
freedom, the concept of authority could be seen as diametri-
cally opposed to reason and freedom: to be, in fact, blind obedience."[10] In a similar spirit John Schaar writes:"I believe that
genuine authority is all but lost to us today, and that perhaps
we have lost even the concept of authority, so that we cannot
know what honorable obedience consists in. This is no small
loss, and no amount of liberation will make up for it, because
if we do not know what authority is, we cannot know what liberty is either. Perhaps that is why so many people today find
themselves as bewildered and unsatisfied after a succession of
liberations as they were before."[11]

Despite differences of argument and accent, Arendt, Gadamer, and Schaar are all agreed that the concept of authority itself has been largely lost to us; that the loss is largely the result of our having inherited the Enlightenment's antinomies—freedom versus authority, reason versus prejudice, and autonomy versus obedience; that the social sciences, and perhaps political science in particular, have for the most part simply assumed and augmented these antinomies even as they have ignored or banished other distinctions; and that their (mis)understanding of authority accordingly consists of an ersatz blend of blind prejudice and raw power.

Might Arendt, Gadamer, and Schaar be mistaken in claiming that authority has disappeared? *Auctoritas* has indeed vanished, along with the scheme in which it was located, and "authority" may well have been corrupted in successive reformulations. Not all conceptual change is for the better. Far from having gone from the modern world, "authority" has assumed newer and distinctly more modern meanings by virtue of its having been redefined and relocated in frameworks that are radically different from the one that Arendt rightly identified as authority's original home.[12] Of the many restatements of authority in its complex and checkered history, two are of particular interest to me here. These two construals of "authority" might best be termed "emotivist" and "epistemocratic." The first functionalizes authority; the second rationalizes it by tying it to claims of expertise and specialized knowledge. The former is predicated upon an emotivist view of the meaning of moral and political concepts; the latter assimilates authority to the model of technical expertise.

Before turning to an examination of these attempts to reconstruct authority, a word of warning: My two models are ideal types that do not yet describe or correspond to political reality. My question is, What would the political world look like if we were to construe authority in these ways? What would it mean for us as agents and citizens to speak of and think about authority in radically new idioms?

THE EMOTIVIST MODEL

What Arendt called the functionalizing of authority was originally a philosophical stratagem that social scientists and political analysts inherited, willingly though perhaps unwittingly, from a certain sort of philosopher. According to the non-cognitivist or emotivist theory of ethics, the terms of moral and political discourse are not cognitively meaningful but serve only to signal the speaker's feelings. Thus to call something good (or just or beautiful) means merely that one approves of it; to label it bad (unjust, ugly) means that one dislikes or disapproves of it for whatever personal or idiosyncratic reason. When Hobbes, for example, said that "tyranny" is merely "monarchy misliked," he advanced an early version of this view.[13] Later, more sophisticated versions of emotivism are to be found in the writings not only of philosophers like A.J. Ayer and C.L. Stevenson but of many eminent social scientists as well. Of course, social scientists are apt to deny any affinities with this or that particular school of moral philosophy. But what generally happens when social scientists attempt to ignore philosophical and ethical concerns is that they nevertheless opt unconsciously, and therefore uncritically, for a particular philosophical and ethical perspective. Their attempts to reformulate moral and political concepts, presumably to make them more precise and scientifically servicable, more often result in bad moral philosophy than in good social science.

Lest this seem like overstatement, consider the way in which a distinguished political scientist (and contributor to the first *NOMOS* volume) attempts to define authority. There are at least three reasons for reconsidering David Easton's contribution to the debate about authority. The first is that "authority" is clearly central to Easton's "systems" approach to the analysis of political phenomena, an approach that he has since qualified but by no means given up; secondly, all the aforementioned themes are to be found in Easton's analysis of authority; and thirdly, while later analysts abandoned Easton's systems approach, their own analyses of authority have followed his fairly closely.[14]

According to Easton's oft-quoted definition, politics is the activity of authoritatively allocating values. And since "all social mechanisms are means of allocating values," it follows that politics is differentiated only by virtue of being "authoritative" in its allocations. Hence "authority" is conceptually prior to "politics" itself.[15] A question that has vexed generations of political philosophers—namely, what is authority and how are we to know it when we see it?—is answered with dispatch. "Although the literature is replete with discussions about the nature of authority," Easton writes, "the meaning of this term can be resolved quickly for our purposes."[16] All the muddle of a benighted, philosophical, prescientific past is swept away with a simple operational definition: "A policy is authoritative when the people to whom it is intended to apply or who are affected by it consider that they must or ought to obey it."[17] Lest this seem a trifle simple, Easton justifies his redefinition "because it gives to the term a meaning that enables us to determine factually whether a group of people do in practice consider a policy to be authoritative."[18] The test of whether a policy is or is not authoritative is behavioral—that is, do those at whom it is aimed obey it, or not? The political scientist need only observe the obedience of the citizenry to ascertain that a particular policy is indeed "authoritative," is promulgated by "authorities," and so on.

Easton does not deny that authority may have a moral dimension. He wishes merely to point out "that the grounds upon which a person accepts a policy as authoritative can be distinguished from the actual acceptance of the authority of the policy."[19] The latter, he adds, "may flow from a number of sources: moral, traditional or customary, or purely from fear of the consequences."[20] In other words, the "moral aspect" of authority, which has to do with the sorts of reasons that people give for obeying (or disobeying) laws or policies, are of no concern to the political scientist qua scientist. "For purposes of . . . political research, whatever the motivations, a policy is clearly authoritative when the feeling prevails that it must or ought to be obeyed."[21] So far as the correct application of the concept of authority is concerned, the reasons, arguments, and justifications offered by those over whom authority is exercised are irrelevant and immaterial. Not reasons for obeying but causes of obedient behavior; not considered judgments but "feelings"— these are the stuff of authority according to Easton.

Several things are striking about Easton's reconstruction of authority. For one, it becomes simply a synonym for what engenders obedience and compliance. This is all the more remarkable when we recall that authority is central to—indeed, constitutive of—Easton's account of politics. We are left, then, with a warmed-over Weberian (or perhaps a reheated Hobbesian) view that command and obedience are the poles of political life. Politics is, in Hobbes's terms, a relation between a powerful or authoritative agent and a passive or powerless patient. Moreover, since authority is operationally reducible to anything that produces obedience, it follows that all obedient behavior provides proof positive of the presence of authority: where there is obedience—whatever its cause, reason, or justification—there also is authority. And if the effect of such compliant behavior is to "allocate values," the relationship is necessarily "political." Hence we may regard the thief who robs me at knife-point as engaged in "political" activity. That I obey because he has a knife in my ribs is beside the point; the political scientist is interested in my compliant behavior, not in my reasons for complying, save for the fact that I do (under the circumstances) feel that his re-allocative "policy" of robbing people "must or ought to be obeyed." And the empirically observable fact that I do obey would suffice to show that the relationship between thief and victim is indeed "authoritative" and hence "political."

By Easton's lights, then, it is difficult if not impossible to distinguish between robbery and politics, or for that matter between politics and almost any kind of coercive activity. And indeed Easton admits as much. In a long footnote, apparently added as an afterthought, he writes:

> My classification of power relationships . . . views the ability to command as one of a number of types. It may be exercised legitimately or illegitimately. If a thief orders you, at the point of a gun, to yield your wallet and you obey him, he has the ability to command you. He therefore can be said to have authority over you even though, because you would challenge its legitimacy, you consider it coercive . . . I am aware, of course, that this diverges from ordinary usage. Authority is usually applied only to situations in which there is a belief in the legitimacy of the orders or commands. Nevertheless it is more useful to broaden the term to cover all command-obedience relationships, discriminating further in each case by reference to the reasons why the exercise of the power or authority is effective.

"This," Easton adds, "is clearly a matter of definition, but it has important theoretical as well as empirical implications."[22] Yet Easton fails to see the even more important *political* implications of his departure from "ordinary usage."

Although the scientific and analytical advantages of Easton's notion of "authority" are nowhere specified, its political consequences are clear enough. Every government wishes to claim the mantle of authority. This they can do, according to Easton, if they can supply their subjects with reasons to obey. Scientifically speaking, it does not much matter what these reasons are. They can rest upon love and respect, or habit and sentiment, or upon fear of arrest, imprisonment, torture, and murder. This "functionalist" conception of authority is explicitly emotivist. For, as Easton stipulates, "*whatever* the motivations, a policy is clearly authoritative when the *feeling* prevails that it must or ought to be obeyed."[23] If Easton had not banished "the state" from the systems vocabulary, one could say that state terrorism, when sufficiently terrifying to be effective, is no less authoritative than milder measures.

The point is not that Easton in any way condones coercion or illegitimate authority; it is, rather, that his emotivist construal of authority makes the distinction between legitimate and illegitimate authority into a subjective one involving "feelings" of approval or disapproval. Just as Hobbes claimed that "tyranny" was merely "monarchy misliked," so Easton implies that illegitimate authority is simply authority misliked. In this respect, at least, Easton is indeed Hobbes's heir.

It is of course true that the tide has long since turned, in most quarters anyway, against extreme behavioralism in political science. My reason for reexamining this particular episode in the history of the social sciences is not to single out Professor Easton for special censure but to trace the political implications of a certain kind of conceptual revision. I mean only to point out the moral and political deficiencies of emotivism, and of an emotivist account of authority in particular. I turn now to a consideration of a second restatement of "authority."

THE EPISTEMOCRATIC MODEL

We need to begin by drawing a distinction between epistemic and epistemocratic authority. Epistemic authority is that which is ascribed to the possessor of specialized knowledge, skills, or expertise.[24] We defer to the physician in medical matters and to the lawyer on legal questions. When we are ill we want to be treated by an authority on the healing arts, and when we face legal difficulties we want to consult an authority on the law. Epistemocratic authority, by contrast, refers to the claim of one class, group, or person to rule another by virtue of the former's possessing specialized knowledge not available to the latter. Epistemocratic authority is therefore conceptually parasitic upon epistemic authority. Or, to put it slightly differently, epistemocratic authority attempts to assimilate political authority to the nonpolitical epistemic authority of the technician or expert.

This distinction is related to one that is commonly drawn between one who by virtue of office or position is *in* authority and one who by dint of specialized knowledge or expertise is *an* authority.[25] Thus the president, though *an* authority on nothing in particular, is nevertheless *in* authority. And a plumber, though *an* authority on taps and drains, is nowhere *in* authority save, perhaps, in flooded basements. Politically speaking, the distinction between being *in* authority and being *an* authority, far from applying universally, is applicable only within a certain kind of society. In the sort of society in which the distinction marks a real difference, political rule and claims of expertise or epistemic privilege are separable, and the roles of ruler and expert are occupied by different persons and justified on different grounds. Yet this distinction is, in modern bureaucratized societies, increasingly blurred if not meaningless. To speak in the Maoist idiom, one might say that in modern societies, communist and noncommunist alike, the Red is increasingly giving way to the Expert, and the amateur deferring to the authority of the professional. More and more, the expert is in authority because he or she is an authority, in medicine, management science, accounting, law, education, or any one of a dozen domains. Our social practices and institutions increasingly exemplify an ideal that is less democratic than technocratic. Or, to coin a neologism, modern societies increasingly resemble epistemocracies ruled by people claiming to possess specialized knowledge and expertise.

It might be objected that there is nothing novel or peculiarly modern about these developments. After all, does not the history of political thought harbor an ancient and recurring vision of the good society in which political authority and expertise are inseparable and in which ruler and expert are one and the same person? It is worth rehearsing that claim in order to criticize it.

The *locus classicus* of the epistemocratic vision is generally held to be Plato's *Republic*.[26] There and elsewhere (e.g., *The Statesman*), Plato relies repeatedly upon analogies between the art *(techne)* of ruling and other arts, particularly medicine and navigation. The variable, ill-informed opinion *(doxa)* of the citizen, the patient, and the passenger is contrasted with the genuine knowledge *(episteme)* of the philosopher-king, the physician, and the navigator. Even so, he warned, one's possessing a *techne* or specialized technical knowledge is not tantamount to having true insight into the good. For this and other reasons, the otherwise understandable temptation to designate Plato as the first proponent of epistemocracy is fraught with anomalies and interpretive problems too numerous and difficult to discuss here.[27] One might then be tempted to turn to Hobbes. For it was Hobbes who first claimed to have set political philosophy on a firm scientific footing, and to have based the undivided authority of the sovereign upon that foundation. But, again, the temptation should be resisted. For nowhere does Hobbes claim that the sovereign is smarter or in any way more knowledgeable than his subjects. Whatever its other features, Hobbes' ideal commonwealth is no epistemocracy.[28]

In its full-blown form, the epistemocratic ideal may most justly be traced to nineteenth-century positivism, and to Saint-Simon and Comte in particular. Holding that "domination should be proportionate to enlightenment," Saint-Simon called for the management and coordination of social and economic relations by twenty-one experts.[29] The authority of *les industriels* rests in particular upon the *kind* of knowledge that they purport to possess. Theirs is, above all, a nomological knowledge of the heretofore hidden general laws governing human behavior. As Comte put it, "Social phenomena are subject to natural laws, admitting

of rational prevision" and, hence, of purposive human intervention, manipulation, and control. Rather than controlling their
own affairs, the citizenry must henceforth defer to the authority of experts. The "elite of the human race" can now be trusted
to manage the affairs of the whole society. Those outside that
elite have no right to engage in the "mischief" of criticizing
those more knowledgable than they. Indeed, "the critical spirit,"
Comte continues, "is directly contrary to that which ought to
reign in scientific politics."[30]

It is altogether too easy to dismiss these as mad utopian fantasies. Modern variations on this epistemocratic theme include
Lenin's notion of a vanguard party, the behaviorist utopia of
B.F. Skinner's *Walden II*, and, still more recently, the vision of
a coming post-industrial "knowledge society."[31]

The only thing wrong with earlier versions of epistemocracy
and epistemocratic authority, say the prophets of post-industrialism, is that they were premature.[32] The sort of knowledge
needed to "steer" (note the Platonic navigational simile) a complex society was not available to anyone in Plato's day, and least
of all to philosophers. Nor was such knowledge needed in order to govern a small society like the Greek *polis*. By contrast,
the steering of large, bureaucratized, centralized societies requires specialized skills and expert knowledge. Questions about
arms control and disarmament, defense expenditures and
weapons systems, foreign policy, public assistance programs,
pollution and toxic waste disposal, alternative energy sources,
the exploration of space, acid rain, and a hundred others seem
more suited for scientists than for citizens. We are therefore
understandably tempted to turn to them, not only to advise
and guide but to govern us. Already those who are nominally
or formally in authority are apt to turn to someone who is an
authority on this subject or that. One who is an authority is
required to fulfill a function that those in authority are unable
to fulfill. The epistemocratic ideal is one in which politicians
are replaced by planners and citizens by clients. It is an ideal to
which political reality in some respects increasingly corresponds.

That the influence of this new class of epistemocrats is increasing has been noted by enthusiasts and critics alike.[33] Enthusiasts like Daniel Bell and the late Herman Kahn see the

emergence of epistemocracy as a hopeful development. Critics like Robert Dahl and Michael Walzer are less sanguine, seeing in this development a danger to democracy.[34] The danger, I want to suggest, is not that we will concede too much authority to experts but that we will come to think of political authority exclusively in terms of expertise. Thus my question is not, How much authority should we give to the experts? but is instead, What would the political world look (and be) like if one of the concepts constitutive of political discourse—that is, authority—were to be construed along epistemocratic lines, as advocated by the prophets of post-industrialism? In sketching the barest outlines of an answer I shall suggest, strange as it may sound, that epistemocracy poses a danger not only to democracy but to political authority itself. Epistemocratic authority is in fact a debased simulacrum of political authority precisely because it is an oxymoron. Let us see why.

In its epistemocratic form, "authority" in matters moral and political is assimilated to the paradigm of epistemic authority: one is *in* authority because he or she is *an* authority on something. This assimilation assumes that politics and ethics are activities in which there are experts, and that most of us are not now, and perhaps cannot even aspire to be, expert in these matters. To see why and in what respects this epistemocratic contention might be mistaken, we could do worse than to consult Aristotle. Although he can scarcely speak to us with the authority that he once possessed, Aristotle did draw some useful distinctions which we ignore at our peril. In Aristotle's distinction, politics is *praxis,* not *poiesis* or *techne.* If politics were a "technical" rather than a "practical" activity, it could be left to the experts. But politics is not, in the nature of the case, an exact science admitting of determinate answers about which there can be no dispute or disagreement, but an art—the art of collective deliberation, dialogue, and judgment. From the fact that politics is a dialogical activity admitting of differences of opinion and judgment it follows either that in politics and ethics there are no experts or, as Aristotle would have it, that each citizen has expertise sufficient to join the discussion, to listen and learn, to hear and to be heard. Or, to put it another way, politics is not essentially an instrumental or goal-oriented activity undertaken for the sake of some separately identifiable end, but is instead the medium of the moral education of the citizenry and the very activity an end in itself.

When the late Carl Friedrich averred that authority involves the "capacity for reasoned elaboration," he did not go quite far enough in the right direction.[35] For the engineer, scientist, technician, physician—indeed any expert to whom epistemic authority is ascribed—can also supply reasons for arriving at a particular conclusion or recommending one regimen rather than another. But when epistemic authority (being *an* authority) is used as a model or template for analyzing political authority (being *in* authority), we misunderstand the essential distinguishing features of the activity of politics and of the place of authority in that practice. The kinds of reasons that are relevant in political deliberation are those internal to that practice and arrived at in the course of that deliberation itself. Politics, as Gadamer reminds us, is a matter of practical reason. To turn to experts and the kinds of reasons that they can give, and which we may or may not understand, is to denature politics by viewing it not as *praxis* but as a *techne*. It is this misunderstanding, more than any other, Gadamer contends, that has deformed and debased the concept of authority. And this deformation is due less to ambitious would-be epistemocrats than to disaffected citizens eager to cast off the burdens of citizenship:

> . . . the problem of our society is that the longing of the citizenry for orientation and normative patterns invests the expert with an exaggerated authority. Modern society expects him to provide a substitute for past moral and political orientations. Consequently, the concept of *"praxis"* which was developed in the last two centuries is an awful deformation of what practice really is. In all the debates of the last century practice was understood as application of science to technical tasks. This is a very inadequate notion. It degrades practical reason to technical control.[36]

This epistemocratic deformation of politics and practical reason, Gadamer continues, "is the peculiar falsehood of modern consciousness: the idolatry of scientific method and of the anonymous authority of the sciences." To recognize that "practical and political reason can only be realized and transmitted dialogically" would be to "vindicate again the noblest task of the citizen—decision-making according to one's own responsibility—instead of conceding that task to the expert."[37]

The epistemocratic rejoinder is that this democratic ideal cannot be realized in modern society. The democratic vision of an active, informed, and responsible citizenry is naive at best, and dangerous at worst. Ill-informed people are apt to make mistakes that are altogether too costly to risk. Better, then, to leave such matters to experts. To this criticism Dahl's reply is eloquent:

> It is true that a democratic regime runs the risk that the people will make mistakes. But the risk of mistake exists in all regimes in the real world, and the worst blunders of this century have been made by leaders in nondemocratic regimes. Moreover, the opportunity to make mistakes is an opportunity to learn. Just as we reject paternalism in individual decisions because it prevents the development of our moral capacities, so too we should reject guardianship in public affairs because it will stunt the development of the moral capacities of an entire people. At its best, only the democratic vision can offer the hope, which guardianship can never do, that by engaging in governing themselves, all people, and not merely a few, may learn to act as morally responsible human beings.[38]

As a vision of political authority, then, the epistemocratic vision of rule by an elite of experts is deficient for reasons that are at once empirical, pedagogical, moral, and civic.

CONCLUSION

To rebuild authority along either emotivist or epistemocratic lines requires dismissal of a number of distinctions. As regards the former, perhaps the most important of these, as MacIntyre says in another context, "is the fact that emotivism entails the obliteration of any genuine distinction between manipulative and non-manipulative social relations."[39] Epistemocratic authority conflates the distinctions between epistemic and epistemocratic authority and between being *in* authority and being *an* authority, in both instances by assimilating the former to the latter. And as our society becomes increasingly rationalized, the social scientist's studied indifference to these and other distinctions assumes added political importance. As Arendt often noted, to conflate conceptual distinctions is to make our language not more precise but less, thereby impoverishing the very medium through which political communities are constituted and reconstituted.[40] To reconstruct "authority" is not merely to alter the meaning of the word but to restructure the world in ways both subtle and ominous. As Arendt and Gadamer and Dahl remind us, politics is a dialogical activity practiced by citizens. Its medium is speech, its form of reason "practical" in the original meaning of that term.[41] As the concepts constitutive of that speech are corrupted—primarily by being confused with other, nonpolitical concepts and practices—the activity it makes possible is also impoverished. That some sectors of our society and many modern governments have an interest in impoverishment of this sort seems beyond doubt or dispute. Political and social scientists, in particular, might do well to ask themselves whether they should be aiding and abetting this process, or resisting and criticizing it.

All tales have a moral and mine is no exception. Language is not a neutral medium but is fraught with moral meaning. As we speak, so we are. To reconstruct the concepts comprising our language is therefore to re-remake ourselves and to see and be in the world in new ways.[42] We had best be wary, then, of the understandable temptation to revise the concepts that are constitutive of moral discourse and human agency. Perhaps, by way of warning, we should say of the emotivist and epistemocratic "models" what George Eliot said of metaphors: "For we all of us, grave or light, get our thoughts entangled in metaphors, and act fatally on the strength of them."[43]

NOTES

For their painstaking criticisms of an earlier version of this essay, I am greatly endebted to Mary Dietz, James Farr, and the Editors. All remaining errors are, alas, my own.

1. Richard Tuck, "Why is Authority Such a Problem?" in *Philosophy, Politics, and Society*, fourth series, eds. Peter Laslett, W.G. Runci-

man, and Quentin Skinner (Oxford: Basil Blackwell, 1972), pp. 194–207. For further details on authority's problematic character, see Steven Lukes, "Power and Authority," in *A History of Sociological Analysis*, eds. Tom Bottomore and Robert Nisbet (New York: Basic Books, 1978), pp. 633–676; and Richard E. Flathman, *The Practice of Political Authority* (Chicago: University of Chicago Press, 1980), passim.

2. For those who find Michel Foucault's terminology more illuminating than I do, these first two approaches might be termed the archaeological and the genealogical, respectively. Their complementarity is emphasized in William E. Connolly, *The Terms of Political Discourse*, 2nd ed. (Princeton: Princeton University Press, 1983), pp. 231–243.

3. One of the best examples of this third approach is Felix E. Oppenheim, *Political Concepts: A Reconstruction* (Chicago: University of Chicago Press, 1981). Unfortunately, Oppenheim considers "authority" only in passing (pp. 22–23).

4. Søren Kierkegaard, *The Concept of Irony*, trans. L.M. Capel (London: Collins, 1966), p. 47.

5. Hannah Arendt, "What Was Authority?" in *NOMOS I: Authority*, ed. Carl J. Friedrich (Cambridge: Harvard University Press, 1958), pp. 81–112, at 81. Subsequent references are to the revised version, "What is Authority?" in *Between Past and Future*, expanded ed. (New York: Viking Press, 1968), pp. 91–141.

6. Arendt, "What Is Authority?" p. 102.

7. Ibid., p. 95.

8. Ibid., p. 96.

9. Ibid., p. 103.

10. Hans-Georg Gadamer, *Truth and Method*, trans. Garrett Barden and John Cumming (New York: Crossroad Publishers, 1984), p. 248.

11. John H. Schaar, *Legitimacy in the Modern State* (New Brunswick, N.J.: Transaction Books, 1981), p. 2.

12. Although "concepts, like individuals, have their histories, and are just as incapable of withstanding the ravages of time," they nevertheless "retain a kind of homesickness for the scenes of their childhood." Kierkegaard, *The Concept of Irony*, p. 47. If I read her aright, Arendt's analysis of "authority" addresses that sense of homesickness by reconstructing several salient features of that concept's childhood. The exercise is not, however, sentimental or reactionary but critical and restorative.

13. Thomas Hobbes, *Leviathan*, ed. C.B. Macpherson (Harmondsworth: Penguin, 1968), II, ch. 19, pp. 239–40. I have argued elsewhere that Hobbes's complaint about the state of nature is pre-

cisely that it is a condition in which something like the emotivist theory of meaning is true, and that this is itself a good (if not a sufficient) reason for leaving that natural state. See my "Hobbes' Linguistic Turn," *Polity* 18 (Summer 1985): 739–760, at 757–759.

14. See, e.g., David Easton, "The Perception of Authority and Political Change," in *NOMOS I: Authority*, pp. 170–196, and "The Political System Beseiged by the State," *Political Theory* 9 (August 1981): 303–325. Compare, inter alia, Harry Eckstein and Ted Robert Gurr, *Patterns of Authority* (New York: Wiley, 1975), and Oran R. Young, *Compliance and Public Authority* (Baltimore: Johns Hopkins University Press, 1979).

15. David Easton, *The Political System* (Chicago: University of Chicago Press, 1981; first pub. 1953), pp. 129–134. Cf. also *A Systems Analysis of Political Life* (Chicago: University of Chicago Press, 1979; first pub. 1965), pp. 21–33, 207–211.

16. Easton, *The Political System*, p. 132.

17. Ibid.

18. Ibid.

19. Ibid.; and the elaboration in *A Systems Analysis of Political Life*, pp. 205–209.

20. Easton, *The Political System*, p. 132.

21. Ibid., p. 133. Compare Easton, "The Perception of Authority and Political Change," pp. 179–182 and 185.

22. Easton, *A Systems Analysis of Political Life*, p. 208, n. 9.

23. Easton, *The Political System*, p. 133; my emphasis.

24. For an explication and defense of the notion of "epistemic authority," see Richard T. De George, "The Nature and Function of Epistemic Authority," in *Authority: A Philosophical Analysis*, ed. R. Baine Harris (University, Ala.: University of Alabama Press, 1976), pp. 76–93.

25. See, e.g., Richard S. Peters, "Authority," and Richard B. Friedman, "On the Concept of Authority in Political Philosophy," both in *Concepts in Social and Political Philosophy*, ed. Richard E. Flathman (New York: Macmillan, 1973), pp. 150–153 and 139–146, respectively; and Flathman, *The Practice of Political Authority*, pp. 16–19.

26. For a recent discussion, see Robert Dahl, *Controlling Nuclear Weapons: Democracy vs. Guardianship* (Syracuse, N.Y.: Syracuse University Press, 1985), chaps. 2 and 3. Dahl's suggestive and illuminating study is slightly marred by his failure to distinguish between Platonic "guardianship" and the later notions of "technocracy" and "meritocracy," the latter after Michael Young's splendid satire, *The Rise of the Meritocracy* (London: Thames and Hudson, 1958). Al-

though clearly related, both, I believe, can be further distinguished from what I call epistemocracy.

27. For a suggestive beginning, see Mary P. Nichols, *"The Republic's Two Alternatives: Philosopher-Kings and Socrates,"* *Political Theory* 12 (May 1984): 252–274.

28. It is instead, I believe, a linguistically constituted commonwealth. See my "Hobbes' Linguistic Turn," op. cit.

29. Henri Comte de Saint-Simon, *Social Organization, the Science of Man, and Other Writings*, trans. and ed. Felix Markham (New York: Harper Torchbooks, 1964), p. 77.

30. Auguste Comte, in *Auguste Comte and Positivism: The Essential Writings*, ed. Gertrud Lenzer (New York: Harper Torchbooks, 1975), pp. 223, 57, 54.

31. See William Barrett, *The Illusion of Technique* (Garden City, N.Y.: Anchor Books, 1978) for an illuminating meditation on these matters.

32. My main source for what follows is Daniel Bell, *The Coming of Post-Industrial Society* (New York: Basic Books, 1976), esp. ch. 6.

33. See, e.g., *The Authority of Experts*, ed. Thomas L. Haskell (Bloomington, Ind.: Indiana University Press, 1984).

34. Cf. Dahl, *Controlling Nuclear Weapons*, ch. 1; and Michael Walzer, *Radical Principles* (New York: Basic Books, 1980), ch. 14.

35. Carl J. Friedrich, "Authority, Reason, and Discretion," *NOMOS I: Authority*, pp. 28–48, at 35 f.; and his later elaborations in *Man and His Government* (New York: McGraw-Hill, 1963), pp. 213–233, and "The Relation of Political Theory to Anthropology," *American Political Science Review* 62 (June 1968): 536–545. Gadamer reaches the same conclusion by a rather different route: *Truth and Method*, pp. 248–249.

36. Gadamer, "Hermeneutics and Social Science," *Cultural Hermeneutics* 2 (1975), pp. 307–316, at p. 312. See, further, Gadamer, *Reason in the Age of Science*, trans. F.G. Lawrence (Cambridge: MIT Press, 1981), pp. 69–87. For a historical sketch of the deformation of the concept of *praxis*, see Nicholas Lobkowicz, "On the History of Theory and Praxis," in *Political Theory and Praxis: New Perspectives*, ed. Terence Ball (Minneapolis: University of Minnesota Press, 1977), pp. 13–27.

37. Gadamer, "Hermeneutics and Social Science," p. 316.

38. Dahl, *Controlling Nuclear Weapons*, p. 51.

39. Alasdair MacIntyre, *After Virtue* (South Bend, Ind.: University of Notre Dame Press, 1981), p. 22.

40. See Arendt, "On Violence," in *Crises of the Republic* (New York: Harcourt Brace Jovanovich, 1972), esp. pp. 142–155; and the powerful title essay in Schaar, *Legitimacy in the Modern State*.

41. Compare de Jouvenel's reminder that "The elementary political process is the action of mind upon mind through speech . . . Even as people belong to the same culture by the use of the same language, so they belong to the same society by the understanding of the same moral language. As this common moral language extends, so does society; as it breaks up, so does society." Bertrand de Jouvenel, *Sovereignty*, trans. J.F. Huntington (Chicago: University of Chicago Press, 1958), p. 308.

42. This point is powerfully made by James Boyd White, *When Words Lose Their Meaning: Constitutions and Reconstitutions of Language, Character, and Community* (Chicago: University of Chicago Press, 1984).

43. George Eliot, *Middlemarch* (Baltimore: Penguin Books, 1965), p. 111.

4

PERSPECTIVES ON AUTHORITY

STEVEN LUKES

What is authority? It is an old question. Indeed, Hannah Arendt in the first *NOMOS* volume asked "what *was* authority?" somewhat nostalgically, fearing that even the answer might be lost in the mists of antiquity. But the question goes on being asked and has recently received much renewed attention from political and legal philosophers.

The question is, on the face of it, at least two questions. It could be the analytical question: what are the elements of the concept of authority and how are they structured? What are the criteria by which we may recognize the possession, exercise, and acceptance of authority? How is it to be distinguished from other forms of influence over persons and from, say, persuading, threatening, advising, and requesting? Or it could be the normative question: what is legitimate authority? What is it that renders authority legitimate? What justifies the claims of authority as being worthy of acceptance? When should utterances be treated as authoritative?

Discussions of authority divide over the issue of how the analytical question relates to the normative question. Some hold that the questions are quite distinct: that we can elucidate the concept of authority and as a separate matter ask when, if ever, submission to it is justified. They may well go on to say that this latter question is not a timeless one: that what is justified in one context and from one point of view may not be so in and from another. Others hold that the questions cannot be divorced in this way. They hold that to do so is to advance a "relativized" notion of authority, according to which "we simply state what authority is had by whom from a certain point of view"[1] and that this "severs the connection between authority and practical reason."[2] For them the nonrelativized notion is primary and is presupposed by the relativized notion. On this view of the matter, to analyze authority is to analyze legitimate or justified authority, to which different people in different times and places lay claim and submit, some rightly, some wrongly. It is on this view not a matter of meaning that a person can have authority, be an authority or in authority only if his authority is recognized by some people whose identity will vary with the nature of his authority (though in practice, especially in political contexts, it will be contingently true that such recognition will be a condition of his exercising his legitimate authority effectively). On this second approach, establishing the grounds on which an authoritative utterance should be recognized as such is prior to all empirical inquiry into beliefs and practices. On the first, it is not. Indeed, on the first view, what is authoritative will not, in any given case, be independent of a whole web of beliefs, some explicit and some implicit in practices. Of course, not anything can be a ground or reason for treating an utterance as authoritative (e.g., that it is loud—though that could be a sign that there is such a reason). But what counts as such a reason will be internal to a web of beliefs.

Both approaches, however, concur in the aim of enabling us to identify relations of authority and distinguish them from others. What I seek to suggest in this chapter is that such identification is an even more complex matter than is often supposed and always involves a process of interpretation. More particularly, I claim that every way of identifying authority is relative to one or more perspectives and is, indeed, inherently perspectival, and that there is no objective, in the sense of perspective-neutral, way of doing so. This feature of attributions of authority has, I think, been far too little attended to in the voluminous literature on the topic, including that compatible with its recognition.

Without analyzing or exploring the notion of "perspective" here,[3] I mean it to refer to a point of view, a more or less integrated set of ways of seeing and judging matters of fact and practical questions, not excluding basic moral and political questions, and incorporating beliefs about the possibilities and necessities of social life, and about how the self, its relation to society, and its manner of reasoning are to be conceived. In this domain, of course, the reality upon which perspectives bear is itself in part constituted by contending perspectives. To speak thus of perspectives is not in itself to embrace any deep form of relativism: some will be, for example, more perspicuous or comprehensive or consistent than others. Typically, different perspectives—and at what points and how much they differ will in turn be variously interpretable—are associated with different positions within a social relation (such as an authority relation), with different social and political roles (e.g., the judicial, the bureaucrat's and the citizen's perspectives) and with different activities (e.g., the actor's and observer's perspectives). How to individuate perspectives is a complex question into which I cannot go here. The question of whether differences of belief and judgment are variations within one perspective or demarcations between two cannot be answered in the abstract and in general. The answer will depend on the reasons for which perspectives are being discriminated. I do not of course mean to suggest that any one person ever adopts only one perspective. We all engage in multiple relations, roles, and activities and accordingly adopt and negotiate multiple perspectives.

For the purposes of what follows, I shall distinguish a number of potentially different perspectives. First, with respect to the authority relation itself, we can distinguish between the exerciser or holder of authority and those who accept or are subject to it. I shall, in the time-honored philosophical fashion, call the first A and the second B and thus speak of *perspective A* and *perspective B*. I shall call the observer (who may or may not be internal to the authority relation or to the society in which it occurs) C and his perspective *perspective C*. Authority relations generally occur within a wider framework of social norms and conventions, legal and customary. Some of these are officially and definitively interpreted by judges, courts, and representatives of the state. I will call this perspective society's official perspective or *perspective SO*. This is likely to diverge at various points from prevalent, unofficial, and informal understandings of such norms, rules, and conventions. I shall call such unofficial ways of understanding *perspective SU*—and, on the plausible assumption that these will be various and conflicting, SU_1, SU_2 . . . SU_n. It is, however, often suggested that there is, in some or most societies, an underlying consensus that will be implicit in, though distinct from, SO and SU_1 . . . SU_n, which may be elicited by a sensitive interpretation or reconstruction of a society's beliefs and practices. This notion of consensus has long played a role in contemporary sociology and has recently surfaced in political philosophy. It is what Michael Walzer relies on in order to determine the criteria that demarcate his "spheres of justice."[4] And it is what John Rawls supposes will result from the confrontation of a society's unreconstructed beliefs with theoretical criticism through "reflective equilibrium." Let us call this third, consensual social perspective *perspective SC*. (We can see it as an amalgam of perspectives SO and SU interpreted from perspective C.) Finally, we may postulate a putative impersonal, "objective" and "archimedean" perspective from which all other perspectives may be assessed. Rawls calls it a standpoint that is "objective and also expresses our autonomy," which "enables us to be impartial, even between persons who are not contemporaries but who belong to many generations." To "see our place in society from the perspective of this position" is, he eloquently continues, "to see it *sub specie aeternitatis:* it is to regard the human situation not only from all social but from all temporal points of view." It is "the perspective of eternity"— not "a perspective from a certain place beyond the world, nor the point of view of a transcendent being; rather it is a certain form of thought and feeling that rational persons can adopt within the world."[5] Thomas Nagel calls it "a conception of the world which as far as possible is not the view from anywhere within it."[6] Let us call this perspective *perspective O*. One central question this chapter seeks to address is whether there is indeed any such perspective.

I now turn to consider some attempts to analyze the nature of authority. All mark out a distinctive mode of securing compliance which combines in a peculiar way power over others and the exercise of reason. On the one hand, authority appears to be part of that network of control concepts that includes power, coercion, force, manipulation, persuasion, etc. As Hobbes said, "command is a precept in which the cause of the obedience depends on the will of the commander" and "the will stands for the reason." Even authority over belief appears to involve an influence that bypasses rational argument. On the other hand, reason is plainly involved: authority offers a reason and operates through reasoning. Moreover, only rational agents are capable of claiming, recognizing and accepting authority. As Friedrich observed, it involves "a very particular kind of relationship to reason," namely "the potentiality of reasoned elaboration."[7]

I shall first consider three accounts exemplifying the first, "relativized" approach presented above, in order to illustrate the different perspectives that they exemplify. I shall then turn to a further account that illustrates the second approach in order to show that even an account that explicitly seeks to avoid perspective dependence fails and must fail to do so.

Consider first Max Weber's celebrated account of authority. Weber was, of course, concerned with *Herrschaft,* or domination, but he was interested specifically in "the authoritarian power of command," as against "domination by virtue of a constellation of interests (in particular by virtue of a position of monopoly"). Domination in Weber's preferred sense indicated the securing of compliance which occurs "as if the ruled had made the content of the command the maxim of their conduct for its very own sake."[8] He wrote,

> "The merely external fact of the order being obeyed is not sufficient to signify domination in our sense; we cannot overlook the meaning of the fact that the command is accepted as a 'valid' norm."[9]

Of course, Weber was well aware that commands may be obeyed for a wide variety of reasons: "the command may have achieved its effect upon the ruled either through empathy or through inspiration or through persuasion by rational argument or through some combination of these three principal types of influence of one person over another."[10] Indeed,

> "In a concrete case the performance of a command may have been motivated by the ruled's own conviction of its

propriety, or by his sense of duty, or by fear, or by 'dull' custom, or by a desire to obtain some benefit for himself." [11]

Yet it is a striking fact that Weber's sociology of domination never explores these possibilities by investigating the question "When and why do men obey?" or looks at authority relations from below, that is, from perspective B. On the contrary, his classification of authority is exclusively from perspective A, in terms of prevailing rationales for obedience—claims typically made by those in command. As Parkin observes, Weber never asks "whether the legitimations put out by traditional, charismatic and legal-rational authorities differed in the degree to which they were actually endorsed by the masses." [12] On the contrary, he proceeds throughout "as though widespread endorsement of all three types of legitimation was typically found among all and sundry." It is "as if Weber simply assumed the correctness of Marx's dictum that the prevaiing ideas in any society are the ideas of its ruling class." [13] I suspect this may be because Weber, as a cynical "realist" concerning power, and despite his talk of the "voluntary" acceptance of maxims, basically saw prevailing principles of legitimation (especially democratic ones) as "myths" injected into the masses by elites. At all events, the Weberian approach, while offering an illuminating classification of authority claims, succeeds in identifying authority relations by only taking account of perspective A. Authority on this view is the securing of compliance by command on the basis of claims, of the three indicated types, assumed to be accepted by the commanded.

Consider next the illuminating analysis of the authority relation offered by Richard Friedman, as consisting in two tiers: first, "that special and distinctive kind of dependence on the will or judgment of another so well conveyed by the notion of a 'surrender of private judgment;' " and second, "the recognition and acceptance of certain criteria for designating who is to possess this kind of influence." [14] This analysis is intended to cover both the cases of "an authority" and "in authority."

In both cases, "we have to see the notion of authority in connection with the idea of a very special sort of reason for action (or belief)"; one difference being that "belief in authority calls for internal assent, whereas the notion of acting in conformity to the commands of authority allows for the dissociation of thought and action."[15]

A claim to the former, Friedman suggests, rests on the ground of "superior knowledge or insight, that makes belief, and not merely external conformity, the appropriate response to authority."[16] It presupposes an inequality of knowledge, insight, or wisdom prior to the authority relation itself; and it presupposes the epistemological claim that such superior knowledge, insight or wisdom is in principle available. It presupposes, in short, "a world of common beliefs and the recognition of inequality in the capacity of men to understand those beliefs."[17]

By contrast, the relation of those "in authority" to those who defer to them presupposes a world in which there is "a complex *recognition* of dissensus and equality at the substantive level over against which men are prepared to step up to the procedural level and abide by the decisions of the person designated as being 'in authority,' whether or not those decisions happen to coincide with their 'private' opinions."[18] Indeed, authority serves to mark off the distinction between private and public in this sense. Such authority is a response to a "predicament" in which "a collection of individuals wish to engage in some common activity requiring a certain degree of coordinated action but they are unable to agree on what the substance of their common behavior should be."[19] In general, according to Friedman, both forms of authority imply "some mutually recognized relationship giving the one the right to command or speak and the other the duty to obey. Authority thus involves a form of influence that can only be exercised from within a certain kind of normative arrangement accepted by both parties."[20]

Friedman's account is decidedly an improvement on Weber's. It hinges on the notion of mutual recognition: what is essential is that perspectives A and B agree in "a certain kind of 'recognition' that the person to whom one defers is entitled to this sort of submission."[21] Legitimation claimed and the according of legitimacy coincide in a shared recognition of entitlement. That recognition may be based on a very wide range of possible "marks" or credentials of authority—"office, social station, property, 'great' power, pedigree, religious claims, 'miracles' (Augustine) etc."[22]

A number of problems are raised by this account. Less seriously, it seems obvious that many cases of "an authority" over belief need not involve mutual recognition of that authority; such authorities can go unrecognized and they can be seen as authorities unwittingly or posthumously. Similarly, persons "in authority" may sometimes properly be said to have it even if those subject to it fail to endorse it, as parents and teachers know well. Second, Friedman's discussion of the "marks" of authority does not successfully distinguish between *signs* and *grounds:* the crown and scepter are the former, the regal office they betoken the latter. But two more serious problems arise. First, what are the criteria by which these "marks" are recognized as marks of authority? Is it just up to the parties in an authority relationship to fix on anyone they wish to recognize as authoritative? And second, what is the nature of that recognition? Is it like a "cue" triggering off "blind obedience" and the "surrender of judgment?" Or is a process of rational judgment involved?

These last two questions are addressed by the third account we will consider, namely that of Richard Flathman. He answers the first by placing the authority relation within a wider "practice" of authority in which shared values and beliefs prevalent in a community play a constitutive part. And he answers the second by firmly resisting the notion of a "surrender of private judgment," maintaining this notion to be "at the very least, seriously misleading."[23]

For Flathman, both "in authority" and "an authority" relations are "grounded in shared values and beliefs to which we are referring as the authoritative":[24] the "partly constitutive character of the values, beliefs, actions and so forth of subscribers . . . to a set of rules, institutions, etc." is "a central feature of our entire theory of authority."[25] But how are these to be identified and just how do they bear on the authority relation? Sometimes, Flathman seems to be referring to perspective SO, as when he, rather oddly, assumes that "the values and beliefs which make up Marxism-Leninism are now among the constitutive features" of the practice of authority in the Soviet Union.[26] Sometimes, he seems to be referring to SU, without any real sensitivity to the systematic divergences it embraces—as when, rather baldly, he remarks that "if we are trying to determine whether Ivan had authority in sixteenth-century Russia we must ascertain the criteria that had standing among sixteenth-century Russians and we must determine whether sixteenth-century Russians thought those criteria were satisfied."[27] Sometimes, as when discussing the shared values and beliefs of modern liberal democracies, as allowing for disagreement and the practice of civil disobedience, he seems to be embracing a version of perspective SC.

But a further and deeper problem is raised by his rejection of the notion of the surrender of private judgment and his insistence that participants in the practice of authority are making "judgments grounded in evidence and reason," that there is within the authoritative "a basis both for grounded, reasoned judgments concerning it and for grounded reasoned disagreements concerning those judgments"[28] and his call for a "critical justificatory theory of authority."[29] Do such judgments transcend the confines of prevailing authoritative beliefs and values? Or, to make the same point conversely, does the "authoritative" in part determine what counts as convincing evidence or a good reason? What kind of a constraint does "evidence and reason" place upon the constitutive character of the "authoritative?" Flathman rejects what he calls "collectivistic subjectivism" but we need to know more about why he does so.

So I turn finally to an account of authority that fearlessly avoids such dangers and temptations by offering a straightforwardly rationalist "critical justificatory theory of authority" on the assumption that this can be done independently of and prior to any "relativized" way of conceiving it, while acknowledging that "the relativized notion is useful because it reveals the views of people or societies concerning non-relativized authority."[30] The account in question is that developed in a number of writings by Joseph Raz. I shall refer here to his 1979 book *The Authority of Law* and to his 1985 article "Authority and Justification"[31] in which the relation between authority and reason and the justification of authority are systematically explored.

Raz, starting from the "basic insight" that "authority is ability to change reasons for action,"[32] sees authority as "a species of normative power" which changes such reasons by exclusion. Thus, orders are both first-order reasons (for acting) and "exclusionary reasons" which "exclude by kind and not by weight:" their impact is "not to change the balance of reasons but to exclude action on the balance of reasons."[33] Accepting authority involves "giving up one's right to act on one's judgment on the balance of reasons;"[34] the authority is legitimate if such exclusionary reasons are valid.

When, then, is authority legitimate? What renders its exclusionary reasons valid? Raz advances what he calls the "dependence thesis," namely that *"All authoritative directives should be based, in the main, on reasons which already independently apply to the subjects of the directives and are relevant to their action in the circumstances covered by the directive."*[35] The "normal" and "primary" way to show that one person should be acknowledged to have authority over another is given by what he calls the "normal justification thesis:" it is to show *"that the alleged subject is likely better to comply with reasons which apply to him (other than the alleged authoritative directives) if he accepts the directives of the alleged authority as authoritatively binding and tries to follow them, rather than by trying to follow the reasons which apply to him directly."*[36] These reasons need not be confined to the furthering of his interests (as when a military officer orders soldiers to defend their country, against their personal interests). Other justifications for accepting authority—such as consent, or respect for the law, or identification with a community—are merely secondary. They are valid only if they accompany the primary reason. Typical of situations where the normal justification holds are those presenting coordination problems, including prisoner's dilemma type situations. Indeed, Raz argues, solving coordination problems is one of the important tasks of political and many other practical authorities. The key idea (especially in relation to politics) is what Raz calls "the service conception of the function of authorities"—namely, that "their role and primary normal function is to serve the governed," which they do when they "help them act on reasons which bind them."[37]

Raz's attempt is to "explain the notion of legitimate authority through describing what one might call an ideal exercise of authority." It is through their "ideal functioning" that the practice of authorities must be understood. This is given by how they publicly claim that they attempt to function, which is "the normal way to justify their authority."[38]

This is an unwarrantably rapid summary of Raz's complex account, which is the most perspicuous analysis of the concept to date and the most systematic attempt I know of to escape the problems we have been investigating, by presenting an analysis of authority relations that purports explicitly not to be an account of "what authority is had by whom from a certain point of view."[39] Does it do so?

I doubt it. For Raz, "the normal and primary way of justifying the legitimacy of an authority is that it is more likely to act successfully on the reasons which apply to its subjects;"[40] accepting legitimate authority offers the advantage of having found "a more reliable and successful guide to right reason."[41] But how are we to ascertain what the reasons that apply to authority's subjects are and in what "success" in acting on them or guiding us to them consists?

There is a whole range of cases where the answers to these questions seem obvious and uncontroversial. The traffic policeman, the tax authorities, legislators, judges, military officers, parents can all be seen as "in the main," at least in certain areas, directing us to act on reasons that independently apply to us, so that we may properly see them as having the right to replace people's own judgment on the merits of the case. Of course the legitimacy of such authorities is (in perhaps ascending order of frequency) questioned, on particular occasions, over whole ranges of cases, and (as with anarchists, pacifists, and revolutionaries) in general. It may be questioned in various ways. They may be held to have a false or misconceived idea of the "reasons which apply to [their] subjects." Lawmakers and judges may be denounced for being out of touch with the interests and needs of those they purport or are claimed to protect and guide (as they have been by blacks in the U.S. or opponents of abortion). Military leaders may appeal to duties and commitments that both soldiers and citizens reject (as in the U.S. during the Vietnam War or Israel during the later stages of the invasion of Lebanon). Secondly, the legitimacy of authorities may be questioned on grounds of "reliability" and "success," the reasons applying to their subjects being taken as given. Corrupt policemen and incompetent military regimes (rarely) lose their legitimacy in this way. But either way, Raz would probably argue, questioning the legitimacy of particular authorities, even in general, in

these ways does not show that they would not be legitimate if
the conditions set by the normal justification thesis were to be
met.

I fail to see how the reasons that apply to authority's subjects,
on which authoritative directives should be based, are to be ascertained in a perspective-neutral manner. The objectives an
authority is to further are not determinable a priori and are
often matters of intense controversy. On the other hand, it is
plausible to suggest that, once such objectives are agreed, the
question of a given authority's "reliability" and "success" (like
that of an investment consultant) could be seen as a matter of
fact. yet even this is not obvious. What is being judged: the
institution or its agents, and over what period of time? Raz's
phrase "in the main" leaves leeway here too for judgment and
interpretive dispute.

The sorts of cases we have considered are plainly those on
which this account of legitimate authority is centrally based and
to which it is most obviously applicable. The most obviously
applicable cases are those in which authority establishes or helps
sustain conventions, seen as solutions to coordination problems,
or enables people to escape prisoner's dilemma type situations.
More generally, this account works best for all those cases where
there is what we might call an extrinsic relation between authoritative directives and reasons they depend on and replace.
Authority on this view is an invaluable device to achieve, more
reliably and successfully, independently given and agreed objectives that would otherwise be less easy or impossible to at-
tain. Even here, as we have seen, there is much room for interpretive dispute as to which objectives are relevant and what
constitutes success.

But what of cases where the relation between authority and
reason is intrinsic: where the objectives authority serves are internal to, that is shaped and sustained by, the authority relation
itself. The examples that come most naturally to mind here are
religious, though the point is far wider than that. The role of
the priesthood is, in part, to lead men along the path of righ-
teousness or truth, as it is interpreted by the priesthood—to
show the way to destinations that people might not have conceived apart from it (that is, apart from the institution and tradition it embodies)—and may not even be characterizable with-

out presupposing it (e.g., living according to the Torah). The fundamentalist preacher, say, and his congregation are in a relationship of self-reinforcing authority, in which the word of God (as he interprets its expression in the Bible) gives them reasons for actions concerning which he is, in turn, the authoritative guide.

Religious examples demonstrate this intrinsic relation with clarity. Here the "primary normal function" of authority is not always best described as "serving the governed." Of course, religions often do have instrumental functions, promising (as magic typically does) to bring benefits in the here and now or (more probably) in the hereafter. But they also have soteriological functions and Durkheimian social functions, both of which involve *transforming* rather than serving their adherents—by leading them to salvation, imbuing them with faith, giving meaning to their lives, and so on. In such cases, the legitimacy of authority does not lie in its reliability and success in securing independently given objectives, as measured against some objective standard, since it itself defines the objectives and sets the standard. And this applies, beyond religious cases, to all cases of intrinsic authority, where Raz's picture of an exclusionary reason justifiably preempting the balance of reasons does not really fit. A better picture might be that of a dominant reason that reduces the significance of other reasons that would otherwise prevail, and removes the point of weighing them. Thus (to take disparate examples at random): charismatic leaders define their followers' goals, the legitimacy resting on "the belief in and devotion to the extraordinary, which is valued because it goes beyond the normal human qualities" and "transvalues everything;"[42] the Party prescribes certain objectives as primary; psychoanalysts (on one view of what they do) transform their patients' self-understanding; women exhibit patriarchal attitudes. In all these cases, it seems that if authority is justified, it is justified from a point of view, namely that of the authority itself, which becomes that of the subject.

It may, of course, be replied that only extrinsic authority is legitimate: only if putative authorities guide their subjects extrinsically to "right reasons" can their claims be justified. In this case, we are owed a doctrine of "right reason," indicating which *are* the "reasons which bind them." Moreover, it is not clear why, on principle, this reply should be given. Are there no cases of legitimate intrinsic authority? More generally, it may be suggested that the analysis proposed is, in principle, neutral between different perspective-dependent accounts within which different reasons, or sorts of reasons, can be judged to be "right reasons." This suggestion would bring Raz's analysis much closer to the position this paper seeks to advocate, since it leaves the answer to the question, When is authority legitimate? perspective-dependent. However, for the reason indicated in the previous paragraph, it is not clear that the analysis itself, with its "service conception" of authority's function, successfully captures the nature of authority as understood in all contexts and cultures.

We are, it is clear, back to the problem with which we began. We are offered a test by which claims to authority that are imposed (à la Weber), mutually recognized (à la Friedman) or culturally given (à la Flathman) are to be judged genuine or spurious. Could such a test be perspective-neutral?

The very idea of such a test is central to our cultural tradition. Since the Enlightenment, we have believed that some such test should be available, distinguishing "right" from spurious reasons, autonomy from heteronomy, self- from other-directedness, and providing a bedrock for practical judgment. This strand of our tradition is deeply hostile to priestly power, paternalism, and mystifying ideologies of all kinds. Basic to it is the image of an autonomous rational individual. Consider now the metaphor at the heart of Raz's account. "Exclusionary reasons," excluding by kind rather than changing the balance of reasons, conjure up the old image of the scales of justice, and therewith an underlying and specific conception of the subject of authority. It suggests, in a word, a distinctly judicial conception of the individual, weighing and balancing, in an impartial spirit, the reasons that present themselves, in order to reach an independent judgment as to what to do or think "all things considered"—but on occasion allowing "binding" reasons to prevail. Yet this picture of the individual is not unique. Other pictures exist to which other styles of reasoning are central[43]— Talmudic, Confucian, Buddhist, etc.—whose relevance to the testing of authority claims merits investigation. Indeed, the thought suggests itself that Raz's aspiration to perspective-neutrality shapes his very notion of the subject, and that this aspiration and notion are no less perspective-dependent than any other.

Indeed, Raz freely admits that his argument is "inescapably a normative argument," "part of an attempt to make explicit elements of our common traditions," a "partisan" account "furthering the cause of certain strands in the common tradition by developing new or newly recast arguments in their favor."[44] The critical justificatory theory of authority he develops is true to "our" concept of authority and behind it to "our" notion of the reasoning subject. It offers a test for legitimacy that is tailor-made for Friedman's "second world," riven by conflicting interests and opinions but with a shared interest in the procedural resolution of coordination problems. It is, unquestionably, worth defending and propagating, in a world in which authoritarian and obscurantist notions of authority are rife and growing. But it is, while compelling, "our" view, gaining its plausibility from the web of beliefs in which it is embedded. For this reason, I agree with Flathman's suggestion that "caution is appropriate in positing—as for example Joseph Raz does—a 'non-relativized' notion of authority that is a presupposition of the 'relativized' notions we in fact find among this or that historical people."[45]

NOTES

1. J. Raz, *The Authority of Law* (Oxford: Oxford University Press, 1979), p. 11.
2. Ibid. Cf. Hannah Pitkin, *Wittgenstein and Justice* (Berkeley: University of California Press, 1972), pp. 280 ff.
3. See my "Relativism in Its Place," in M. Hollis and S. Lukes, eds., *Rationality and Relativism* (Cambridge: MIT Press, 1982).
4. M. Walzer, *Spheres of Justice* (New York: Basic Books, 1983).
5. J. Rawls, *A Theory of Justice* (Cambridge: Harvard University Press, 1972), p. 587.
6. T. Nagel, *Mortal Questions* (Cambridge: Cambridge University Press, 1979), p. 208.
7. C.J. Friedrich, "Authority, Reason and Discretion," in C.J. Friedrich, ed., *NOMOS I: Authority* (Cambridge: Harvard University Press, 1958), p. 35.
8. Max Weber, *Economy and Society*, ed. G. Roth and C. Wittich, 2 vols. (Berkeley: University of California Press, 1978), pp. 943, 946.

9. Ibid., p. 946.
10. Ibid.
11. Ibid., pp. 946–7.
12. F. Parkin, *Max Weber* (London: Methuen, 1982), p. 78.
13. Ibid.
14. Richard B. Friedman, "On the Concept of Authority in Political Philosophy," in R. Flathman, ed., *Concepts in Social and Political Philosophy* (New York: Macmillan, 1973), pp. 131, 134.
15. Ibid., p. 135.
16. Ibid., p. 143.
17. Ibid., p. 146.
18. Ibid., pp. 145–6.
19. Ibid., p. 140.
20. Ibid., p. 134.
21. Ibid., p. 131.
22. Ibid., p. 133.
23. Richard E. Flathman, *The Practice of Political Authority* (Chicago: University of Chicago Press, 1980), p. 124.
24. Ibid., p. 26.
25. Ibid., p. 231–2.
26. Ibid., p. 87.
27. Ibid., p. 228.
28. Ibid., p. 234.
29. Ibid., p. 232.
30. J. Raz, *The Authority of Law*, p. 11.
31. J. Raz, "The Justification of Authority," in *Philosophy and Public Affairs* 14 (Winter 1985): 2–29.
32. J. Raz, *The Authority of Law*, p. 16.
33. Ibid., pp. 22, 23.
34. Ibid., p. 26. However, "there is no reason for anyone to restrain their thoughts or their reflections on the reasons which apply to the case" ("The Justification of Authority," p. 10) and one may always challenge a putatively authoritative directive on jurisdictional grounds by questioning whether it has violated the conditions of its rightful power.
35. J. Raz, "The Justification of Authority," p. 14.
36. Ibid., p. 19.
37. Ibid., p. 21.
38. Ibid., p. 27.
39. *The Authority of Law*, p. 11.
40. "The Justification of Authority," p. 20.
41. Ibid., p. 25.
42. H.H. Gerth and C. Wright Mills, *From Max Weber: Essays in Sociology* (New York: Oxford University Press, 1948), pp. 296, 250.

43. See M. Carrithers, S. Collins and S. Lukes, eds., *The Category of the Person: Anthropology, Philosophy, History* (New York: Cambridge University Press, 1985).
44. J. Raz, "The Justification of Authority," p. 27.
45. R. Flathman, *The Practice of Political Authority*, p. 77.

5

GOVERNMENT BY
CONSENT

JOSEPH RAZ

The idea that the legitimacy of government rests on consent is deeply embedded in Western thought. The role of consent in the legitimation of government is the topic of this chapter, and its theme is that this role is only marginal and secondary.

The first section explains the nature of the problem within the context of the wider issues of the justification of government. The argument begins in the second section with one of the familiar paradoxes of authority, the conflict between authority and autonomy. The attempt to escape from the paradox by basing authority on consent leads to a consideration of the ability of consent to form the foundation of any political authority.

AUTHORITY AND DOMINION

It is common among philosophers to regard the problem of the justification and limit of governmental power as identical with the legitimation and limits of governmental authority. Governments exercise authority by giving binding instructions. But their power is not bounded by their authority. Governments like everyone else have rights under private law which enable them to own property and make contracts. In contemporary industrial societies two processes go hand in hand. Governmental economic power continues to increase. In many countries they are the largest employers, the biggest customers of advanced technology, and so on. At the same time governments have a growing tendency to use their economic power to achieve goals that used to be regarded as requiring governmental authoritative action, legislative or executive. Partly they do so in order to evade the complex machinery for controlling governmental action, which, in many countries, is stricter and more efficient regarding their activities as public authorities using authoritative powers. Partly they do so because use of economic muscle enables governments to achieve many objectives more efficiently than the use of their authority, with its often inevitable reliance on the inefficient and not infrequently counterproductive criminal penalties.

A theory of the justification of government should encompass both aspects of governmental power. A just government is one that conducts itself justly in both its capacities. It is tempting to say that in their use of economic power governments are just like any other person, that only their public authority is subject to the principles of justice that apply to states. But this would be a formalistic view, assigning too much importance to the means by which power is exercised. What matters is the power governments have over people, their actions in exercising these powers, and the goals that inform those actions. In all these respects, since governments tend to regard the choice of methods they employ, i.e., the invocation of public authority on the one hand or action as a private agent in the market on the other hand, by and large as a matter of expediency, it is plain that both methods, both kinds of power should be subjected to the same principles of justice.

This is not meant to deny that each aspect of governmental power raises unique moral issues. In particular I do not wish to obscure the fact that exercise of authority involves a claim that those subject to it have a duty to obey it. This raises the special problem of the legitimacy of authority, which is but one aspect of the wider issue of the justification of government. Explaining the conditions under which, and the ways in which, governments may operate as property owners involves setting principles defining the goals they may pursue and the ways in which they may manipulate the environment in which we live in order to achieve them. Both questions are pertinent to the justification of authority as well. But here a new question arises: What can justify holding some people to be duty-bound to obey others? Under what conditions can some have a right to rule others?

Consent theories are those that find the answer to these questions in the consent of the subjects to the authority of the rulers. Consent theories are not and cannot be complete accounts of the justification of government. They are addressed to the question of the legitimacy of its authority, not to the issue of the justification of its dominion. Their dominance, at times, in writings on the justification of government is evidence of the narrow perspective through which theorists often see the problem of government.

Having said that, I will concentrate on the role of consent in legitimizing authoritative power. Consent may enter the theory of legitimacy in three ways. It may be a condition, or the condition of holding legitimate authority. Or, though not a condition of legitimacy itself, those conditions may be such that only a government based on the consent of the governed meets them. Finally, legitimate government may deserve the consent of its subjects. They may have a duty to give it their consent. In popular political thought government by consent often means a government whose constitution and policies enjoy the support of the majority of the population. This is not the sense of consent in traditional consent theories of authority. They are concerned with the conditions for holding binding authority, and whether having the consent of a person is either a necessary or a sufficient condition of having authority over him. This is the problem to which we must now turn.

AUTHORITY AND AUTONOMY

One may start by recalling one of the familiar paradoxes of authority, the conflict between authority and autonomy. Authorities, argue some philosophical anarchists, are there in order to decide for their subjects. Therefore to admit that an authority is legitimate, which entails that its directives are binding, is to hold that those subject to its authority must surrender their judgment to that of the authority. This is inconsistent with their autonomy. Therefore one cannot have legitimate authority over autonomous persons.[1]

Many of the attempted refutations of this argument miss its point. They argue that all that follows from the fact that an authority is legitimate is that its subjects ought to give its directives some weight in their deliberations. The directives of a legitimate authority are valid reasons for action. But that, so the attempted refutations proceed, does not mean that one surrenders one's judgment to the authority. There is nothing more problematic in giving authoritative directives weight on one's deliberations than in giving similar weight to the needs or desires of other people. In both cases one's action should be affected by the way other people are or behave. But in both cases it is up to one to decide for oneself how to act. Autonomy implies an independent exercise of judgment in determining one's conduct in the light of right reason. It does not imply that what is right for one is unaffected by the conduct of others. The anarchist confuses the issue of who decides with the question of what are the valid reasons that the decision should take into account.

Appealing as this response sounds it fails to meet the anarchist challenge, for it ignores its source. It ignores the fact that authority is justified only if its directives make it more likely that those subject to them will, if they acknowledge the legitimacy of the authority, better conform to reasons which apply to them anyway, i.e., reasons which should guide the action of the subjects if the directives are not issued.[2] If this is so then authorities function by displacing their subjects' judgments. They function, and can only legitimately function, by substituting their own judgment for that of their subjects. I will not argue for these conclusions here.[3] But it may be worth noting that they are strongly supported by the common belief that it is the duty of governments to govern in the interest of the governed, and that a degree of success in doing so is an important element in any justification of political authority.

If these premises are accepted then it follows that authoritative directives ought to be such that in conforming to them their subjects will be acting as they should act in virtue of reasons that apply to them independently of the authority's action. Sim-

ilarly it follows that an authority is legitimate and its directives
are binding only if they meet this condition to such a degree
that its subjects will better conform with reasons that apply to
them if they try to follow the authority's directives than if they
do not. I shall therefore refer to it as the condition of legitimacy. Finally, it follows that normally authorities should issue
directives after considering how their subjects ought to act and
what would be best for them, in order to judge which directives
might conform most closely with the above condition.

There is only one respect in which these conclusions diverge
from the premise that government is legitimate only if it is in
the interest of the governed. This common premise excludes
the right of governments to pursue moral objectives when these
are not in the interest of the governed, or perhaps only when
they conflict with it. On this conception it would appear that if
an active anti-apartheid policy is not in the interest of Americans, not even in their long-term interest, then the U.S. government should not pursue anti-apartheid policies. This result is
paradoxical, at least if one assumes that each American ought
to contribute his share to the struggle against apartheid. If the
most effective means of doing so is by the government taking
action in the name of its citizens why should it be barred from
doing so by endorsing anti-apartheid policies that will help its
citizens do their moral duty? One can avoid the paradox by
claiming that though the U.S. government's duty to its subjects
is to look after their interests and nothing more, it has another
duty to protect human dignity wherever it is infringed, and
that is why it ought, within bounds, to adopt anti-apartheid
measures.

I find this an unsatisfactory conception, for it assumes that
the duty to protect human dignity conflicts, in the apartheid
case, with the government's duty to its citizens. It seems to me
more plausible that if individual Americans need not contribute to the protection of human dignity outside their country
their government has no reason to do so either. That is, it seems
plausible to regard the government in this as in other matters
as acting for its people. Individual Americans contribute their
share to the protection of human dignity throughout the world
in part by getting their government to act in a way consistent
with that aim, and by supporting it when it does so. This point

does not, however, make any difference to the argument below. Those who disagree could still accept the argument of this chapter once they replace the above condition that authoritative directives should be such (that in acting on them their subjects would be pursuing reasons which apply to them anyway) with the narrower condition that the directives should be such that by conforming to them their subjects will be serving their interests better than if they do not.

As was noted above, in normal circumstances this condition of legitimacy can be best satisfied, can indeed be satisfied at all, only by authorities that act having done their best to establish what is the right or the best way for their subjects to behave. There are exceptions to this rule. Sometimes the best way to achieve a certain result is not to aim at it, just as in order to hit a moving target one should aim not at it but in front of it. Advocates of the virtues of the market often argue that one of them is that by aiming at one's own good one does, in a free market, serve the interests of the community better than in any other way. They typically contrast the market with attempts to achieve the same goals through the actions of authorities that specifically aim at them. Be that as it may, it is common ground that authorities try to establish what is the best course for them to pursue. And since that is the issuing of directives which, if followed, will enable their subjects to conform to reasons that apply to them better than they otherwise can, authorities typically engage in trying to establish what those reasons are.

This fact, which is at the heart of our understanding of authority, gives the lie to the claim that valid authoritative directives are just ordinary reasons with (prima facie) force to be added to the balance of reasons when considering what is to be done. Governments decide what is best for their subjects and present them with the results as binding conclusions that they are bound to follow. A government does not merely say to its subjects: "Here are our laws. Give them some weight in your considerations. But of course you may well be justified in deciding that on balance they should be disobeyed." It says: "We are better able to decide how you should act. Our decision is in these laws. You are bound by them and should follow them whether or not you agree with them." Take taxation, for example. Let us assume that its justification is in the moral reasons individuals have to contribute to the provision of certain communal services. The government assesses the just rate of contributions and demands that each of us should pay as assessed. It does not say: "We think that that is the just rate, but we will understand if you refuse to pay, provided you did so after giving careful consideration to the balance of reasons, our demand included." They say: "It is for us to decide what is the just rate of pay. You must pay the sum we prescribed unless you fall into one of the exceptions we allowed for."

We all know that the claim I have just described is not the expression of one government's excessive zeal. It is part of the notion of government, part of the way in which, by their very nature, all governments operate. Whatever else they are, they claim the right to rule us by right reason, i.e., to take over from us the job of deciding what we should do, on certain matters. Does it follow that the anarchist is right and that there cannot be a legitimate government over autonomous people? Yes, if one assumes that autonomy requires that one does not hand over to anyone the right to decide for one. But if so, then one abandons one's autonomy when one authorizes an agent to represent one in a sale or in some complex commercial negotiations. One surrenders one's status as a moral agent when joining a trade union which has the power to reach binding agreements concerning one's wages and conditions of employment. And one cannot appoint an attorney to conduct a lawsuit without losing one's status as an autonomous moral person. For all these are just a few of the innumerable occasions on which people find it reasonable to give up their right to decide for themselves on certain matters, in certain circumstances. True, in none of them is one put under an authority that claims such an extensive right to rule as do governments. We shall return to this point below. But it does not bear on the argument against the anarchist.

The anarchist claimed that submission to authority is inconsistent with autonomy. We saw that his argument is not guilty of the confusion with which it is often charged. The anarchist regards an authoritative directive not as a consideration to be added to the balance of reasons but as a decision by another that displaces his right to act on his own judgment on the merits of the case. In this he finds the disturbing and problematic aspect of authority. And in this he is right. He further claims that autonomy implies always deciding every issue for oneself on the merits of each case. This is an unargued-for misconception. One way of wisely exercising one's autonomy is to realize that in certain matters one would do best to abide by the authority of another.

GOVERNMENT BY CONSENT

The argument above may give the impression that the conciliation between autonomy and authority is to be found through consent. This is a popular mistake. But it derives from a powerful picture, whose force must be acknowledged. Autonomy is a notoriously slippery notion. But whatever else one may say of it, it has to do with controlling one's life by one's own decisions. To consent is to take a decision for oneself. Therefore, whereas duties appear problematic from the autonomy perspective, for having a duty to perform an act denies one's freedom to act as one wishes, obligation assumed through consent appears to point to the only source of obligation that is consistent with autonomy.[4]

The flaw in this view is familiar. It presupposes that consent is a valid source of obligations but does not explain why. One requires an explanation why one's decision now should bind one later. One cannot dispose of the point by saying that whatever one does structures one's future options, and that many of one's actions or inactions restrict future options. This shows that if consent is a valid source of obligation then it is not the only case by which a person's present actions limit his future options. But this is no way to explain why consent is a source of obligations.

The need for an explanation finds no parallel in ordinary acts. There is no special need to explain why if I lock myself in a room and throw the key out of the window my options for the immediate future are rather limited. But there is a need to explain why consent to stay in a room restricts my options. For it does so only if it is a valid source of obligations. And what is and what is not a valid source of obligations is not a brute fact. It is an intelligible fact that can be explained and which is what it is because of the availability of the explanation.

Many explanations were of course offered for the binding force of obligations undertaken through voluntary consent. If consent is binding then those who can so bind themselves have an additional asset that is a marketable commodity. They can undertake obligations in exchange for some other benefits. It is in their interest to have that asset, and rules that serve people's interests are valid rules. Therefore, consent is binding. Another explanation emphasizes that consent is a way of incurring special obligations, i.e., a way of incurring obligations over and above the common duties that every person owes anyone else, or which he owes all other members of his community. In that sense voluntary obligations help in the formation of special bonds between people. Since it is desirable that people should form special ties, consent is a binding way of creating obligations.

Both explanations are good ones, or rather they point to the way sound, complete explanations can be developed. There are other good explanations for the validity of consent. There was never a problem in finding good explanations. The problems lay elsewhere. One was the tendency of many to assume that there can be only one true explanation. Those who fall into this trap assume that they have refuted all other accounts of the binding force of consent by producing an account of their own. They then proceed to argue that consent does not have certain features or consequences because it does not have them in virtue of their account of it.

Another surprisingly common fallacy is the assumption that consent, i.e., truly voluntary and informed consent, either does not bind at all or can bind one to anything one consents to. In fact, each justification of consent validates certain categories of acts of consent but not others. And while by multiplying justifications one can extend the binding categories, there is plenty of reason to believe that not all kinds of consent are binding. Take consent to perform a moral atrocity. It can be used to foment or express a special bond between people, or to gain benefits for the agent. But it is not the sort of relation that people should have, nor is it desirable that they should gain advantages by such means. As it seems unlikely that any other justification of consent will extend to this type of case it is not a case of valid consent. Those who consent to perform atrocities are not bound by their consent.

Doubts about the range of valid consent are particularly pressing when considering the question of authority by consent. A voluntary undertaking to obey a government, which is the major part of consent to its authority, is evidently unlike the common or garden variety of voluntary undertakings, such as agreeing to babysit for a neighbor, to prepare the first course for a party organized by a friend, to go on a three days' march in support of a campaign calling for a nuclear freeze, and so on. The nearest common undertaking is that of the marriage vows. It is a lasting commitment, encompassing many aspects of one's life. But marriages are closely regulated by law and by custom. The many uncertainties that the future holds notwithstanding, one's commitment in marriage is bounded by law and custom in a way in which consent to a government is not. It is considerably more comprehensive and more open-ended.

Governments typically claim authority to govern any and all aspects of their subjects' lives. They do in fact interfere with their education, their relations with their parents, with their children and spouses. They decide which sexual activities are allowed and when and where. They decide how many children one may have, how many spouses, and of what age and race. They decide whom one can visit and befriend, and where and how much, which religion one may follow and where, and in what form, which ideas one may propagate and by what means. One can go on forever with horrendous illustrations of the range of powers that governments claim the right to, and which they in fact exercise over people's lives. You may say: but my government does not control me in these ways, mine is a liberal and enlightened government. I think that most people who are tempted by this response will discover, if they take trouble to study the matter, that their government interferes with the life of its subjects in much more far-reaching ways than they imagine. But be that as it may. It is true that my list of examples is drawn from the activities of many states, some of them in far-away parts. But it is equally true that all of them are matters that each of our governments claims the right to decide. Whatever activity or pursuit you may think of, whether or not it is now forbidden by your law, your government claims the right to forbid it. In just about all states there are legal means to change any law, and to pass any conceivable or inconceivable law.

If consent to authority is consent to respect the claim the authority makes for itself, then it is hard to see what justification there can be for the binding force of consent to the authority of governments, given the extremely extensive powers modern governments claim to have. At this point some may feel that consideration of a long-overdue objection to my train of thought can no longer be postponed. I have dismissed the idea that consent is the only way in which authority and autonomy can be reconciled on the ground that the fact that obligations created by the agent's own consent are consistent with his autonomy is no explanation of why consent is binding. This is true, but it should not obscure the fact that autonomy provides a straightforward additional account of the validity of consent as a source of obligations.

The two justifications of consent sketched above consist in pointing out (a) that if consent is valid it increases the opportunities available to people, and (b) that the addition is likely to be to their advantage, i.e., to enhance their well-being. An autonomy-based explanation of consent also proceeds from (a), but it does not depend on (b). Instead it argues that increasing people's opportunities enhances their autonomy, for it gives them greater control over the course of their lives. Here as before we are not concerned with the precise shape of the notion of autonomy at work. It may well be that the present argument is based on an understanding of autonomy considerably at odds with that which underlies some of the other claims in the name of autonomy that were mentioned above. None of this matters to us as it does not affect the validity of the present argument. Its distinctiveness is in being rooted in autonomy and not in personal well-being. Even if people's use of consent is likely to detract from their well-being it is, according to this account, valid, for it enhances their autonomy. Autonomy is intrinsically valuable. One can use it in a way detrimental to one's interest, or in a way contrary to reason. This is no reason to invade or restrict one's autonomy. It is no mere means to rational action or to personal prosperity. Hence the autonomy-based account of consent shows that it is valid even in cases to which the previously delineated accounts do not apply.

This seems to vindicate the belief that autonomy and authority can be reconciled if, and only if, authority rests on consent. Authority then derives its legitimacy through an exercise of the autonomous power of its subjects and is therefore not in conflict with autonomy. That submission to authority is not in the interest of the subjects is irrelevant to the validity of their consent in so far as it rests on considerations of the value of autonomy. The last point should indeed be conceded, but the argument is flawed nonetheless, and for very familiar reasons. Consenting to be ruled by a government, when understood as the granting to it of the powers it claims to have, is not only an exercise of autonomy, it is also a submission to a power that may at any time take away all one's autonomy.

This is not the anarchist argument that was refuted in the first part of the chapter. I am not resting the claim on an alleged incompatibility of autonomy with authority as such. I am relying on the claim to unbounded power that authorities of one particular type, i.e., governments, make. My argument is that to the extent that the validity of consent rests on the intrinsic value of autonomy it cannot extend to acts of consent that authorize another person to deprive people of their autonomy. Whatever else one may gain by such submission to authority, no autonomy-based reason is served by allowing another to violate one's autonomy.[5]

QUALIFIED CONSENT

But is not the argument against the possibility of regarding consent as conferring authority on a government based on an unjustified all-or-nothing approach? Let it be assumed that there is a government that rules in a liberal and enlightened spirit. Let it further be assumed that all its subjects consented to its authority. Does not the autonomy account of consent justify holding their consent to be effective for as long as the government continues to rule in the same liberal and enlightened way?

I have not considered that possibility so far, for it is often assumed that consent to authority is an all-or-nothing affair. Either one consents to the claims that an authority makes for

itself or one rejects them. No halfway house exists. If so, I argued, consent cannot be regarded as the foundation of the authority of governments at all. It cannot even be the foundation
of the authority of governments that are behaving in the most
just way, for they all claim the power to rule in all respects. It
is now time to examine the suggestion that a qualified and
hedged consent to the authority of governments may be valid.[6]

The first question to arise is what qualifications are required
to render the consent valid. A ready answer is offered by the
condition of legitimacy explained in the first section: authoritative directives ought to be such that their subjects will be acting as they should act in virtue of reasons that apply to them
independently of the authority's action, and an authority is legitimate and its directives are binding only if, by and large,
they meet this condition to such a high degree that its subjects
will better conform to reason if they try to follow the authority's directives than if they do not. It was argued that when this
condition is met submission to authority is not inconsistent with
autonomy. Does it not follow that any consent to authority that
is subject to the qualification that it is valid only if the condition
of legitimacy is met is consistent with autonomy and is therefore binding in virtue of the autonomy account of consent?

At this point the anarchist is likely to protest. It is far from
clear that the condition of legitimacy that refuted the philosophical anarchist's challenge to the possibility of any authority
is able to resolve the doubt about the legitimacy of any political
authority. The reason should by now be clear. The condition
of legitimacy is concerned with one's success in following right
reason. An authority is legitimate, it says, only if by following it
one is reasonably successful in following right reason. What is
left out is what the believer in autonomy cares about most, i.e.,
that one should decide for oneself. In the first section above we
rejected the philosophical anarchist's claim that to be autonomous one must decide everything for oneself. Autonomy, we
said, is consistent with authorizing your lawyer to decide how
to handle your suit against your landlord, and authorizing your
doctor to decide upon examination whether mastectomy or ra-
diation therapy is most advisable, and to proceed to remove the
breast if he so decides, without further authorization. The doubt

remains whether autonomy is consistent with handing over to the government the right to decide everything for us, even if giving it this right will improve our conformity with reason.

Every government, as we saw, claims unbounded power to decree whatever it decides. The condition of legitimacy only says that it cannot have that power unless its use of it leads its subjects to conform to reason. This condition protects against one kind of danger. But does it protect our interest in autonomy? Is it enough that we can decide how to conform with the law, even if the law never tells us to do anything that we would have decided not to do had we decided how to act by ourselves, and had we been successful in following reason? Clearly, sometimes it is more important that we should decide for ourselves than that we should decide correctly. It is, e.g., generally thought that, at least within limits, it is more important that we should choose our friends and conduct our relations with them ourselves, than that we should do so wisely or successfully. So our first condition of legitimacy has to be supplemented with a second to the effect that governments can have legitimate authority only over matters regarding which acting according to right reason is more important than deciding for oneself how to act.[7] Since we saw that such matters exist, the anarchist's challenge is met. Government within the bounds set by the two conditions of legitimacy is consistent with the autonomy of its subjects.

But rebutting the anarchist's objection only leads to another objection. Is not the fact that an authority meets the conditions of legitimacy sufficient to establish its legitimacy? If so, what room is there for consent? It appears that one can validly consent only to an authority that is legitimate anyway on independent grounds. It is important to see that the objection is not repeatable against consent generally. It is peculiar to the case of consent to authority. The reason is that such consent, if valid without qualification, surrenders one's autonomy. This is not the case with ordinary consent. It means that consent to be governed can be binding only if limited so as to be consistent with autonomy. That entails that it must be consistent with the two conditions of legitimacy. But it seems that the two conditions are in themselves sufficient both to show that the governments that meet them are consistent with autonomy and that they are legitimate. There seems to be nothing that consenting to be governed can do. It imposes no duty and confers no right except those that exist independently anyway.

In common political discourse government by consent often means no more than democratic government. That is, the expression is used to refer to any structure of political authority with legal arrangements ensuring that the composition and decisions of the government are sensitive to the wishes of the adult population. It is arguable that in some countries some democratic constitution or another is better than any non-democratic alternative in the sense of satisfying the two conditions of legitimacy to a higher degree. The doubts just raised about the place of consent are not doubts about the advantages of democratic constitutions. We assume that some system of government, whether democratic or not, meets the two conditions of legitimacy. The question arises whether the fact that one or all its subjects consent to be governed under that system of government adds to its legitimacy.

CONSENT AND TRUST

At the very least consent cannot be denied one modest role. Those who consent to be governed by an authority that is anyway legitimate have strengthened their obligation, which now rests on two sources even if the one is a precondition for the existence of the other. In this way consent strengthens the bond between subject and government. But can consent do more? Can it make the difference to the legitimacy of an authority so that an authority that is not otherwise legitimate is so if its subjects consent to be ruled by it? The question boils down to this. The two conditions of legitimacy concern the value or otherwise of being subject to authority. What if consent to be governed is itself valuable? Would it not then be binding because of its own value, thus, indirectly as it were, lending legitimacy to the government one consented to?

This strategy seems impeccable.[8] But one may doubt whether it will ever yield the desired result. After all, we are considering consent to an authority that does not meet the two conditions of legitimacy. Consenting to its claim to unbounded rule has such far-reaching consequences that conflict both with one's welfare and with one's autonomy interests that it is hardly imaginable that it can have some other independent value which will compensate for these drawbacks. This observation seems to me right in general. But what if the authority concerned, though not meeting the two conditions of legitimacy, nearly does so? Here, you may say, consent sacrifices very little. It is possible that consent itself will be valuable to a degree that will justify holding it to be valid and thus conferring authority on a government that would lack legitimacy without it.

It is perhaps a trivial conclusion that if but a trivial gap blocks the argument for the legitimacy of an authority any trivial advantage in consenting will tip the balance. But I would like to mention one intrinsic value of consent to be governed that is not trivial, and is, to my mind, at the heart of the connection between consent and authority. Consenting to be ruled by someone expresses confidence in that person's ability to rule well. It is easier to see this if we think of personal relations. Think of a person putting his affairs in the hands of a friend when he goes abroad, or while he is ill in the hospital, or a person entrusting his children to the care of a friend. Consenting to be ruled by a friend is an expression of great trust, and as such is often greatly cherished. One may be deeply touched that one was so chosen. That very fact can help to cement the relation and to deepen it. As an expressive act consent has here an intrinsic value. People are aware of this and may entrust themselves or their affairs to the care of another because he is the one toward whom such a gesture of trust is most becoming, even though they know of another who is willing to take charge and will do so more successfully.

The same is true, and is recognized to be true, in our relations with our governments. It is seen in some of the attitudes people have to related actions, such as naturalizing in a country they emigrated to, or giving up the citizenship of a country they left. Naturalization normally involves an oath of loyalty. Given that consent to be governed is not a common event, it is one of the ways in which people come close to it in the course of ordinary life. Another is an oath of obedience and loyalty which one has to take upon assuming certain offices, e.g., judicial offices, or membership of the legislature of a country. In all these cases the oath is an expression of confidence and trust.

And in being such an expression it strengthens the trust that it expresses. It is no arbitrary legalism that one way in which in many countries a duty of loyalty to the state, and a right to protection by the state are created, is the taking of an oath of allegiance.[9]

If one believes, as I do, that loyalty and trust should mark the relations of a citizen to his government, in part because one's attitude to one's government is an aspect of one's attitude to one's society, then consent to be governed is intrinsically valuable as an expression of such an attitude and a way of strengthening it. Indeed the expressive value of consent may be considered to be of such importance as to refute the earlier suggestion that it can make a difference only when the conditions of legitimacy fail by no more than a small margin to establish the legitimacy of the government in any case. This would be a mistake. It overlooks the fact that trust is valuable only where it is deserved. There is no value in people trusting their fate to an immoral government, and such trust speaks poorly of the discrimination and the moral character of those who so misplace it. In these circumstances the expression of trust cannot be regarded as valuable either, and consent is not binding. Therefore, consent has an expressive value only where the conditions of legitimacy are satisfied or are nearly satisfied.

This point alerts us yet again to the dual nature of the argument from trust. On the one hand trust is owed to a just and humane government that has legitimate authority in virtue of the conditions of authority in any case. Since it is owed, acts that express and foment the attitude of trust are valuable. They are acts that one has reason to perform because of their intrinsic value.[10] Since they are intrinsically valuable there is reason to perform them even where no other reasons justify their performance, i.e., even when the conditions of legitimacy are insufficient in themselves to endow an authority with legitimacy. That is why such acts of consent are binding and why they can give legitimacy to an authority that does not have it for other reasons. On the other hand, since the value of such consent is due to the fact that it expresses and cements a relation of trust, and since trust is valuable only if it is not misplaced, the consent is binding, at least in so far as these considerations are concerned, only if the authority substantially meets the conditions of legitimacy in any case. Hence consent has an independent, but auxiliary and derivative, place as a source of legitimacy.

One final consideration: in as much as the validity of consent to authority rests on its contribution to an attitude of trust to the authority, consent must be regarded as a marginal special case since that attitude does not depend on consent, and is only exceptionally formed by it or expressed through it. It is arguable, and I have argued the point elsewhere,[11] that the very existence of an attitude of trust in the government includes as a constituent element an acceptance of an obligation to obey the government. And this can endow it with authority over the people who have that attitude, under the conditions we examined above. Such attitudes of trust and respect are normally formed not through deliberate decisions, let alone formal acts of consent, but through the normal habit-forming processes of education and habituation. They are none the worse for that. Such habit-forming processes can but need not be blind to reason. They can be responsive to right reason. In any case, where the attitude they give rise to is morally valuable it is so even if not acquired as a product of deliberate choice.

Consent represents merely one end of the spectrum in the myriad of processes and actions that lead to the formation of and that express this attitude of trust in one's government. It represents the deliberate and relatively formal end of that spectrum. This makes it particularly suitable for some circumstances, such as a public attestation of loyalty by officials. But inevitably it can have no more than a marginal ceremonial, as well as an auxiliary and derivative, role. So Hume understood the matter better than Locke.

Notes

1. The best defence of philosophical anarchism is in R.P. Wolff, *In Defense of Anarchy*, (New York: Harper & Row, 1970) though my discussion does not attempt to follow the details of his argument. Cf. my "Authority and Justification," *Philosophy & Public Affairs* 14 (1985):3, and Part One of my *The Morality of Freedom* (Oxford: Oxford University Press, 1986), for a more extensive discussion of the issues involved in the justification of authority. I there sup-

port the anarchist argument against attempts to claim that an authority can be legitimate even if its directives are not binding.

2. I shall assume thoughout this discussion that authority comes with a claim of legitimacy. Governmental authorities do not merely command their subjects. They also claim the right to do so. To acknowledge the legitimacy of an authority is to agree that it has that right. By normal usage mere de facto authorities, authorities who rule over their subjects but do not have a right to rule, are included among authorities. Many saw this as proof that an authority cannot be distinguished from a gunman by reference to a right to rule, for both may lack it. This is a non sequitur. While both may lack it, de facto authorities are characterized by their claim to have it, a claim that is typically acknowledged, sometimes unjustifiedly acknowledged, by at least some of the population they govern. Only those who claim authority can have it, one might say, remembering that it is the claim of legitimacy that is a condition of the possession of de facto authority.

3. See the references in note 1 above for the detailed argument.

4. I will concentrate exclusively on consent as a source of voluntary obligations. For an analysis of other aspects of consent and its relations to promising, see chapter 4 of my *The Morality of Freedom*.

5. It is generally agreed that the intrinsic value of autonomy is the value of an autonomous life, and not the value of one autonomous act throwing away one's autonomy once and for all. Whether or not a person reaching the end of his life may surrender the autonomy of the rest of it, and other similar questions, cannot be considered on this occasion.

6. A qualified consent, e.g., I will abide by whatever you say unless it adversely affects my interests, differs from an unqualified consent, valid only if certain conditions obtain, e.g., only if the authority's directive does not conflict with the subject's interest. But I will disregard this difference and will avoid considering which is the better view of the matter.

7. This brief discussion of autonomy shows that conformity to reason is not everything: how we decide what to do is, sometimes, of independent value. The value of autonomy comes to saying that sometimes there is intrinsic value in a person deciding for himself. But other considerations may make it desirable that others will decide for him, even though this will not improve his conformity with reason. This may free him to attend to other things, or it may relieve him of the anxiety that the need to decide for oneself imposes on many people. Such considerations show, as was pointed out to me by Professor Donald Regan, that the first condition of

legitimacy is not strictly speaking a necessary condition. I suspect that its satisfaction is in fact necessary for the legitimacy of any political authority, since the other reasons to abandon deciding for oneself generally in a whole class of cases are unlikely to apply in the relation of a subject and his government.

8. It would not seem so to someone who thinks that autonomy is a matter of all or nothing, and that its preservation has lexical priority over all else. I am assuming, however, that autonomy, in the sense relevant to this part of the argument, is a matter of degree and that other gains can justify compromising it to some degree.

9. It is not part of my claim that this is the only way in which trust and loyalty can be expressed or forged.

10. The argument of the text depends on regarding the relation between a valuable attitude and the actions that express it as an internal one. They are part of the attitude, constitutive of it, and not merely causal consequences of its existence, nor causes of it.

11. See Part 4 of my *The Authority of Law* (Oxford: Oxford University Press, 1979). I there refer to the attitude as one of practical respect, but its analysis makes clear that it is the same attitude that is under discussion here.

6

COMMENT ON LUKES

MARK TUSHNET

Steven Lukes's interesting paper begins with a reference to Hannah Arendt's question, "What was authority?" I wish to begin there as well, taking Arendt as suggesting that authority is a normative concept related in a complex way to actual social practices, and that it is always open to question whether a practice to which it refers now exists. I find that Lukes's perspectival account of authority, with one interpretation of which I largely agree, shows that "authority" has today a severely restricted scope, and that it is likely to shrink further.

Because my field is constitutional law rather than philosophy, I use a certain kind of rhetoric about the Supreme Court as my frame of reference. My attention is directed to the Supreme Court by three interrelated considerations. The first is Lukes's quotation from Carl Friedrich, who defines authority as intimately connected to "the potentiality of reasoned elaboration." Friedrich said that he drew this phrase from "a discussion group of Harvard faculty members, mostly from the Law School, who met [at the initiative of Lon Fuller] during 1956–57."[1] In the legal academy an entire school eventually grew up around the proposition that the Supreme Court engaged in the reasoned elaboration of something or other. But the doctrines of that school have been so undermined that no serious scholar can any longer maintain allegiance to it with a straight face.

Criticism has taken three forms. The earliest is the most straightforward.[2] Anyone who wants to engage in reasoned elaboration has to have some premises that are to be elaborated in a reasoned way. It was only the feeling that, during the 1950s, the United States experienced an "end of ideology"[3] that allowed people to think that authority flowed directly from reasoned elaboration. Once it became apparent that the selection of premises could be challenged, there was no reason to accord authority to reasoned elaboration unless one was prepared to give authority to those premises as well.

The second criticism is that the criterion by which one determines whether something counts as a reasoned elaboration in fact fails to sort out ways of presenting conclusions in a useful manner.[4] Whenever someone presented an argument that a Supreme Court opinion failed to satisfy the requirements of reasoned elaboration, it turned out to be rather easy to demonstrate that, even according to the critic's own standards, the requirements really were satisfied.

The third criticism of reasoned elaboration as linked to authority is for me the most important. Much as the first criticism began with the observation that premises could be questioned, the third criticism asserts that much of the discussion of reasoned elaboration appears to be concerned with judicial craft. I have suggested elsewhere that sometimes, what are criticized as departures from judicial craft are actually attempted innovations in judicial method.[5] For example, Justice Blackmun's opinion for the Court in the abortion cases[6] is widely regarded as unsatisfactory on "reasoned elaboration" grounds.[7] But one might have treated it as an effort to create a new sort of judicial opinion, which might be called the patently legislative opinion. If it succeeded, Justice Blackmun would have altered the criteria for determining what counts as an authoritative reasoned elaboration by the Supreme Court. Success of innovations can be determined only as time goes by. But some reason exists to think that Justice Blackmun's effort did indeed succeed. Recently the Supreme Court has engaged in similar legislative decision-making, as it assesses whether some statute or regulation actually does a reasonable job of what it seems intended to do.[8] The overall effect of these innovations is to place the notion of reasoned elaboration in question, a point to which I shall return.

These three criticisms of the idea of reasoned elaboration leave it gravely wounded. People frequently pay lip-service to the idea,[9] but when pressed abandon it so quickly that it is clear it no longer has any real intellectual force.

I find also of interest in discussions of the authority of the Supreme Court the frequent claim that its authority, as a social practice involving the effective articulation of norms, somehow rests on what it says. This is of course tied to the first charge, in that the claim usually was that the Court's authority, in the sense just defined, rests on its reasoned elaboration of the text of the Constitution, the norms embedded in the text, the norms expressed in the relevant precedents, or whatever. This claim combined a normative with a social proposition, and the latter has always been questionable. The social proposition is that, unless the Court's decisions are well reasoned, they will in fact lack the social efficacy that authoritative decisions ought to have. On its face this proposition is dubious. It is hard to believe that public acceptance of or acquiescence in a Court decision depends in any important way on how well the majority presented its case. Research on both public attitudes toward the Court and processes of implementing decisions bears this out.[10] Only a restricted group of people pays careful attention to the the Court's reasoning. Reasoned elaboration may create authority for that group, although even here I am skeptical. And that group may transmit some of its view to a larger group, as to which *it* has some authority. But as the message gets transmitted, it loses most of its connection to the criterion of reasoned elaboration.

The third development is related to the second. Political scientists have examined the conditions under which people and institutions comply with Court decisions.[11] I think it fair to say that, though they have discovered a lot of relevant variables, one that plays no role whatsoever is the degree to which the opinion satisfies the criterion of reasoned elaboration. From Lukes's perspective B, then, and perhaps from most perspectives SU(i), reasoned elaboration, that is, authority, has little to do with social practice.

Why is this so? Here I wish to present an argument that ultimately connects with Lukes's criticism of Raz. It begins with a summary of the criticism of the "reasoned elaboration" school in the legal academy. The debate developed with some critics asserting that a particular opinion failed to provide a reasoned elaboration of its conclusion. Defenders of the decision, if not always the opinion, responded by showing that the purported failure actually occurred because the majority of the Supreme Court placed more weight on some values than its critics did.[12] This line of defense connected the critique of reasoned elaboration to debates over balancing as a technique of adjudication. Here is what I regard as the best formulation of what balancing involves: "[B]alancing . . . [is] a mandate to perceive every . . . interest in a situation and to scrutinize every justification for restriction of individual liberty. Moreover, . . . [it] str[ives] for unifying principles that might guide future decisions. . . . [It] is rich in sensitive, candid, and articulate perceptions of competing concerns, and in overarching approaches which retain their capacity to instruct."[13]

That sounds nice, but when you look closely, it turns out that the words really mean very little. They provide guidance to a judge, or a critic, only in certain circumstances, of a sort identified by Lukes. To make sense of them, you have to be an insider to the process of adjudication. You have to agree, as Lukes puts it, that while there are conflicts of interest in the particular case, there is a shared social interest in its procedural resolution. To make sense of the idea of reasoned elaboration in adjudication, we need people who understand what it is. They share perspectives A and SO.[14]

I call this group a class. Of course, in every adjudication someone—the loser—could adopt a different perspective. The loser might deny the authoritativeness of the decision on the ground that, even accepting the insiders' criterion of reasoned elaboration, the decision lacks authority. If authoritativeness is denied on this ground, the concept and social practice of authority remain unchallenged. But another ground for denying authoritativeness would be that the loser rejects the insiders'/winners' criterion of reasoned elaboration. Here the concept and practice are directly challenged. This is the line taken by the third critique of reasoned elaboration mentioned earlier.

It then remains to ask how one could go about rejecting reasoned elaboration, and under what social circumstances. Here I adopt one version of Lukes's perspectival account,[15] and make the insider/outsider metaphor crucial. To reject the criterion of reasoned elaboration, the loser must see herself as a more or less permanent outsider, and reject the insiders' criterion of reason itself. Among legal academics, of course, the sense that the criterion of reason is unchallengeable is extremely strong. But that feeling ought to be undermined by challenges from two directions. First, some philosophers and anthropologists insist, in my view convincingly, that the criteria of reason are embedded in a matrix of social practices such that altering the practices can alter what counts as reason and, of course, vice versa.[16] Second, there is the feminist challenge, which I take it goes directly to the judicial conception, metaphors of balancing, and images of judgment as distanced from action. Feminists would substitute metaphors of webs and images of connectedness to describe the process of reasoning.[17]

This brings me, finally, to the question of the social conditions for the existence of authority. The first assault on the concept of authority appears to have occurred, at least for purposes of this discussion, at a time when the consensus underlying Lukes's perspective SC began to dissolve. The concept was successfully reconstructed for a while, by a variety of techniques, to produce nonrelativized conceptions. These techniques all made the notion of transcendent reason central to the concept of authority. The next assault on authority will occur, or is occurring, as the meaning of reason is brought into question. And that will occur, or has occurred, as losers in the particular begin to see themselves as outsiders in the general stream of things. That, at last, is why I used the word "class" earlier.

Notes

1. Carl J. Friedrich, "Authority, Reason, and Discretion," in *NOMOS I: Authority* (Cambridge: Harvard University Press, 1958), pp. 35, 40.

2. Arthur Miller and Ronald Howell, "The Myth of Neutrality in Constitutional Adjudication," *University of Chicago Law Review* 27 (1960): 661.

3. Daniel Bell, *The End of Ideology: On the Exhaustion of Political Ideas in the Fifties* (New York: Free Press, 1962).

4. I take my formulations of the second and third criticisms of reasoned elaboration from my own work, "Following the Rules Laid Down: A Critique of Interpretivism and Neutral Principles," *Harvard Law Review* 96 (1983): 781. Despite this, I believe that the formulations do capture a general belief in the profession.

5. Ibid., pp. 818–21.
6. 410 U.S. 113 (1973).
7. For a brief discussion, see "Following the Rules Laid Down," pp. 820–21.
8. See, e.g., Supreme Court of New Hampshire v. Piper, 470 U.S., 105 (1985).
9. See, e.g., Michael Perry, "Why the Supreme Court Was Plainly Wrong in the Hyde Amendment Case," *Stanford Law Review* 32 (1980): 1113.
10. See, e.g., Austin Sarat, "Studying American Legal Culture," *Law & Society Review* 11 (1977): 427.
11. See, e.g., Theodore Becker, ed., *The Impact of Supreme Court Decisions* (New York: Oxford University Press, 1969).
12. The best examples are Henry Hart, "The Time Chart of the Justices," *Harvard Law Review* 73 (1959): 84; and Thurman Arnold, "Professor Hart's Theology," *Harvard Law Review* 73 (1960): 1298.
13. Gerald Gunther, "In Search of Judicial Quality on a Changing Court," *Stanford Law Review* 24 (1972): 1001, at 1013–14.
14. This argument is elaborated in Mark Tushnet, "Anti-Formalism in Recent Constitutional Theory," *Michigan Law Review* 83 (1985).
15. It is possible, and some of his comments suggest that he is willing to do so, to treat Lukes's account as a simple story about relativism. But his account is more interesting, and I think more accurate, if, instead of claiming merely that people will differ on what authority is depending on where they stand with respect to particular exercises of authority, it claims that people will differ on what authority is depending on how they are situated systematically with respect to exercises of authority generally.
16. See, e.g., Bryan Wilson, ed., *Rationality* (New York: Harper & Row, 1970).
17. See, e.g., Carol Gilligan, *In A Different Voice* (Cambridge: Harvard University Press, 1982).

7

STUDYING AUTHORITY: KEEPING PLURALISM IN MIND

NANCY L. ROSENBLUM

INTRODUCTION: A GENERATIONAL PERSPECTIVE

The World War II generation of scholars identified authority with legitimacy. For them, Max Weber's typology of the claims rulers make to get themselves recognized and obeyed dominated the theoretical literature. The typology Weber provided for thinking about authority was political as well as analytic. Since he had not considered democratic authority a possibility, and since traditional authority had been eclipsed, it seemed as if rational-legal authority would have to bear the full burden of social cohesion. The alternative—the threat in the event that legalism was frail—was charismatic authority.[1] At the heart of this generation's work was a single urgent problem that Weber helped them to address: the stability of liberal democracy.

Altogether different questions are asked about authority today. Where Hannah Arendt had refused to consider the concept "authority" in general, the post-war generation of analytic philosophers does just that.[2] They identify its main elements. They debate whether some neutral or ideal concept is discoverable. These studies tend to be apolitical, strikingly so. They contemplate the meaning of authority apart from questions of acquisition, legitimacy, purpose, effectiveness, and institutions.

This turn to systematic conceptual analysis has occurred for good reasons. For one thing, in post-war liberal democracies the principal experience of authority may not be political at all. Authority is felt at home or school, in a labor union, athletic association, or church, or in our dealings with experts of all sorts. Certainly for women, the presence of state authority may be less imposing than male authority in settings like the family and work. As for government, its chief business is negotiating and bargaining, informing and inducing, planning and promising, so that what is most keenly felt is not authority per se but responsiveness or efficiency.[3] For most of us, the everyday experience of public authority is more likely to be as recipients of benefits than as subjects obligated to obey. It makes sense to replace a typology based on how rulers get subjects to obey commands with one that applies to authority throughout the full range of social contexts. This is the virtue of the main conceptual distinction currently in use, the distinction between authority of office and authority of expertise.

The tenor of much of the recent work on authority can also be traced to the fact that in a complex liberal society authority is pluralistic. Political authority is various and diffuse. Official policy often cannot be traced to an identifiable source or justified with a single rationale, or even with several noncontradictory ones.[4] Moreover, authorities throughout the various secondary associations of society are seldom congruent with political authority or with one another. Weber's classic typology simply does not suffice even as an introduction to this diversity, and in its place we have Harry Eckstein and Ted Gurr's exhaustive array of categories for studying patterns of authority, and innumerable empirical case studies, which seem to mirror rather than order diversity.[5] Surely the recent philosophical literature is in part an intellectual reaction against this daunting complexity. After all, identifying the universal elements of the concept "authority" is remote from identifying pluralistic authorities in practice.

In this chapter I discuss the current typology—authority of office and authority of knowledge or belief—in Part 1, and perspectives on legitimacy in Part 2, referring selectively to the recent literature on authority. The common thread running through these sections is pluralism, and the intellectual costs of the distance political philosophers put between their systematic definitions and what we know about the complexity of authority from other sources. These sources remind us that however precise philosophers may be in defining authority, authority relations, like other human relations, are messy and psychologically ambiguous. I go on to outline an unconventional defense of messy pluralistic authority in Part 3—"unconventional" because it is motivated neither by the perennial liberal preoccupation with autonomy nor by the wartime generation's preoccupation with the stability of democratic authority.

My defense of pluralistic authority in Part 3 has a personal cast. In a sense, it is a "romantic" defense. It associates pluralism with individuality and with desires for self-development and self-expression. It presents variety and ambiguity in authority relations as positive goods. My propositions are speculative. I hazard them because they provide fresh reasons for keeping pluralism in mind, reasons that I believe are shared by scholars of my generation whose formative political experiences occurred in the 1960s and 1970s. The connection between authority, and self-development and self-expression, suggests that compelling reasons for studying authority remain even in the absence of a crisis of democratic authority, and even when systematic analysis has done its work.

1. CONCEPTUAL ANALYSIS

a. Surrendering Judgment

Classical liberal theorists opposed the elements of authority associated with tyranny. They opposed the embodiment of political authority in persons rather than offices on account of the danger of arbitrariness, and they opposed a single hierarchy of offices on account of the danger of unlimited and efficient coercion. Political authority was circumscribed, divided, and diffused. But liberal theorists have always been more concerned with the way some authorities control beliefs, with their formative or manipulative ethos and the way they invite a particular kind of internal assent. In liberal theory, pluralism begins here. Political authority, which constrains action but is neutral or impartial in respect to loyalty and belief, is differentiated from authority that molds beliefs and inhibits judgment.

Contemporary conceptual analysis echoes this conventional

liberal distinction. Philosophiers begin by arguing that authority in general means not having to give reasons as a condition for being obeyed. Authority exists where subjects "surrender judgment." Already this definition of authority is resonant of liberal individualism, with its focus on the fate of judgment and the way "surrender" brings its opposite, victorious independence, immediately to mind. Philosophers go on to draw the distinction between someone "in authority" and someone who is "an authority on" some matter. In Richard Friedman's account, deference to the authority of superior knowledge does not exactly entail surrendering judgment because the experiences necessary for judgment do not exist.[6] Individuals believe what they are told without reflection or interpretation. We might wish that Friedman had refined this category. "An authority" relations seem to include everything from superstitious subordination to a cult leader to untutored subordination to expertise. It unites absence of judgment arising from an innate sense of inferiority, from fatalism, and from faith. But that is precisely Friedman's point. He wants to construct a typology that contrasts "an authority" and "in authority." Authority based on office is vulnerable to judgments of entitlement and correctness; only action on these private judgment is inhibited. The purpose of this type of authority is coordinated action, not common opinion. Constraint applies to behavior, not thought.

Recent conceptual analysis makes the status of judgment central just as traditional liberalism had, but without having recourse to epistemology, as did John Locke, or to a logic of judgment, as did Immanuel Kant. Not that the traditional liberal tendency to differentiate types of authority on the basis of control over belief was always psychologically sophisticated. It did not have to be, so long as it sufficed to separate out religious from political authorities. But traditional liberal *is* marked by considerable sophistication when it comes to subjection to political authority. Here, liberals added concepts of trust and distrust to judgment in discussing authority, and contemporary philosophical discussions of surrendering judgment seem thin by contrast.

The standard argument is Locke's. If neither constitutionalism nor a system of representation can determine the scope of political office once and for all, then discretion is a vital aspect of government and trust is inseparable from the exercise of public authority. Discretion means that even limited authority is open to partiality and abuse, so distrust is built into authority relations too. Paradoxically, trust buys subjects the time and distance they need to judge public authority.[7] Contemporary philosophy does not reflect this complex dynamic of trust and judgment. Even a journalistic description of the democratic citizen—"called on to pursue contradictory goals . . . active, yet passive: involved, yet not too involved; influential, yet deferential"—suggests ambivalence and movement and appears positively subtle next to the grim finality of "surrendering judgment."[8]

"Surrendering judgment" needs refining. In the context of the division of labor between pubic officials and private citizens we may want to describe trust as a suspension of judgment about the content of directives, but suspension does not evoke "surrender." Trust also differs from other situations when we do not insist on examining what we are asked to do, and defer to authority on account of apathy, or collective inertia, or because we distance ourselves by assuming the posture of spectators at a political drama rather than subjects. None of these cases conforms well to the formal definition of authority, which says that attributing authority to a command provides the determining reason for obedience.

And with Locke in mind, a further question arises: what makes us act on our judgments of authority when we do form them? For Locke, generalized distrust was a necessary condition for organizing resistance. Wherever structural opportunities for action matter, as they almost always do, inaction by itself may not signify recognition of authority. Yet the conceptual literature on authority has little to say about the objective external conditions under which judgments are made or surrendered, acted upon or not, or, fatally, how our actions appear to others. It is as if judgment were a purely internal affair.

In Locke's writings, authority and trust coexist in a complicated way. Effective authority ensures trustworthiness and promise-keeping among heterogeneous, often anonymous men and women who are not bound to one another by loyalty or common agreement. John Dunn observes that for some liberals only trusted authorities are effective in this, while for others only certain authorities deserve trust even though they may be appreciated and obeyed on other grounds.[9] That is what judgment is about: whether trust is deserved. Authorities may not have to give reasons for what they do, but they must convince subjects that they can be trusted and that they will fulfill expectations, which attach to many features of authority besides just expected outcomes. Contemporary definitions of authority relations neglect this element. For example, Richard Flathman's elaborate argument about justifiable authority relations follows classic liberalism closely, but without considering trust or observing that the object of judgment in liberal democracies is only sometimes authority's conformity to a formal system of rules or to an underlying web of shared beliefs. Expectations and judgment often have to do with character.[10]

Trust in authority involves personal trustworthiness. In addition to judging formal entitlement and the content of commands, which Friedman singles out, we judge character and intentions. We respond to personal qualities in public officials, beginning with honesty and moving on to more elusive elements of personality like decisiveness or responsiveness. We are always on the alert for signs of hypocrisy, too. These estimates are affective; they may not be reducible to principles at all. And it seems as if judging character is something we are unable to surrender. Romantic concern for authenticity and psychological sophistication about the motives of others combine to make preoccupation with personality irresistible. And democratic institutions reinforce this by inviting us to size up individuals all the time. Government actions are regularly dramatized and personalized by the media. Moral sentiments apply to character before anything else. Judging is not always done in the spirit of responsible citizenship, though. Politics as spectacle plays its part. When Friedman says that the claim to obedience made by a person "in authority" does not derive from any special personal characteristics, he defines authority in a fashion calculated to ignore a crucial aspect of democratic authority.

The dilemma posed by the need for both "eternal vigilance" and trust has played a large part in the political literature of the past two decades. Lockean liberalism emphasizes the need for distrust. By contrast, in response to political volatility in Western democracies during the 1960s, commentators were impressed with what they saw as massive distrust of authority, and they emphasized the need for surrender of judgment. Between these two positions lies more than just changed circumstances and the continuous search for a balance of scepticism and faith. In these contemporary writings, distrust is not associated with independent judgment but with alienation, normlessness, and irrationality. Distrust is taken to be a sign of vulnerability to extremist forces rather than political self-protection. Citizens are said to have surrendered judgment, not to authorities as they should have, but altogether and irrationally. Samuel P. Huntington pointed to a "democratic distemper."[11] When political scientists spoke of the need to restore habits of deferring to authority, it was apathy they had in mind, and not Walter Bagehot's traditional deference, Locke's trust, or analytic philosophers' "recognition of entitlement."

Political scientists in the 1960s and 1970s saw apathy as the counterpart of distrust. And they looked to apathy as a remedy for crises of authority for two reasons. First, it was considered a realistic response to the impossibility of participatory democracy. Given what they took to be the structural inevitability of powerlessness, uninvolvement was the alternative to continual crises of ungovernability. Second, apathy must have seemed to them to constitute a kind of proof that strong authority is still liberal, since apathy is not the same as unreasoning assent, and since widespread apathy is proof that authority does not compel belief or exact displays of loyalty and political enthusiasm. For these writers, appeals to obligation or to weighing the desirability of authority against the advantages or disadvantages of particular performances were futile. After all, what was most feared was incapacity for judgment and self-control.

When the motive for studying authority is to get more of it, it does no good to answer the question, "Why should I obey authority?" with the systematic philosophers' answer "Because that is what authority means." Instead, we see the question formulated as it had been for the wartime generation: what causes political authority to be believed in? Except that where the earlier generation had sought the answer in historical theories of legitimacy or in shared beliefs, political scientists in the 1960s looked to the political efficacy of elites. New studies emphasized the way skillful authorities could make pragmatic policy and at the same time manipulate symbols to arouse the necessary minimum of endorsement from a generally apathetic people.

The current conceptual literature ignores this work on symbolic politics. Yet studies on the power symbols have to evoke both cognitive and affective associations raise doubts about whether "surrender of judgment" is one single thing. Authority has both an instrumental and a symbolic face; our attitude toward one can be passive while at the same time we are insistent on satisfaction from the other. Our judgments of the two aspects of authority may diverge. Indeed, this is not unlikely, since authorities may not be equally successful at making pragmatic policy and invoking symbols and legitimating norms. The discrepancy between experience and symbol—in one example, "bureaucracy," a negative symbol—may explain why most Americans describe their own encounters with bureaucrats as positive (eighty percent feel they are treated fairly), but only 42 percent think that government agencies treat most people fairly.[12] Writings on political symbolism also challenge the usefulness of the conceptual distinction between judgments of entitlement and judgments of content. We know that people respond to public policies on the basis of symbolic presentation, so that identical programs proposed by the same formal authority have met with both acquiescence and resistance.[13]

The limitations of systematic conceptual analysis are most striking if we reverse the usual question and ask when it is that refusal to surrender judgment and the decision to act on our private judgments signifies failure of authority. We know that in business or government resistance by subordinates can be a dramatic way to inform superordinates, and that it may even strengthen their authority, and the organization as a whole. In Albert O. Hirschman's familiar terms, "exit" and "voice" can be as constructive as "loyalty."[14] Even if we accept that action on private judgment is subversive, at what point on the spectrum of distrust-passive obedience-disobedience-revolution does authority cease to have meaning?[15]

During the 1960s and 1970s political scientists assumed that distrust was a direct and sufficient cause of political activism, and that mobilization was identical to a crisis of authority. In fact, we know very little about the relation between attitudes toward authority and political action. The public opinion literature demonstrates the coexistence of distrust and discontent on the one hand and pride in the system on the other—proof that the psychology of authority relations is just as messy as it is for all our other relations. The withdrawal of general loyalty from political authority may still allow for pragmatic acquiescence. Or it may signal party realignment and new participatory institutions. But is rapid and radical institutional change the same as the failure of authority? The reverse is familiar too: authority may have a "reservoir of diffuse support" yet be the object of civil disobedience because "specific support" is lacking. Little of this ambiguity makes its way into the conceptual analysis of authority.

For this, we must turn to theorists of civil disobedience, who invite us to discriminate among political authorities, between a single authority and its performance in specific instances, and between isolated acts of disobedience and systematic disobedience, between refusal and revolution. They construct political theory out of familiar psychological materials, the fact that neither our sentiments of loyalty and affiliation nor our perspectives on authority are of a piece.

The observation that authority is not simply "there" for us or "not there" and that instead we move in and out of authority relations in careless ways and by indeterminate degrees is nothing new. Jeremy Bentham noted that "habits of obedience" are difficult to discern and can change from day to day. It should not be surprising to find imprecision tolerated here by a thinker normally obsessed with exactness. Concerned as he was with the ordinary business of government, Bentham knew that the instances when political authorities command subjects and when authority can be said to be measured by concrete acts of obedience—in wartime, mainly—are extraordinary. As a utilitarian, Bentham was also sensitive to the way public policy itself changes from day to day, so that expressions of authority become diffuse and banal. Once authority presents such a mundane face to us, it is especially unlikely that compliance can be identified with "recognition" and "surrender of judgment" rather than apathy, habit, utilitarian calculation, or some other elusive reason why men and women obey, or do not disobey.

Thus, the analytic literature arouses expectations of a logic of judgment and action that are not fulfilled. Its positive contribution is to move us beyond the original liberal differentiation of political from religious authority by creating a typology that applies to authority in general.

b. The Troublesome Relation Between "In Authority" and "An Authority"

By itself, the distinction between "in authority" and "an authority" is of limited interest. Its significance has to do with the relation between these types. What made the distinction powerful in classical liberal thought was that it evoked conflict between political authority and authorities of knowledge and belief. Many liberal thinkers anticipated and abetted the erosion of authorities that form our minds. Liberation from intellectual authority, and subjection only to legally limited authority of office, was what "enlightenment" was all about.

But other liberals have been less intent on eliminating authority over belief or authority of superior knowledge than on multiplying authorities of every kind. The "Millian" argument has it that pluralism ensures disagreement among authorities, which is necessary if they are to achieve self-understanding and correction. Authorities that are forced to recognize differences and to change are more deserving of trust than closed, hereditary ones. In the complementary "Madisonian" view, autonomy does not mean the absence of authority but instead not being subject to only one authority. By itself, public liberty does not solve the problem of private despotism. Freedom requires pluralism for individuals in practice, occasions to move in, out of, and among a variety of authority relations. "Spreading deference around" assuages the liberal fear of control over beliefs, since any single authority's attempt to inhibit judgment is likely to be undermined somewhat by the sheer dissonance of other claims. It is too much to say that by itself subjection to plural authorities consistently produces scepticism. But pluralism does provide impetus for the conclusion that no single source of legitimating norms extends everywhere.

When political philosophers write about "an authority" today, professional or scientific experts come to mind before religious or moral ones. And here it is fair to say that authority does mean "surrendering judgment." Here, the liberal dynamic of trust, distrust, and judgment is irrelevant. Deference to the superior knowledge of experts is just that, and stems from both a sense of inferiority and faith. Despite increased moves to seek "second opinions," the authority of scientific experts is often taken as a matter of faith in a way that political authority is not. Titles of authority can produce "surrender" by themselves. Whatever their deficiencies as models of social science research, Stanley Milgram's experiments remind us of what we know, or fear, about ourselves.

Perhaps the most important result of the current typology is that it draws our attention to the critical matter of the relation between authorities. Today, the urgent question is, when does authority based on office defer to expertise, and vice versa? This question becomes increasingly problematic with the rise of public paternalism and the growth of public policy about technology, ecology, and economics. The principal problem for liberal thought has shifted from how to contain abuses of authority to the Millian question, when is it good for people, *and their officials,* to be subject to the authority of superior knowledge?

Nearly everyone approves of paternalism for some purposes, but which ones? From the orthodox liberal standpoint, the cost of paternalism is loss of autonomy, which is vigorously defended by appeals to moral rights.[16] But when authorities disperse knowledge and benefits that increase opportunities for individuals, paternalism appears in an altered light, as it does in John Rawls's work. Besides, "the modern welfare state intermingles benefits, dispensations, and transfers to such an extent that it is practically impossible to separate dependents and nondependents."[17] Justification of paternalism—of everything from compulsory social security to enforcement of ecological standards—are supported less by demonstrations of increased liberty than by evidence that the most efficient way to achieve complex technical ends is for public authorities to defer to experts.

The current dilemma of representation illustrates the strain on democratic theory caused by the relation between authority of office and expertise. None of the traditional theories of representation accommodate the distinction between experts and "consumers" of their knowledge, including officials. Three problems come together here. First, who is an expert for the purposes of forming a health planning board, say—doctors, administrators, officers of medical associations, providers of insurance? Second, who is subject to the authority of health-care providers? What consumers require representation—the sick, or all taxpayers, or should representatives mirror the ethnic composition of the community served?[18] Finally, matters are complicated by the fact that political jurisdictions do not correspond to technical and economic problem areas, so the basis of even official representation must be rethought. Disputes over representation have been enough to stalemate planning boards even before substantive issues are taken up, because the question of deference to experts by both officials and private citizens is focused there. And in some policy areas like the disposal of nuclear waste, there is no time for local experimentation and incremental change.

Studying which authority defers to the other is the business of comparative politics.[19] Relations between these types of authority vary among liberal democracies, and among democracies, "authoritarian" states, and revolutionary regimes (like China under the Red Guards). Virtually any public policy issue, public health for example, tells us as much. Scientists have been most successful in arguing that education and creativity can solve problems if only the "republic of science" and not government or the market is trusted to determine what areas of investigation show promise and merit support; consider the history of the National Science Foundation or of agriculture research. The latest genre of expert to claim deference from political officials is that of public policy analysts—analysts who use cost-effectiveness studies to find the most efficient program; organizational experts, analysts who evaluate policy in terms of market demand, and so on.[20]

But if the question which authority defers to the other is a matter for comparative politics, the question who is "an authority" does belong to conceptual analysis. Defining characteristics should aid in identifying who possesses authority, but current ones like "surrender of judgment" are not always enough to determine when we are relating to an authority, and neither is the idea that we recognize certain "marks" of authority, since these are not always as clear as professional licenses. For example, public officials defer to the judgment of businessmen and industry representatives all the time, not only because they constitute an important, perhaps the crucial, interest group in a capitalist society but also as "authorities on" productivity and economic growth. When industrialists have information vital to governing, or when their cooperation is necessary for program success, clientele relations arise. Is the claim to authority by businessmen anything more than the wealthy and powerful wanting to be honored for superior knowledge too? Can political officials attribute authority to business executives at will? The desire to represent oneself as occupying a pure realm of truth or common good is not unfamiliar; scientists do it all the time.[21] But can parties to a relation of authority simply ascribe authority to one another? Since systematic definitions of authority do not have much to say about the sources of recognition or marks of authority, nothing argues against this possibility. Perhaps designating someone "an authority" arises as a problem only when the claim that officials should defer to some expert provokes strong political opposition.

It does for democratic theorists, of course, who are always intent on limiting the authority experts exercise over both officials and private citizens. They raise two kinds of objection to the authority of superior knowledge. One is the difficulty of holding experts accountable. The other objection is to the insolence of experts, and the way knowledge translates into unacceptable social inequality. Michael Walzer sees both problems: he wants legal authority to circumscribe the authority of knowledge; he also wants experts to exhibit humility.[22] Walzer encourages us to think about the fact that the solution to these separate problems may not be the same, but for most democratic theorists the two problems converge. On occasions when "the claims of expertise, seniority, experience and special talents may override the claims of democracy as a way of constituting authority,"[23] democratic theorists insist that the public must be convinced, not merely informed. For them, citizens' estimate of their own political role is crucial; it matters whether deference is dazzlement or recognition of the rationality of a particular course of action. It matters whether authority is delegated or alienated.[24] In any case, sceptical attitudes are never entirely absent. There is the deeply ingrained democratic fear of being deceived, and there is the familiar observation that experts have their own interests and disagree among themselves. These factors are sometimes strong enough to cause people to withhold from authorities the overt recognition and rewards they are accustomed to, but not even scepticism enables us to avoid surrendering judgment.

The difficulty with the democratic intention to constrain experts is clear if we consider the trouble we have interpreting the public's "right to know." Once associated mainly with military secrets or with the press's access to judicial proceedings and to information that touches on the privacy of individuals, it now appears in an entirely different guise. As technological knowledge plays a larger and larger part in public policy, an effective "right to know" requires other kinds of information than the media appears capable of providing. It may point to new obligations for authorities to originate and publicize information. Indeed, the right to know may involve more than access to information. It may require institutional innovations in the process of public policymaking, with a view not only to education and convincing citizens what the best policy is, but also to convincing citizens to trust experts to choose the best policy for them.[25] Robert Dahl has proposed mechanisms for representing a "minipopulus" of randomly chosen but well-informed citizens in the policy process. These difficulties have inspired other philosophers to devise more drastic remedies, such as Robert Goodin's suggestion that it ought to count against certain programs like nuclear power production that citizens do not have the necessary competence to make policy.[26]

Some theorists are not content with the standard democratic appeals to popular representation and expert accountability. They redefine citizenship entirely, insisting that neither complexity nor bureaucracy can eclipse our responsibility for judging the meaning of technology "in its full implication" for collective life; as Ronald Beiner says, "here the expert can claim no special privileges."[27] The most striking thing about Beiner's position is not, as one might think, the explanation he offers for why disinterested "reflective judgment" is an adequate substitute for expertise; he offers none at all. Instead, what is striking is the motive behind Beiner's devaluation of authority: revulsion at the banalization of politics by experts. His hope is that deliberation by citizens will eliminate dullness and restore to politics its dramatic dimension. "Reflective judgment" is an heroic ideal. The idea is that we will realize that human judgment cannot master all possibilities, that our faculties and our purposes conflict, and we will begin to think of ourselves as spectators to a tragic drama.[28] Judgment does not promise better decisions than authorities could make, but it does promise compensatory moral and esthetic rewards.

We all judge and act under conditions of uncertainty and ignorance all the time. Ordinarily this doesn't evoke tragedy. It simply indicates why "an authority" is such an important concept, for most issues fall between the ones that anyone can know about and the ones that are unknowable. Differential knowledge and uncertainty exist, and "dialogue" cannot eliminate them. Walzer denies that this differential is absolute: "in principle, I can learn what they [experts] know . . . Even by myself and as I am, I know enough to question the advice I get from the experts I consult . . . the distribution of socially useful knowledge is not a seamless web, but there are no enormous gaps."[29] In fact, it is an empirical question whether technological literacy can ever close enormous gaps where they exist, in what areas, and for whom. Some hierarchies are very steep. It remains an open question, answerable only with concrete evidence, what kind of technical knowledge can be widely distributed, and if it is, whether this makes popular decision-making possible or desirable. Even if we agree with Dahl that democracy is preferable to "guardianship," another difficulty remains: the potential gap between our *capacity* to make judgments and our *disposition* to form opinions about matters of public policy, especially when we are aware that outcomes are not only risky but genuinely unstable, as they are in nuclear weapons control.

Political philosophy must go further than it has, in sorting out "surrender of judgment" to superior knowledge from what it means to lack the faculty of judgment altogether (a possibility Arendt raised in her essay on Eichmann), and these from incapacity for particular kinds of judgments (moral, esthetic, technical, etc.) and from judgment that is simply uninformed. But refining the typology of ways we relate to "an authority" is not all that is needed. It seems to me that democratic theory, with its focus on the right to know and on experts' accountability, is insufficient, too. What is needed is not only a better theory of the responsibility technical authorities have *to* people, but also a theory of responsibility *for* them, which is quite different.

Material for thinking about a political philosophy of service and care exists in writings on paternalism, on professional ethics, and on the moral considerations that enter the thinking of men and women whose business it is to foster and preserve objects and relations. None of these sources have been fully exploited by political theory. From the subject's point of view, when an authority takes decisions on our behalf the important questions may center more on trust than on judgment. Neither Locke's thoughts on political trust nor Niklas Luhmann's functional approach is of much use here; a suitable theory of trust remains to be constructed.

c. The Challenge of Practical Experience

Contemporary philosophers create a typology of authority that draws our attention to the relation between "an authority" and "in authority". But from outside the systematic literature come serious challenges to the distinction between authority of office and belief. One is Michel Foucault's argument that authority has disappeared and is replaced by "discipline" and therapeutic forms of social control that are not amenable to recognition or judgment, properly speaking, at all.[30] Another challenge emerges in feminist writings. For some feminists, authority patterns throughout society seem to converge. That authority is almost always male, to say nothing of patriarchal, overwhelms differences between authority of office and knowledge. Women also appear to have a distinctive psychological relation to authority of any kind.

Recent work on the moral thinking of women identifies a "different voice."[31] For women, the typical moral ideal is cooperation and interdependence rather than fulfillment of a formal obligation. The implication for authority is that women are less likely than men to allow understanding authority as a relation of obedience and command to govern their reading of situations or their actions. Women's "contextual relativism" suggests that authority, rules, and procedures will be less imperative for them than empathy or the impulse to be responsible for maintaining concrete personal relations.

But other sources paint a different picture. Classical psychoanalytic writings identify an anatomical basis for female passivity, dependence, even masochism. A relative lack of castration anxiety means that women lack this powerful drive to develop a strong superego. Male authority is idealized. Later psychoanalytic writings remove the emphasis on biology but still point to the way human law is embodied in the father and to the existence of a rigid female view of authority. Sociological approaches explore the cultural sources of women's innate sense of inferiority and habitual submissiveness, which affects everything from patterns of learning in school to availability for political mobilization.[32] They remind us that historically, women have been expected to surrender judgment and defer to superior knowledge in *every* context. Subjection to authority that controls belief as well as conduct was considered the inevitable accompaniment of gender difference.

Whether women moderate and compensate for authority by thinking about it "in a different voice," or defer to it, the experience of authority as male may eclipse for them distinctions like authority of office and expertise. In the extreme view, authority as male is so embedded in a culture of women as the "second sex" that orderly philosophical accounts of recognizing a particular authority are irrelevant. Authority seems to lose its significance as something distinct from power or sheer coercion. This is not a common view, even among feminists. But surely it *is* common for women to have the sense—often just a flash or intermittent conviction—that a professional or official relation is being experienced as one of habitual deference to authority because it is male, or as sexual domination. The reaction to these simultaneous perspectives on authority may be confusion, unease, and guilt; or women may be accustomed to complexity and negotiate it without undue strain. This phenomenon is revealing because it suggests that authority is neither "there" nor "not there" for us in any simple sense. In this, the experience of women is instructive. We all move in and out of recognizing authority and shift in and out of judgmental modes all the time, and we have recourse to an array of legitimating norms that encompasses contradictory ones.

Feminism reminds us that the authority in terms of office and belief is not the only way to think about authority. When we survey it from the perspective of legitimacy, the full force of pluralism emerges. So does the fact that our relations to pluralistic authority are messy and ambiguous.

2. PERSPECTIVES ON LEGITIMACY: MESSY PLURALISM

Legitimacy brings together three aspects of pluralistic authority. One is the absence of congruence among patterns of authority. Authorities in schools and families, churches and unions, hospitals and government departments have diverse claims to entitlement. Second, political authority itself has more than one source of legitimacy. Not every historical set of values is compatible with a given political society, of course, and liberal democracy rests on secular, nonhierarchic values. Even so, a wide range of perspectives remain: Does the legitimacy of liberal democratic authority rest on popular sovereignty, impartiality, or equal opportunity and social mobility? Or is its legitimating rationale economic growth? Liberalism also harbors residues of historical practices and expectations, which are sometimes associated with particular groups and sometimes widespread in political culture. For example, the enduring attraction of traditionalism, especially for lawyers, explains the identification of the American system of political authority with a heroic founding and the elevation of the Federalist papers into authoritative texts on the Constitution.

Even a single political authority can have diverse grounds of legitimacy. All of the following can be said of the American presidency: that it is purely functional; that its ground is constitutional; that its authority is inseparable from personality. This latter idea contains variety too, since the point of personal authority may be to have an object of deference or to provide effective leadership. To take another example: what gives a planning board its legitimacy? One answer is formalism: its de jure status and its adherence to due process. Alternatively, the answer could be that it is representative. On still another view, authority rests on its newly identified paternalistic purpose: it cares for the environment or some other collective good and for the needs of future generations. Friedman's definition of authority as a relation of mutual recognition of entitlement is correct, but claims too little; recognitions can be diverse. That is why rituals, dignified displays of authority, and symbols are most powerful when they are designed to let men and women attach multiple associations to them, when their resonances are diverse.

Disputes about what makes authority legitimate are generally thought of as crises that bring obligation and obedience into question. But divergent perspectives can coexist in support of a structure of authority without weakening its capacity to govern or provoking charges of betrayal. Nor do we have to take polemics about legitimacy as a sign that we must agree on shared meanings for authority to fulfill its purpose. Authority does not require consensus. Institutions and individuals have a considerable capacity to bear complexity and ambiguity. In any case, divergence among perspectives on legitimacy is ordinarily latent, since in liberal democracies authority rarely demands professions of loyalty and since acts of obedience can rarely be interpreted as legitimating rather than passively acquiescing.

Still, the idea that authority must be understood as the batching of plural perspectives always provokes resistance. Traditionally, political philosophers looked for a single identifiable authority, for sovereignty, or for a unified system of neutral principles. At present, reaction against messy pluralism takes the form of a search for the "authoritative." The idea is that authorities may be diverse and diffuse, but common sense about the authoritative is a condition for the existence of rules bestowing authority in the first place.[33] For Richard Flathman, the authoritative is that "web of overlapping, sometimes conflicting, sometimes complementary and mutually reinforcing values and beliefs that inform, influence, and, to varying degrees in various situations, support" authority.[34] Flathman is careful not to say that the authoritative amounts to consensus. Still, his use of the notion of authoritative recalls older ideas like legitimacy, as well as recent ones like "shared meanings." His definition conforms to the social science notion of cohesive norms. It raises the same epistemological problems as other attempts to elicit shared meanings from practices when these underlying meanings are "deep" and unacknowledged. More troublesome still, it fails to allow that not only structures of authority but the "authoritative" too can be pluralistic.

In fact, Flathman's notion of the authoritative gets in the way of his central argument, that individual agency must be respected for authority to be justifiable. We are left wondering where critical judgments come from if agents are confined within a web of common values and beliefs? Some philosophers appeal to a transcendent perspective or to the notion of "critical distance" or to authority's failure to be "faithful to shared meanings." But it also happens that plural traditions of authority coexist in liberal society, providing material for criticism from within.

In this volume, Steven Lukes proposes "an inherently perspectival interpretation" of authority that promises to incorporate pluralism into current analysis. Beginning with the standard relativist argument that every community has its own definition and normative grounds for authority, Lukes goes on to say that even within a system of authority a variety of perspectives exists. He would distinguish the perspectives of officials from a range of unofficial societal perspectives, and each of these from the perspective of the sensitive philosophical observer who is able to elicit and reconstruct society's underlying values. For Lukes, the meaning of authority can only be understood as a "composite" of these.[35]

A third aspect of pluralistic authority enters where Lukes leaves off. He writes as if specifying perspectives entails no empirical problem, and as if perspectives are neatly compartmentalized. This is not so. Perspectives are not parcelled out to discrete individuals or groups depending on their social situation. The contexts in which we find authority relations are not separated from one another by firm boundaries—and individuals do not always respect boundaries when they do exist. It is not only that men and women have more than one perspective on authority, but that perspectives on authority leak from one realm and role to another. We experience and attribute different meanings to a given authority depending not only on the structural context the authority governs but also on whether in a given context we identify ourselves as private citizens, bureaucrats, property-holders, or religious consciences; as parents or members of a political group. Recall the example of women in relation to male authority, alternately recognizing authority in context (submitting to a medical expert, for example), deferring because of deep cultural norms that accustom women to surrender judgment to male authority, and perceiving the relation in terms of sexual domination rather than authority of any kind. Perspectives coexist for us all in an inchoate way, so that they are blurred, hesitant, transitory, and contradictory.

That is why it is difficult to imagine men and women engaged in the measured process of identifying "exclusionary reasons" that Joseph Raz elevates into the defining characteristic of justified authority.[36] We are seldom lawyerly, uncovering the reasons authority makes determinative, ascertaining whether authoritative directives are based on reasons that relate independently to our actions, and only then allowing these directives to preempt reasons for acting that apply to us directly. Instead, we bring a host of modes to authority relations, including trust, loyalty, apathy, utilitarian calculation, fear, and guilt. And of course authority relations may be decisively affected by matters that have no obvious bearing on them at all. Apart from preoccupation with analytic rigor there is no reason to think that authority is "tainted" by these other connections.

Civil disobedience illustrates the inescapability of plural perspectives. The standard argument for why acts of civil disobedience are moderated is tactical, to separate the illegitimacy of official acts or policies from the system of authority as a whole, to deny revolutionary intent, to recall the public to common principles, and so on. But in practice, civil disobedience may also be moderated by the fact that we are not just consciences or citizens exercising judgment. We are also workers and mothers or fathers. We may associate civil disobedience with economic hardship, social ostracism, and psychological isolation. None of this is adequately encompassed by the view that sees civil disobedience in a moral framework of conflicts of obligation. Simply, our judgments and actions vis-à-vis authority are affected, even eclipsed, by these other things that we are.

3. THE PERSONAL USES OF PLURALISTIC AUTHORITY

Pluralistic authority is intolerably unsystematic to some, and to others it is politically fearful. But we have good reasons to bear conflict, diversity, and ambiguity here at the heart of the political concept traditionally associated with unity, clarity, and assent. Clutter and confusion can become elements in a defense of pluralistic authority from a peculiarly personal point of view.

In liberal society, where so many legitimating norms appear to be activated and so many perspectives on authority accommodated, pluralism may tend to political stability. I am not reiterating the conventional pluralistic arguments, which say that by dividing authority conflicts will be partial and claims of illegitimacy contained, or that redundancy is stabilizing since if one rationale for authority fails there are backups, or that "cross-pressures" on individuals moderate expectations. I have in mind a different connection between pluralism and stability. At its heart are the many vivid expectations individuals have about how authority should look and feel, expectations built up from personal experiences with authority in a variety of contexts. Where political authority is pluralistic and has multiple resonances, these expectations are less likely to be disappointed. Along with legal formalism there is some leadership and personality, some consent, some traditionalism, some deference. This is important, especially in a democratic society. Just as diverse interests demand satisfaction, diverse expectations about the rituals, moral language, and practices that make up authority relations do too. Here, stability has to do with sublimating rather than containing conflict. To pluralistic political mechanics I add a psychological dynamic—satisfying strong expectations.

Harry Eckstein's familiar thesis appears to argue against this, by portraying political stability as the result of congruence among patterns of authority. Eckstein studied mainly the way public authorities were modeled on local government; he paid less attention to congruence among nonpublic authority structures like the family. More importantly, he found in Norway that rare thing, a profound sense of community where sentiments toward structures and members are "intimately emotional," and he traced community to the unusual survival of primordial attitudes from the Viking past.[37] Eckstein's work succeeds in show-

ing what congruence is and how it functions within a system of
public offices. But it does not show what incongruence is, and
it does not support his claim that incongruence produces an-
omie or that it is destabilizing. His structural-cultural analysis
does not disprove my notion that for individuals, messy pluralism may actually enhance opportunities for the satisfaction of
deep expectations about authority.

Another objection to my proposition has it that since all complex societies have differentiated spheres and since most are
not stable, pluralism does not ensure that expectations will be
met. But here too political science may be missing the point
since it is not pluralism per se—the existence of secondary associations—that satisfaction depends upon but rather access to
a wide range of authority relations. It is simply not the case
that in every complex society pluralistic authority is an actuality
for most men and women. This happens only when each social
context is home for more than one authority or authoritative
ground, when individuals move freely among these various
contexts, and when men and women harbor mixed and changing perspectives themselves.

My chief interest in pluralistic authority is inspired by concern for individuality rather than satisfaction and stability,
though. It has personal development and self-expression at its
heart. Authority is something besides a vital functional or moral
relation; after all, it is also constitutive. We seldom hear today
that authority per se stems from universal traits deeply rooted
in the human mind. Instead, psychologists describe stages of
individual development, associating each stage with the need
for a particular type of authority. Some liberal theorists seem
to have had this insight. John Stuart Mill argued that paternalism enables children to reach the maturity of their faculties. He
also assigned certain authorities a constructive part in liberating
adults from other authorities, namely closed traditional ones,
so that even for adults deference can ultimately lead to intellectual independence. Today, we are aware that diversity of authority serves personal development in an even broader sense.
It maximizes contexts for working through crises of personal
identity and averts some of the conditions that make for getting
"stuck." Writings on mentor relations, for example, describe how
authority can facilitate the transition from apprenticeship to re-

sponsibility. Deep needs for various authority relations continue into adulthood, which is now said to have its own stages and tasks. At different times in their lives and depending on the context, people feel more secure, confident, and self-respecting in one sort of authority relation rather than another. And individuals require different situations for expressivity and creativity. We know that some people work most productively within a hierarchy and others under conditions of cooperation or even isolation; less apparent is the fact that the same individual may need all of these. It bears mentioning that it is not always weakness, infirmity, or moral cravenness to choose to be subject to authority, even in situations where autonomy is expected of us or considered ideal.

This is not to say that pluralism provides a market in authority relations, though in many areas of life it does just that. When we select a psychotherapist we enter into one or another kind of authority relation. This is done more deliberately still when we choose a teacher or private school for a child. And we can shop for a physician-patient relation that is paternalistic or collaborative. We may recognize our own foolishness or recklessness in some area and seek out authority to control our own irrational propensities. We may even wish not to have the desire to submit to strong authority we do, and search out situations in which we are not permitted to surrender judgment. Of course, sometimes we choose without being conscious of this impetus at work, as in marriage or a voluntary association. Our perspectives are the results of life stage and of the (often accidental) contexts to which we have access. Our desires for authority have histories. We enter and leave authority relations emotionally encumbered, and some of our preferences for authority are "settled." But they are not fixed—they change, and we negotiate our perspectives and shift involvements among authority contexts carrying this array of perspectives with us, sometimes finding satsifaction for ourselves.

From the point of view of personality, pluralistic authority is not always considered benign. It has been suggested that where patriarchal authority does not exist, men and women will try to escape from ambiguity and from the intolerable burden of choice. Or that the "collapse" of strong parental authority has such an adverse effect on superego development that the consequence is anarchism or rampant hedonism.[38] Liberal society is full of authority, though. Differentiation is not absence, and complexity is not anarchy. Still, it is possible that too many experiences with incongruent authorities produces strain and the desire for "escape." The trouble is, since we necessarily inhabit a variety of spheres, we never encounter a single encompassing authority. It is not to be found outside of religious cults. Fragmentation is inescapable. Daniel Bell singles out the tension between capitalist productivity, which requires discipline, and modernist culture, which excites the return of the repressed.[39] Actually, economic and cultural contexts are more pluralistic than Bell allows. From the point of view of men and women personally, it has not been shown that dissonance always results from experiences with pluralistic authority or that dissonance is always bad. It is just as plausible to say that differentiated spheres and pluralistic authorities provide individuals with occasions for development and, equally important, with safe occasions for regression and displacement.

What is not speculative is the close connection between my propositions about pluralism and personality, and liberalism. Advantages to personality are not guaranteed, but they are only imaginable where differentiated authority is recognized and valued, as it has been from the first in liberal thought.

The favored themes of my generation of political theorists are autonomy and communal affiliation, not authority. Yet contemporary interest in autonomy and community typically stems from just what I have been discussing—concern with personality, with individuality and "the self." Autonomy and community are regarded as the conditions for personal identity and expressivism. My point is that autonomy and community do not exhaust the conditions necessary for self-development and self-expression. Personality requires authority too. Indeed, authority relations can be viewed as scenes of political and psychological creativity. Discovering, inventing, and making personal use of patterns of authority go on all the time. Recreating authority in associations originally intended to be egalitarian and cooperative was a common experience for many men and women during the 1960s and 1970s, and the considerations that led them to reconstruct authority were not purely functional. They also had to do with the personalities and expressive needs of members.[40] For a generation whose vocabulary fuses the political and personal, authority is surely an exemplary case.

The perspective on authority I have proposed can be called romantic on account of its preoccupation with expressiveness and self-development. But this does not mean that political theory written from this perspective is romantic. Notions of self-development and self-expression are no more elusive than autonomy or community. Nothing bars their being related to patterns of authority in a rigorous fashion. Certainly, concern for individuality provides both fresh motives for studying authority and independent criteria for evaluating the way access to diverse authorities is distributed. It gives us good reasons for keeping pluralism in mind.

NOTES

1. Carl Friedrich's insistence that authority is the ability to issue communications "capable of reasoned elaboration" was the counterpart of Carl Schmitt's call for personal authority. See Carl J. Friedrich, "Authority, Reason, and Discretion," in *NOMOS I: Authority*, ed. Carl Friedrich (Cambridge: Harvard University Press, 1958), p. 29.

2. Hannah Arendt, "What Was Authority?" *NOMOS I, Authority*, ed. Carl Friedrich (Cambridge: Harvard University Press, 1958), p. 82.

3. Within authority structures too, social policy works through innumerable state and local agencies by means of financial inducement, not direct control.

4. Edward Banfield's biting criticism of the National Endowment for the Arts for having confused and conflicting goals is weakened by the fact that this is commonplace for large-scale policy programs. See his *The Democratic Muse* (New York: Basic Books, 1984).

5. Harry Eckstein and Ted Gurr, *Patterns of Authority*, (New York: Wiley, 1975).

6. "The recognition of alternatives and the experience of tension and conflict between established practices and independent moral standards" does not exist. Richard Friedman, "On the Concept of Authority in Political Philosophy," *Concepts in Social and Political Philosophy*, ed. Richard Flathman (New York: Macmillan, 1973), p. 136.

7. For the similar way trust operates between executives and subordinates within official structures, see Hugh Helco, *A Government of Strangers* (Washington, D.C.: Brookings Institution, 1977).

8. London *Sunday Times,* July 15, 1973, cited in Vivien Hart in *Distrust and Democracy* (Cambridge: Cambridge University Press, 1978) p. 4.

9. John Dunn, "The Concept of 'Trust' in the Politics of John Locke," in *Philosophy and History,* eds. Richard Rorty, J. B. Schneewind and Quentin Skinner (Cambridge: Cambridge University Press, 1984). For a contrasting functionalist account see Niklas Luhmann, *Trust and Power,* (New York: Wiley, 1979).

10. Richard Flathman, *The Practice of Political Authority* (Chicago: University of Chicago Press, 1980), chapter 5.

11. Samuel P. Huntington, "The Democratic Distemper," *The Public Interest* 41 (1975): 9–38.

12. Study by Robert Kahn, et al., cited in Charles Elder and Roger Cobb, *The Political Uses of Symbols* (New York: Longman, 1983), p. 26.

13. See Charles Elder and Roger Cobb, op. cit., pp. 4–6 on welfare proposals by Richard Nixon and George McGovern in 1972.

14. For business see Albert O. Hirschman, *Exit, Voice, and Loyalty* (Cambridge: Harvard University Press, 1970); for government see Hugh Helco, *A Government of Strangers,* op. cit.

15. The question has, of course, both an internal subjective and an objective answer. Objectively, not everyone's recognition of authority is equally important; in many instances the trust of elites matters most. For the U.S. see James Wright, *The Dissent of the Governed* (New York: Academic Press, 1976); for the Soviet case see Seweryn Bialer, *Stalin's Successors* (Cambridge: Cambridge University Press, 1980).

16. See the essays in *Paternalism,* ed. Rolf Sartorius (Minneapolis: University of Minnesota Press, 1983).

17. Hugh Helco, *Comparative Public Policy* (New York: St. Martin's Press, 1975), p. 276.

18. Theodore Marmor and James Marone, "Representing Consumer Interests: Imbalanced Markets, Health Planning, and the HSAs," *Health and Society* 58, (1980): 125–54.

19. Hugh Helco points in particular to the way the relative prestige of professions is related to their closeness to the public sector; in the U.S. professions employed in the public sector, like teaching, suffer in contrast to Germany. Hugh Helco, *Comparative Public Policy,* pp. 269–70. See also Srewyn Bialer, op. cit., pp. 170–71, note.

20. Expertise affects office: using the budget process to allocate resources puts into place a planning system that strengthens the upper tiers of the executive hierarchy and affects relations between

the executive and Congress. See Charles Schultze, *The Politics and Economics of Public Spending* (Washington, D.C.: Brookings Institution, 1968), p. 16.

21. For example, see Michael Polanyi, *Science, Faith, and Society* (Chicago: University of Chicago Press, 1946).
22. Michael Walzer, *Spheres of Justice* (New York: Basic Books, 1983), p. 135.
23. Samuel P. Huntington, cited in Vivien Hart, *Distrust and Democracy*, op. cit., p. 191.
24. Hart, op. cit., p. 141. It is worth noting that these arguments operate against "scientific socialism" as well as against scientists. The best discussions of authority in terms of the difficulty of demonstrating rationally the adequacy of a course of action remain those of Carl Friedrich. See "Authority, Reason, and Discretion" in *NOMOS I, Authority*, op. cit., and *Dictionary of the Social Sciences* (New York: Free Press of Glencoe, 1964), p. 42.
25. For a futuristic account of the possibilities of the media see Robert Dahl, *Controlling Nuclear Weapons* (Syracuse: Syracuse University Press, 1985). See also Dennis Thompson, "Philosophy and Policy," *Philosophy and Public Affairs* 14 (Spring 1985): 217.
26. Robert Dahl, *Controlling Nuclear Weapons*, op. cit.; Robert Goodin, *Political Theory and Public Policy*, cited in Dennis Thompson, "Philosophy and Policy," op. cit., p. 213.
27. Ronald Beiner, *Political Judgment* (Chicago: University of Chicago Press, 1983), pp. iv, 3.
28. Beiner, *Political Judgment*, op. cit., pp. 141, 161.
29. Walzer, *Spheres of Justice*, p. 155.
30. Michel Foucault, *Discipline and Punish* (New York: Vintage, 1979).
31. See especially Carol Gilligan, *In a Different Voice* (Cambridge: Harvard University Press, 1982).
32. A sample of this literature includes Juliet Mitchell, *Psychoanalysis and Feminism* (New York: Vintage, 1964); Jean Baker Miller, *Towards a New Psychology of Woman* (Boston: Beacon Press, 1976); Sheila Rothman, *Woman's Proper Place* (New York: Basic Books, 1978); Sara Evans, *Personal Politics* (New York: Vintage, 1980).
33. See Richard Friedman, "On the Concept of Authority in Political Philosophy," op. cit., on the two tiers of authority.
34. Flathman, *The Practice of Policial Authority*, op. cit., p. 88.
35. Above pp. 59–75.
36. Joseph Raz, *The Authority of Law* (Oxford: Oxford University Press, 1979) and Joseph Raz, "Authority and Justification," *Philosophy and Public Affairs* 14 (Winter 1985): 3–29.
37. Harry Eckstein, *Division and Cohesion in Democracy* (Princeton: Princeton University Press, 1966), pp. 79, 112.

38. Christopher Lasch, *The Culture of Narcissism* (New York: Warner Books, 1979).
39. Daniel Bell, *The Cultural Contradictions of Capitalism* (New York: Basic Books, 1976).
40. For two studies on this see Jane Mansbridge, *Beyond Adversary Democracy* (Chicago: University of Chicago Press, 1980) and William Schonfeld, *Obedience and Revolution* (Berkeley: Sage Publications, 1976).

8

AUTHORITY AND THE INDIVIDUAL IN CIVIL ASSOCIATION: OAKESHOTT, FLATHMAN, YVES SIMON

TIMOTHY FULLER

I

In thinking about authority, two ways of structuring the modern political situation must be kept in mind. The first meditates on the tension between understanding man as a self-determining being and the residually present understanding of the Classical-Christian outlook. The thesis that civilization may advance materially while declining spiritually is, to many, vividly dramatized by the circumstances of our time. The rhetoric of progress is less compelling now. Many wonder what utterances or actions can quality as authoritative.

The second affirms an ideal of civil association, emphasizing individuality and diversity, presupposing that human beings are intelligent agents. This is a world of selves among selves, disclosing themselves to each other in pursuing their self-chosen aims. The conduct of affairs can be intelligible and manageable without trying to answer questions about the *summum bonum* or *finis ultimus,* provided only that there are some mutually recognized procedures or practices to impart modest stability to the restless transactions of individuals with each other. The self-sufficiency of this civil association precludes a search for authoritative pronouncements about the spiritual conditions of life. From this perspective, the function of authority is severely circumscribed and certainly does not extend to any assessment of the "spiritual condition" of mankind.

In both of these, however, there is a positive and affirming conception of the function of authority. We will see both the convergence and divergence between them in considering Yves Simon and Michael Oakeshott.

On the other hand, what I shall call "resolute irresolution" is a noticeable feature of contemporary liberal politics. This attitude, which I shall illustrate by consideration of the work of Richard Flathman, arises out of reluctance to pay any tribute to authority. Authority is treated with ambivalence as a negative necessity to be exercised with apology and regret. To commentators like Flathman, the continued necessity of authority shows a failure of human ingenuity to have devised means to achieve a social spontaneity that would circumvent relations of authority or at least diminish them to a barely perceptible presence.

II

To Oakeshott, the focal feature of the civil condition is association in terms of noninstrumental "moral practice": "In respect of this practice *cives* and subjects are not joined as comrade expeditionaries in a communal adventure . . . or in some notional and banal agreement to be equally advantaged or not unequally disadvantaged . . . but in that relation of somewhat 'watery fidelity' called civility."[1] His aim is to show the logic of an association that is specifically civil and not anything else. In this he follows, at least in part, Aristotle when he distinguishes the civil association as a relationship obtaining only among human beings, more or less equal, subscribing to some constituting instrument, altogether composing a complete, self-sufficient structure.

Within this association, the interaction of agents appears in two modes. The first, "enterprise association," involves "intermittent transactional association of reciprocity in which agents . . . seek the satisfaction of their wants in the responses of one another . . . It is a relationship of bargainers. . . ."[2] This sort of relationship does not describe association in terms of "civility" or "civil association." Civil association is association in terms of the conditions of a practice illustrated principally in "a common tongue and a language of moral converse."[3] A practice does not "prescribe choices to be made or satisfactions to be sought; instead, it intimates considerations to be subscribed to in making choices, in performing actions, and in pursuing purposes . . . it postulates 'free' agents and it is powerless to deprive them of their freedom."[4]

Individuals in civil association are agents who mediate between their particular circumstances and the generally acknowledged procedures. Practices are not principles from which we could derive courses of action.

No particular actions define human conduct. Individuals must always choose, from among alternatives that occur to them, what they take to be fitting illustrations of acknowledged moral practices in responding to contingent circumstances. Practices qualify, but do not determine, actions. Relationships arising from common subscription to a practice without specification of a joint purpose, product to be produced, or end to be reached, suggest what *civil* association is.

Oakeshott wants to describe a relationship among individuals that does not override their self-identification. Following Hobbes, he imagines how orderliness may come to be among selves who inevitably measure the world according to their own lights.

The ideal expression of civil association is derived from setting out a consistent interpretation of the requirements of order for human beings jealous of their individuality (in themselves what they are for themselves). Citizenship is association in the recognition of a rule of law, not of necessary interests, needs, wants, or common dispositions.

Authority is found in the exercise of the duties of an office, under agreed-upon terms to make rules to which the citizens may subscribe. This categorically distinguishes power from authority. The associating aim of citizens is to establish and maintain authoritative rule. It is the commitment, existing in the thinking of individuals, to conduct themselves as *cives* in a *civitas,* that supersedes relations of mere power. For Oakeshott, the high achievement of modern Europe is the replacement of systems of command and obedience by arrangements of rules,

adjudication, and voluntary subscription—relations of authority and acknowledgment in civil association.

Practically speaking, the categorical distinction of authority
from power is not a fixed and final achievement. The distinction is hard to establish and easy to lose. But even though individuals do not perfectly act in accord with the distinction, the
distinction is indispensable to conceive civil association. To perceive power and authority as separable and, as a consequence,
to exercise ingenuity in making the distinction a practical reality, is the realization, albeit imperfect, of the ideal civil association.

The categorical distinction vanishes when authority is defined in terms of building consensus, proclaiming unifying goals,
or constructing coalitions of interests. To make consensus pre-
requisite to the establishment and exercise of authority is to fail
to see that authority is required by the absence of consensus
and cannot be employed to create or recreate consensus.

Setting out the ideal expression of civil association, and the
authority that goes with it, clarifies what we are already seeking
(for Oakeshott philosophizing is saying in explicit terms what is
already implicit in our experience). In the process, some things
we think we are pursuing have to be set aside. It is the austerity
of the conception of authority and civil association that constitutes a barrier to its acceptance far more than anything else.
Moreover, the question of how to achieve civil association and
relations of authority and subscription is entirely left aside. Their
possibility (reminiscent of Plato) depends fundamentally on the
clarity of our vision of them.

III

Despite Oakeshott's effort at clarification of the elements of
modern political order in terms of civil association and relations of authority and acknowledgment, there remains a strong
tendency to explain or ground these relationships in some more
material, tangible way, rejecting Oakeshott's position that human order is an interpretation of circumstances, a form of self-
understanding or self-interpretation alone. To speak of human
order any other way is to speak of something categorically different or to disguise what is distinctively "human" and hence

"civil" or "political." At best one may construct an amalgamation of elements from different categories of understanding. An example of this is to be found in the extensive analysis of authority in the recent work of Richard Flathman.

In *The Practice of Political Authority*,[5] Flathman embarks upon his own effort to distinguish the exercise of authority from the exertion of coercive power, to distinguish "authority" from the "authoritarian." To do so, Flathman reviews and summarizes the literature on authority as falling into two large categories: the first theorizes authority in substantive purposive (S-P) terms and is exemplified, in his view, by Plato's *Republic;* the second theorizes authority in formal-procedural (F-P) terms and is exemplified by Hobbes's *Leviathan*. In the by now well-established formulation, the distinction is between "an authority" and "in authority." Flathman's primary interest lies with "in authority" since that is the dominant concept within modern liberalism.

In earlier works as well as in this one, Flathman has discerned an impasse between claims of rights and the exercise even of "in authority" relationships.[6] Flathman's preference for what we may call self-critical traditionality is endangered by the disordering effects of rights claims in conflict with the discretionary judgments of office-holders. The balance of "order" and "progress" developed by J.S. Mill as a proper conception of social balance in a free society, and in a different vocabulary expressed by Flathman, is thought by him to be close to falling apart. Furthermore, Flathman does not find any clear resource to employ in maintaining the symbiotic relationship between these contending factors of social life.

Flathman addresses himself directly to the problem in his discussion of "authority and the 'surrender' of individual judgment."[7] By "surrender of individual judgment" what is meant is that an individual, in submitting to someone's exercise of authority, withholds his own assessment of the merits of what is proposed to be done in favor of the assessment emanating from whoever is in authority. The submitting individual does not at this point demand a justification that would move him to act in the prescribed manner on his own in the absence of an authoritative pronouncement. In short, the exercise of authority by A must be presumed to have altered the conduct of B from what it would have been had A not exercised authority.

Now, if I understand Flathman correctly, he wishes to show that a relationship of authority between A and B cannot properly be understood in terms of the debate over whether B surrenders judgment and whether that surrender is good or bad. For Flathman, A can exercise authority in relation to B without B surrendering his "judgment" even if B's conduct alters from what it would have been. Flathman is trying to mediate an abstract dichotomy between the proponents of extreme claims of rights for whom "surrender of judgment" is *prima facie* wicked, and the proponents of unquestioning submission to authoritative pronouncements for whom the exercise of authority is the only salvation from the war of all against all.

If B submits to the pronouncement of A, thereby altering his conduct, he may be thinking that A is authorized to pronounce to this effect on B but B may still think that what A pronounces is not good and should not have been pronounced. B may act in conformity with A's exercise of authority while not "believing in it." For B to submit to the pronouncement of A is not to be taken as a sign that B now believes something to be "true" or "good" whereas he formerly believed it to be "not true" or "not good" (or perhaps "indifferent" or "uncertain"). All that may be said is that whereas B's conduct might have gone one way it will now go another.

But does this analysis relieve the earlier impasse? Even if the alteration of conduct does not require a surrender of judgment, what can be the ground of altering one's conduct without changing one's judgment if not the calculation that order is preferable—in this case—to disorder? And what basis is there for any B to continue to make this calculation in favor of order? One is strongly tempted to answer this question by resort to an argument from habits. Bs will either accept, or not accept, as authoritative, pronouncements from As, as the case may be. Moreover, perhaps the exercise of "in authority" takes on, through habits of compliance, the appearance of "an authority" until some jarring eventuality reminds people of the arguments against "an authority." One might say, on behalf of the argument that to submit to authority is to surrender one's judgment, that it forthrightly acknowledges the tenuousness of all political order and the paradoxical basis upon which the indispensability of authority is established. It has the force of Hobbes's clarity as opposed to the appealing indecisiveness of Locke.

Flathman has provided a strong argument for the possibility of maintaining one's "spiritual autonomy" while submitting to authority. So far then we have an incipient defence of the political order as a "necessary evil," but do we have Tocqueville's "common belief" from which social well-being may spring? Flathman has defended authority from a prima facie charge of wickedness, but it remains to this point a burden to be borne: "Is the fact that a rule or command carries *in* authority itself a conclusive reason for B qua B to have an obligation to conform to the rule or to obey the command?"[8]

Flathman's answer here is that the obligation to conform obtains when the command is "valid." Questions of validity, however, "do not decide themselves. They are decided through the exercise of judgment by parties to the *in* authority relationship."[9] Moreover, the basis for such judgments consists in "some array of values and beliefs that has acceptance in the society or association of which it [authority] is part. For values and beliefs to give such support, a kind of congruence must be thought to exist between them and the actions and requirements of authority. The initiatives, the leadership, in maintaining such congruence may indeed rest largely with the As. But the Bs must believe that the congruence exists, and this belief requires judgments on B's part."[10]

The difficulty with this is that it tends to duplicate authority. Behind A lurks something even more authoritative than A's authoritative pronouncements. As Flathman states it, B may appeal to the authoritative background as well as A. Indeed, B must do so in order to exercise judgment on the pronouncement of A. However, if it is the very meaning of the authoritative background which is at issue (as in principle it must be in every case of A's judgment and pronouncement) then there must always be an incipient crisis of authority, as Hobbes would surely have seen immediately. Is Flathman not in danger of reintroducing a disguised natural source of authority?

It would seem that the genius of Hobbes's solution to the duplication of authorities, which in his time manifested itself in the conflict of theological and political authorities, and which Hobbes saw would show itself in eloquent appeals to private revelatory experiences, has been overthrown by Flathman. The appeal to the authoritative background is Flathman's up-to-date restatement in secular, historical terms of Locke's "appeal to heaven," which anyone can exercise at any time. In a way, then, Flathman seems close to admitting that the relationships of political life can be recorded as the endlessly evolving pursuit of intimations of the authoritative—it is human responses to their sociology. Who, then, is authoritative with respect to the authoritative background? Why cannot B go beyond the question of whether A holds the office of authority, to the "substantive merits" of A's pronouncements? Is not B entitled to claim that he is "an authority" on the exercise of "in authority"? Indeed he is, as Hobbes would say, if he is willing to put himself back into the state of nature.

Thus, B must choose to surrender his judgment in some important respect. B must do so in the sense of separating his private opinion from his public conduct. This is unavoidable. Those who object to the exercise of authority as demanding surrender of judgment correctly perceive that, in the relationship between "in authority" As and the objects of authoritative pronouncements, the Bs, there is a genuine inhibition on Bs externalizing their contrary beliefs in action. Flathman wants to defend this inhibition as necessary, but he equally does not want to be seen in the uncomfortable role of hard-headedly defending real, perhaps painful, restrictions on self-determination. He criticizes theorists who do not mind that role, most notably Hobbes and Michael Oakeshott: "The argument for self-discipline in effect contends that for purposes of action Bs confronted with an A or an X must proceed as if B is the only role they play and as if the characterization 'an A' or 'an X' is the only characterization that they may consider. This is not 'implausibly circumspect' (Oakeshott), it is impossibly limiting. There is no such thing as a person who is nothing but a B, and there is no such thing as a formulation that is nothing but an A or an X. In thought and action the several roles that any person plays and the several characterizations of which any formulation allows inevitably coexist and interact in a variety of ways. As important as they are, role conceptions and distinguishing characterizations do not and cannot (if only because they are commonly defined in part by reference one to the other) form hermetically sealed compartments or windowless monads that are or could be altogether isolated from one another."[11]

The latter is a rhetorically powerful statement but it does not dispose of any of the difficulties. It is precisely because no one is ever only an A or a B, and because no role is ever invulnerable to the nuance of meaning given to it by anyone who plays it, that the elucidation of the authoritative relationship between As and Bs is among the hardest of accomplishments and the most easily eroded. The erosion works both ways. On the one side, the office-holder is in danger of either overstepping his bounds or failing to exercise the duties of his office when they are painful; on the other side, the one who must submit to authority is in danger of wanting someone in authority to be an authority (thus relieving B's ordeal of being conscious and self-enacting) or of "appealing to heaven" merely by being a clever enough sophist to know that A's interpretation of the "authoritative background" of social life can always be made to look arbitrary in some respect.

The problem is not whether we need the "ideal type" of the relations of authority. We do need it inevitably if we are to clarify what we understand to be the requirements of political life. On Flathman's own terms it would seem that we need to know how to recognize when we are acting toward the implementation of the ideal of authority and of citizenship and when we are not. But Flathman, in my opinion, fears that to put the issue this way is to come perilously close to acknowledging that the preeminent requirement is the exercise of authority by the office-holder and not the claim of independent judgment on the part of the individual who will be subjected to the authoritative pronouncement. Common sense suggests that the hallmark of the civic order in a liberal society would be self-discipline or self-regulation. The alternative that forces itself upon us is self-assertion or demand for support on our own terms, or refusal to accord legitimacy to any exercise of authority that does not have prior approval from our point of view (which would be tantamount to making ourselves authorities on the exercise of authority, or making *ourselves* the authoritative background of the exercise of authority).

Flathman states that many are convinced "that citizens have a positive *duty* to make continuing assessments of the substantive merits of X's [requirements emanating from authorities] and a positive duty to make action on these assessments an integral part of *in* authority relations."[12] No doubt this is a widely held view. What foundation it has other than that it is widely held is by no means clear. Why does any B have this duty? Who may impose this duty? Who may assess the manner of its discharge? Can there be a "positive duty to take action on these assessments" in an "in authority" relationship? Can someone "in authority" command us to assess the pronouncements he issues in the form of actions that will exhibit our attitudes toward them? Does he not have to insist that we resound by acting in accord with such pronouncements? If not, then what is his authority for?

Because the issue of whether continued allegiance to authority depends on our independent assessment of the fruits of its exercise has not yet been unequivocally settled, Flathman acknowledges that he has not so far provided "a conclusive argument for or against rejecting authority as such."[13] This is the case because so far all we have as means to settling our attitude to authority are our calculations of its advantage or disadvantage for us. This seems to be a consequence of the fact that, for Flathman, no substantive determination of good for a society is possible. The latter would require articulating a nonarbitrary (the right) opinion on what is good or just amidst the myriad opinions that present themselves. Failing "an authority" we are led to philosophical skepticism on the question of "good," and to "in authority" as the skeptic's solution. But if any "in authority" is arbitrary (i.e., its pronouncements are not the right opinion but only putatively the rule), would it not be better to have no authority? What of the one who willingly submits to the "condition of mere nature" and the possible "war of all against all"?

So far, I think, Flathman has absolutely no answer to such a person. Like Locke, once he has accepted the "appeal to heaven" (B's appeal to the authoritative background values against A's interpretation of them in rules), he can only hope that people will generally feel no compulsion to appeal to heaven. Thus, like Locke, Flathman would have it two ways at once: the threat of the appeal to heaven will help keep the authorities skittish about the exercise of authority, and most people will perhaps find it to their advantage to be governed by those who are skittish about governing.

This may be clever but it is ineluctably contingent: "widespread and continuing approval, or at least the absence of overly emphatic and insistent disapproval, of the X's is a condition of *in* authority (and hence of any 'surrender of judgment' thereto). In short, the existence of *in* authority is a condition of decisions to obey X's is a condition of the existence of *in* authority."[14] Is this remark different in its actuality from the following: "The constitutional histories of European states have some brilliant passages; but, for the most part, and not unexpectedly, they have been the stories of somewhat confused and sordid expedients for accommodating the modern disposition to judge everything from the point of view of the desirability of its outcome in policies and performances and to discount legitimacy."[15]

Nor does even building civil disobedience into the system of "in authority" relations resolve the dilemma. After a lucid account of how the civil disobedient proposes to remain a B while nonetheless refusing to obey the authorities, Flathman concludes: "A showing that the idea of civil disobedience is compatible with *in* authority can be justified."[16] What is clear is that such a complex version of the "in authority" relationship (one making room for civil disobedience) is acceptable to Flathman personally. This version pays its respects to the anarchist and to the Hobbesian simultaneously.

Does Flathman wish authority to disappear altogether? Perhaps it would be more correct to say that he would like to see it totally transformed. The general tendency of his discourse assumes that there is something embarrassing at least, ominous at worst, about the exercise of authority. Although he sees a necessity for authority, he thinks that there is always an incipient illegitimacy in its exercise, or at least that people will tend to perceive authority as suspect. The prescription might be to democratize authority, yet "restricted forms of democratization are likely to diminish the value of the authority itself while reproducing, in what may seem to be only minimally altered forms, the very difficulties that the devices are intended to remedy."[17] Any radical democratization, while "intended to induce participation that is more widespread, vigorous and efficacious than is encouraged or even allowed by more restricted modes of democracy" and thus to "reconcile authority and individual agency," will "in an association of any size" cause conflict between the two: "Either the participation is intense but less widespread and the arrangement becomes hard to distinguish from restricted democracy, or it is widespread but lax or thin, thereby failing to enliven identification with and acceptance of substantive outcomes. And in both cases its formal properties leave the association subject to the veto power that the scheme puts at the disposal of all members."[18]

Even if democratization would have value for making the exercise of authority more palatable (which is certainly not obvious), the issue of the substantive merits of the outcomes of exercising (democratized) authority would remain. In short, even here under conditions of democratization Flathman insists on maintaining a distinction between the authoritative background values and the pronouncements of officials as to the meaning of the authoritative for purposes of action. Any claim to merge authority and the authoritative must be rejected.[19]

But the point must be raised again: Is this position not reintroducing the criterion of substantive merit as the means to assess the exercise of authority (the criterion of self-interest, rhetorically projected as an elucidation of authoritative background values)? Can the civil disobedient claim to remain a B while seeking to establish an alternative authoritative interpretation of the authoritative? Flathman insists on this because he thinks that to do otherwise is to open oneself to "imposition and domination seeking to clothe itself in the normative garb of authority."[20] If I understand this, it seems to lead to the proposition that the best way to prevent "imposition and domination" is to invite clashes over the substantive merits of the actions of those holding offices of "in authority." This confusion must arise to the extent that Flathman both wishes to have moral progress (see p. 241) bespeaking some concrete actualization of good, and also fears every concrete determination of good that is in fact brought forward.

In fact, Flathman's is a theory of the inevitability of clashes over substantive merits of governmental action. As such, it is a real denial of the "in authority" relationship as primary, or, to put it differently, it is a revisionist interpretation of the theory of "in authority" in the form of a politicization. So far the politicization does not have any clear programmatic content. But it seems reasonably obvious that for Flathman the pure theory of "in authority" is distasteful because it sharply distinguishes the exercisers of authority from those upon whom the exercise will fall, or at least it seems to do so (see pp. 241–3). On the other hand, Flathman cannot dispense with "in authority" because of the fundamental philosophical skepticism that underlies his conception of, and commitment to, the liberal political tradition. His aspiration is that the distinction between As and Bs should ultimately collapse.

It would seem that the pure theory of "in authority" accepts this conclusion as well. After all, theorists like Hobbes and Oakeshott do not argue that the historical background of a society is definitively explicated by those who exercise authority. What they argue is that we can only rescue ourselves from the arbitrary and the capricious by reliance on some exercise of authority to avoid the war of every interpretation against every interpretation. Thus, it is difficult to see that Flathman has any solution to the problem posed by the ever available "appeal to heaven." He has to maintain the possibility of such an appeal while urging every effort to mitigate authority's offensiveness to those who know that they can appeal to heaven.[21] "As a response to most if not all of what has been accepted as political authority in human history, the judgment that 'it is not as bad as might be thought' is about the most that could be sustained."[22] Even more startlingly: "the conclusion Rousseau drew in the eighteenth century remains correct in our own day; political authority is in principle a justifiable human practice, but at present that practice is nowhere actualized in justifiable form."[23]

It is hard to avoid concluding that for Flathman what is "authoritative" is the impasse from which he started and to which he seems continually to return. Flathman's key to political life is resolute irresolution.

IV

Resolute irresolution is a noticeable trope of contemporary liberal politics. To be sure, this is not how Oakeshott understands authority. To the contrary, for Oakeshott relations of authority and acknowledgement in civil association are the highwater mark of the political imagination. Yet to other commen-

tators, such as Flathman, there is an unresolved question of the
right or the just coupled with a desire for some, as yet unde-
fined, spontaneity of relationship that would circumvent the need
of relations of authority, or diminish them to a barely perceptible presence.

To this Oakeshott might reply that an association of agents
may create and protect a sphere of spontaneity only by way of
establishing relations of authority, and agree with Hobbes's "brisk
and decisive" answer that "authentic *lex* cannot be *injus*. This
does not mean that the legislative office is magically insulated
form 'unjust' law. It means that this office is designed and authorized to make genuine law, that it is protected against in-
dulging in any other activity and that in a state ruled by law
the only 'justice' is that which is inherent in the character of
lex."[24]

It is clear that the "authoritative" of which Flathman speaks
resolves no issues of the "jus" of "lex" and may only exacerbate
them in the clash of interests to which debate over the "jus" of
"lex" gives rise. Nonetheless, the questions of purpose or of the
goals or ends of life do not disappear. It may be objected to
Oakeshott that, while he has an affirming view of authority, his
affirmation is merely of a circumstantial achievement, an appreciation of a certain relationship for its own sake. Let us consider, then, a theorist of authority who explicitly seeks an unequivocally positive theory of authority, Yves Simon.

Simon's thinking on authority is conditioned by his structuring of the modern political context from a perspective formed
from sources outside it, the natural law tradition as it thinks in
terms of the ascent of the soul as opposed to the progress of
society: "Political and social consciousness, in modern times,
evidences an obscure belief that the progress of freedom is syn-
onymous with social progress . . . that social progress is identical with the progress of liberty . . . conceived as implying a
decay of authority, so that three terms, social progress, the progress of liberty, and the decay of authority, are currently identified."[25]

One may note that this describes an unmistakable tone in
Flathman's analysis. It cannot describe Oakeshott insofar as
Oakeshott rejects in toto "progress" as a meaningful theoretical
concept. It touches Oakeshott too, however, insofar as Oake-

shott is a modern individualist, which Simon is not. Yet even if Simon is not a modern individualist, he assumes the reality of the individual in the Aristotelian-Thomistic tradition: Authority is exercised "through a practical judgment to be taken as a rule of conduct by the free-will of another person . . . no authority can ever take the form of an impersonal necessity."[26]

It is exactly here that many begin to distrust authority in either the Oakeshottian or Simonian versions. There is something arbitrary about practical judgments since it is always possible that they could go some other way. In other words, one way of assessing authority is to say that it only substitutes for an as yet undiscovered certainty that surmounts "practical judgment" in the Aristotelian sense.

Simon objects to this on the ground that it mistakenly interprets political authority as if it is the prelude to scientific or theoretical wisdom, thus failing to remember Aristotle's insight in maintaining the separateness of practical and theoretical wisdom. But beyond this, such a view obscures the discovery of any essential function of authority, i.e., some function important to human beings which can be fulfilled in no other way. If such a function can be sighted then it will be possible to circumvent the view that authority is only a necessary evil, perhaps a temporary necessity of civilization's development so far, but ultimately dispensable. The latter view encourages attacks on authority as if the attacks were a sign of enlightenment long after, following Oakeshott, authority has successfully replaced coercion as central to political order. Or, to put it another way, the continued necessity of authority comes to be seen as a deficiency: "It means that the amount of authority necessary in a society is inversely proportional to the perfection reached by that society . . . the law of progress would take the form of an asymptotic curve at whose unattainable term there would be a complete elimination of authority."[27]

In search of this essential function of authority, Simon proposes a thought experiment. Let us imagine "a community of adults, intelligent and of perfect good will" and let us consider what is required for the common life of such a community. If we do not assume inevitable unanimity (not a logical necessity even with "perfect" good will), how will this community assure unity of action?

Simon's response is that unity even under these ideal conditions requires authority; even the perfectly "enlightened" society will require authority. The correct direction of action cannot be demonstrated "because we are unable to overcome the
mysteries of contingency."[28] Moreover, a decision that is perfectly valid (to travel by car to a vacation resort) may be undermined (by an unforeseeable car crash). The truth of a practical
judgment does not "refer to its conformity with the reality of
things," but to "conformity with the requirements of a will which
is supposed to be sound, healthy, honest . . . not the truth of
a cognition but the truth of a direction."[29] An association of
individuals of perfect good will can never avoid this limitation
even with the best will in the world: "it can never be shown
evidently that this or that practical judgment, to be taken as a
rule for our common action, is the best possible one."[30] With
respect to practical judgment it is possible to act in a better or
worse state of awareness of the requirements of judging well in
contingent circumstances, but it is in principle impossible pro-
gressively to master and transcend the precarious and variable
relation of judgment to the reality of things. Thus in the temporal succession of human experience good judgments are not
perpetuated and they do not accumulate. A movement from
sound judgment to sound judgment cannot be a movement in
the form of better to better still. The latter is wishful thinking.

Those associated in perfect good will cannot depend on unanimity and, as the number increases, the experience of unanimity should decline in frequency. But action must be taken.
People of good will must acknowledge the need of authority
and establish it. It is a function of good will to do so. It is, one
may say, the natural consequence of adequate human reflection
on human relations. It is not "defectives" or "primitives" who
require authority, but those most fully and self-consciously human.

These most fully human beings, being real individuals, have
both the inclination to associate and also to accomplish their
own ends. But these ends include that of association. What is
good from an individual's perspective may or may not be received as good by others. Conflict over goods to pursue is not
a symptom of wickedness (for we are still supposing individuals
of perfect good will), but the natural consequence of the lim-

ited perception of the possibilities of good that is available to any individual. Individuals of good will must see this and thus the very desire of their own good carries them beyond themselves toward the others for confirming or qualifying response. The effort to confirm that individual goods are not incompatible with the larger range of goods is a continuous development from the desire for particular goods to the desire for good. What is good is neither merely abstract, because the first intimations of it are in particular material desires of real individuals, nor merely particular, since the desire is for something "good," it is not just desiring, and that it may be good depends on common acknowledgment in some degree of more or less.

But since unanimity is not only precarious and infrequent but also overrun by the fecundity of possible goods, where individuals are recognized to be real, authority will be required. It will be required not so as to suppress the spontaneous diversification of individual perceptions of good, but to establish some manageability where every good thing cannot be pursued simultaneously. One imagines here an inversion of the Hobbesian notion of the *bellum omnium contra omnes*.[31] Thus the natural movement toward identifying one's good and thence good as such brings forth the desire for authority as the practically necessary condition of fulfilling the quest for one's good and the good. Authority, so far from standing in opposition to human diversity, is *essential* to its rational ordering in qualifying as an attribute of the good itself. Some putative "progress" beyond the need of authority is, in fact, a retrogression masquerading as an abstract "ideal."

To avoid misunderstanding, however, it must be added that it would be entirely mistaken to take this as an argument merely in service to the "powers that be" as if every existent exercise of rule exemplified authority. Pursuit of good carries to sight the need, if good is to be rendered practicable in a really existing polity, of authority, that form of rule which responds to what underlies and constitutes it and may be acknowledged by its subjects as referable to what they require (which is not saying they must "approve" or "agree" with everything it says or does even if they observe it). What is carried to sight is not the "authoritative" (although historians and sociologists may think they are discovering this retrospectively) but a practical judg-

ment determining the "good" for purposes of practical action.
If anything is "authoritative, it is this judgment and it cannot
be subordinated to a "condition" of its appearance.

V

To conclude just here would perhaps suggest to the careful
reader a convergence, despite idiomatic differences, between
Oakeshott and Simon in their positive affirmations of authority
when its function is lucidly set forth. But significant divergence
must be mentioned and it will return us to the point with which
we began.

While it is true that both Oakeshott and Simon begin from
the reality of the individual and the individual's "free will" (Simon) or capacity for intelligent response to contingent circumstances (Oakeshott), their conceptions of the "liberty" enjoyed
by this individual ultimately diverge in a way that affects their
theories of authority. Simon follows Jacques Maritain in distinguishing "initial" from "terminal" liberty, or the capacity to
choose from the attainment of choosing good as opposed to
evil. Here we must recall the difference between "progress of
society" and "ascent of soul."[32] "Initial liberty" is akin to Oakeshott's "intelligent response," but for Oakeshott there can be no
meaning to "terminal" liberty apart from "self-enactment" in
an individual agent. "Self-enactment" means, in effect, the attempt on one's part to live one's life in a manner consistent
with the direction one has chosen for it. This is separable from
"self-disclosure," which is the series of actions and utterances
of one perceptible to others and which they may or may not
take to be consistent with one's self-enactment so far as they
have awareness of both.

For Oakeshott, no common meaning of "self-enactment" can
be established. Selves cannot become simply transparent to each
other. Efforts to achieve this must tend to fall into ideology or
at least misunderstanding. Thus Oakeshott maintains the absolute dichotomy between good and what agents pursue in their
"imagined and wished-for outcomes." Authority cannot therefore operate as a coparticipant in the lives of individuals, guiding them, however indirectly, to that enactment which would
no longer be strictly a *self*-enactment. No such thing lies in the

capacity of anyone exercising authority. Indeed, for Oakeshott, this would be tantamount to reintroducing a command which one must obey even though its implementation might continue to have features of practical judgment. And even if this command were associated with a divine revelation emanating from a sovereignty that is not constituted by our consent, the belief that such a sovereign command is possible *is* constituted by consent.

Insofar, then, as Simon, who has traveled a long way down the road of modernity with Oakeshott, subtly reintroduces a notion of the "progress of society" in the form of a "spiritual ascent," articulated through authority which would assist us to move from "initial" to "terminal" liberty, he must diverge from his travel companion. Of course, it is clear that what Simon (and Maritain and, lately, John Finnis) has in mind is not at all what Flathman means by the "authoritative." The latter can never be other than the cultural conditions of society in some epoch of its temporal progression. Equally clear, to an Oakeshottian, would be the danger, or likelihood, that the conditions of terminal liberty could never be extricated from the "authoritative" of Flathman. The point, then, is not to deny the possibility of universal, spiritual good. The point is never to forget what the limitations of earthly authority are. To my knowledge, Oakeshott has never denied the former nor forgotten the latter. To put it another way: as against Simon's Thomism, one may array Oakeshott's Hobbesian version of Augustinianism. In either version, authority is the creative achievement of the human spirit which "redeems" the liberty of choosing or the procedure of intelligent response to contingency.

Here is where the philosophical conversation on authority might approach the profundity it deserves. Oakeshott brings forth what might be called the pure theory of authority, disengaged in the farthest degree from considerations which mask its categorical attributes. In many respects Simon, and other representatives of his tradition of thought, need not quarrel with Oakeshott's achievement. Nor would Oakeshott fail to appreciate Simon's desire to establish a substantive meaning for good, not as cultural "behavior" but as a natural inclination toward fulfillment which could be translated into "ends" to aid us in the pilgrimage of life. Nevertheless, for Oakeshott, the pilgrimage is a "predicament" and not a "journey." This is not Oakeshott's attempt to refute the alternative but an attempt to say indicatively what can be said. To speak indicatively is to remain consistent with his theory of civil association and of authority and to keep other reflections in the realm of the private.

To Oakeshott, the inclinations which "by nature" move all human endeavor can only be understood as imagined and wished-for outcomes in a state of constant revision in the sequences of individual experience, and authority offers a certain stability of procedure but no independent criteria of enactment pertinent to preferences among self-enactments. Simon, in his emphasis on the essentiality of practical judgment, converges with Oakeshott in upholding the procedural achievements of modern democratic polities. They may agree to disagree, as friends occasionally do; they disagree on the metaphysical premises of the conduct to which they mutually agree to subscribe.

NOTES

1. Michael Oakeshott, *On Human Conduct* (Oxford: Clarendon Press, 1975), p. 147.
2. Oakeshott, *On Human Conduct*, pp. 112–113.
3. Oakeshott, *On Human Conduct*, p. 119, p. 59.
4. Oakeshott, *On Human Conduct*, p. 79.
5. Richard Flathman, *The Practice of Political Authority* (Chicago: University of Chicago Press, 1980).
6. See Richard E. Flathman, *The Practice of Rights* (Cambridge: Cambridge University Press, 1976).
7. Flathman, *Practice of Political Authority*, ch. 5.
8. Flathman, *Practice of Political Authority*, p. 104.
9. Flathman, *Practice of Political Authority*, pp. 104–5.
10. Flathman, *Practice of Political Authority*, p. 106.
11. Flathman, *Practice of Political Authority*, pp. 107–8.
12. Flathman, *Practice of Political Authority*, p. 108.
13. Flathman, *Practice of Political Authority*, p. 109.
14. Flathman, *Practice of Political Authority*, p. 114.
15. Oakeshott, *On Human Conduct*, p. 193.
16. Flathman, *Practice of Political Authority*, p. 122.
17. Flathman, *Practice of Political Authority*, pp. 195–6.
18. Flathman, *Practice of Political Authority*, p. 199.
19. Flathman, *Practice of Political Authority*, p. 205.

20. Flathman, *Practice of Political Authority*, p. 124.
21. Flathman, *Practice of Political Authority*, pp. 218–19.
22. Flathman, *Practice of Political Authority*, p. 220.
23. Flathman, *Practice of Political Authority*, p. 229.
24. Michael Oakeshott, "The Rule of Law," in *On History and Other Essays* (Oxford: Basil Blackwell, 1983), pp. 130–31.
25. Yves Simon, *The Nature and Functions of Authority* (Milwaukee: Marquette University Press, 1948), pp. 5–6. See also Yves Simon, *A General Theory of Authority* (South Bend: University of Notre Dame Press, 1980).
26. Simon, *Nature and Functions of Authority*, pp. 6–7.
27. Simon, *Nature and Functions of Authority*, p. 15.
28. Simon, *Nature and Functions of Authority*, p. 23.
29. Simon, *Nature and Functions of Authority*, p. 24.
30. Simon, *Nature and Functions of Authority*, p. 27.
31. "That virtuous people, as a proper effect of their very virtue, have the common good and subordinate their choices to its requirements is an entirely unquestionable proposition. Thus, *in a certain way at least*, the volition and intention of the common good are guaranteed by virtue itself, independently of all authority." Yves Simon, *Philosophy of Democratic Government* (Chicago: University of Chicago Press, 1953), p. 39.
32. Simon, *Nature and Functions of Authority*, p. 40.

9

ON AUTHORITY: OR, WHY WOMEN ARE NOT ENTITLED TO SPEAK

KATHLEEN B. JONES*

The standard analysis of authority in modern Western political theory begins with its definition as a set of rules governing political action, issued by those who are entitled to speak. Descriptions of those who act as public authorities, and of the norms and rules that they articulate, generally have excluded females and values associated with the feminine. This seems to be an unexceptional observation. After all, few women have been rulers in any political system of any epoch. But what if we argue that the very definition of authority as a set of practices designed to institutionalize social hierarchies lies at the root of the separation of women-qua-women from the process of "authorizing?"[1] If we argue further that the dichotomy between compassion and authority contributes to the association of the authoritative with a male voice, then the implication is that the segregation of women and the feminine from authority is internally connected to the concept of authority itself. It is this structural implication that I want to explore.

Feminist scholars have argued that the roots of the dichotomy experienced by women between being in authority and being subject to it stem from the separation of public life and

*The author gratefully acknowledges the support of the National Endowment for the Humanities Summer Seminar Program, and the critical comments of William Connolly, Tom Dumm, Richard Flathman, Jane Jaquette, Kingsley Widmer, and the editors of NOMOS.

political authority from private life and the passions. As a corollary, they claim that the discourse of political theory identifies women with the private sphere and affective life.[2] Since women are excluded from the public realm, they do not learn how to lead others in authoritative ways. They are not originators of orders, or high in the hierarchy of commands, ritualistic or real.

To a certain extent these arguments have merit. Feminist scholars have revealed how the practice of authority depends in many ways on patterns of socialization established in the private sphere, and that these patterns educate women in subordination. They have clarified how conceptual analyses of power have excluded women systematically by rendering female power invisible, either because it is different from male power, or because it is wielded in the private sphere. They have not, however, extended this criticism to the idea of authority. Indeed, all too frequently they have allowed power to stand for authority, despite the fact that political thought has long recognized not only a distinction between power and authority but, at times, a fundamental antithesis.

While building on their work, I will argue that the feminist critique of authority as a specific form of male privilege has not focused enough on the limitations of traditional concepts of authority. When these scholars argue that women have not learned how to be in authority, they accept the adequacy of the concept of authority itself. In contrast, I would suggest that authority currently is conceptualized so that female voices are excluded from it. Following the genealogical method of Michel Foucault, we may see how the dominant discourse on authority silences those forms of expression linked metaphorically and symbolically to "female" speech. It is my claim that this discourse is constructed on the basis of a conceptual myopia that normalizes authority as a disciplinary, commanding gaze.[3] Such a discourse secures authority by opposing it to emotive connectedness or compassion. Authority orders existence through rules. Actions and actors are defined by these rules. Compassion cuts through this orderly universe with feelings that connect us to the specificity and particularity of actions and actors. Authority's rules distance us from the person. Compassion pulls us into a face-to-face encounter with another. If it is legitimate to contend, as Carol Gilligan has in her studies of women's moral development,[4] that women approach ethical dilemmas and make decisions with a fundamentally different language and logic, then the female voice of would-be authority may speak in compassionate tones inaudible to listeners attuned to harsher commands. Hence, in the dominant discourse, much of compassion is taken as nonauthoritative, marginal pleadings for mercy—gestures of the subordinate.

With this issue, we might follow the course of what Foucault has called the project of genealogy. Its purpose is to explore the constraints and discipline involved in traditional constructions of authority. It is meant to be subversive, substantive, in a literal way: it looks below the dominant meanings of texts to consider meanings and knowledge hidden or disqualified. To deconstruct authority is to discover the ways that a particular conceptual framework restricts our knowledge of it. For example, an overemphasis on the "rationality" of authority, i.e., the radical separation of the realm of cognition from the realm of belief and feeling, arbitrarily restricts authority to formal rules. In addition, the logic of defining authority as a system of "conflict resolution" sees decision-making less as consensus-building and more as a process of adjudicating competing private claims of self-interest. Moreover, since adjudication requires some "surrender of private judgment," traditional notions of authority incorporate an acceptance of an internal conflict between authority and personal autonomy. Finally, the norms that constitute authority as an association of inequality and control are understood to be unmodified by emotive connectedness or compassion. Authority, like judgment, is necessarily hierarchical and dispassionate.

Each of these aspects of authority helps define it as a system of rules for social control within the context of social hierarchies. To the extent that authority is understood to order social behavior, making it predictable and manageable because it is rule-governed, then even those social relationships that seem to operate more arbitrarily—as in the case of parenting and the judgments of juries—gain authority insofar as the actions of those in authoritative positions are explicable in relation to rules. In the Anglo-American tradition, a jury responds with mercy toward a defendant, in the legal sense, because the defendant's behavior fits the category of excuses for crimes established by statutory and case law. Or they excuse a particular defendant because the individual lacks the mental capacity to behave in conformity with the law, also as defined by statutory and case law.[4] Even parenting is a relationship of authority to the extent that the parent's judgments have more than mere compulsion or whim to rationalize them. Consider the case of the state operating as protector and legitimate authority *in loco parentis* in instances where the actual parents have reduced their authoritative claims to rule over the child to power relations, as in cases of child abuse.

But this definition of authority as rules normalizes an androcentric view of authority. Although it comes to be associated with systems of rule that are themselves genderless, this form of sociality is at least arguably male. "Male hegemony in the culture," writes Jessica Benjamin, "is expressed by the generalization of rationality and the exclusion of nurturance, the triumph of individualistic, instrumental values in all forms of social interaction."[5] Even when the attempt to make authority compatible with agency modifies this view, the ideal of autonomy and participation in rational discourse excludes certain forms of expression, linked metaphorically and symbolically to "female" speech, from those which make authority coherent. For example, sociolinguists recently have argued that female patterns of speech reveal a different expressiveness than do male patterns. Rhythms, nuance, emphasis, and assertiveness, in tone and syntax, appear to vary with gender. Nevertheless, we define the masculine mode of self-assured, self-assertive, unqualified declarativeness as the model of authoritative speech. "Female" hesitancy and other-oriented language patterns, considered as the marks of uncertainty or confusion, are derogated.[6] Consequently, we purchase the distinction between authority, coercion, and persuasion at the expense of recognizing certain dimensions of human action and speech that would make authority more humane, although more ambiguous.

Following Thomas Hobbes, the standard view of authority is of a mode of discourse that gives expression to rank, order, definition, and distinction, and hides dimensions of human reality that disorient and disturb. The problem here is to consider the ways that the subject of authority is constituted so that "female" bodies, gestures, and behaviors are hidden by authority's gaze.[7]

Can it be that the exclusion of the "female" from the practice of authority contributes to the tendency to identify authority with rationalized compulsion?

In Western political philosophy it is common to regard authority as a distinctive type of social control or influence.[8] Sometimes the differentiation between authority and force is not clear.[9] But generally, theorists have attempted to distinguish authority as a peculiar form of getting people to obey social prescriptions short of compulsion.[10]

Most theorists of authority also would agree that some sort of surrender of private judgment—at least in the weak sense of submitting to the judgment of another without making conduct dependent on one's assessment of the merits of the command—is entailed in any concept of authority.[11] For them, recognition of authority is sufficient for accepting the prescriptions produced by authority systems. Put differently, if authority is defined as a "mutually recognized normative relationship giving the one the right to command or speak and the other the duty to obey,"[12] then any justification of authority depends only on clarification of the criteria whereby authority is recognized in the first place. One does not have to be persuaded to particular obedience to those in authority, nor is one coerced into obeying. One obeys those in authority because they are, in general, entitled to obedience.

This notion of authority seems to separate the obligation to obey from any judgment about the substantive merits of specific acts one is required to perform.[13] But the particular act of recognition that establishes authority in the first place can neither originally nor over time be dissociated from the network of common beliefs which constitutes the identity of those in authority, or those subject to it. Although many political theorists concede that communal beliefs establish the criteria for recognizing authority originally, they contend that the idea of authority requires that subjects suspend disbelief once a leader's right to rule is established. But this conceptual stress on the rationality of deferential obedience hides the ambiguous and contentious ground out of which obedience springs. The idea of authority as traditional hierarchy makes sense so long as we accept on faith that the need for an ordered, efficient social system takes precedence over any other form of social organization. But this may be a variable condition. The identification of authority with some form of hierarchy is based, although not intentionally, on what Carol Gilligan has called a peculiarly male approach to decision-making: the willingness to sacrifice relations to others in the face of established rules; or, to put it differently, to exchange the uncertainty of human relationship for the certainty of rules. It may be interesting to consider the ways that a "female" stress on relationship over rules or abstract rights modifies the ways that authority is constituted and practiced.

Recall that in conventional rule-oriented definitions, the need for authority is made identical with the need for some hierarchical system of decision-making that defines social cooperation within the context of necessarily stratified relations. To institutionalize authority is to institutionalize vertical hierarchies of differential rights, privileges, and duties in order to facilitate the accomplishment of some common project. This conception of authority depends upon an instrumentalist view of political life and political action. Heavily influenced by some variant of the Hobbesian view of human nature ("the war of all against all"), authority, from this perspective, stabilizes social interaction, marking human action by tolerable, rule-governed levels of sociality. Since, in Hobbes's view, "every man has a right to every thing," human social behavior is intrinsically bellicose and, ironically, in the state of nature, it appears inherently anti-social. Authority enables groups of individuals, necessarily in conflict with one another, to resolve their conflicts by appealing to the rules that specify priorities of rights. The rules of authority systems provide sanctuary from the dangers of social intercourse. Hobbes's methaphor, in *Leviathan*, of the Sovereign as an artificial man, and his definition of the commonwealth as a society created by convention become literal descriptions of the perspective on community reflected in nominalist discourse on authority. The community *is* an artifice: a mask of rules and roles that covers the face of *real* humanity—the autonomous Self.

This instrumental view of human community, and the identification of authority with hierarchy, may be based on peculiarities of masculine need. In her study of the psychodynamics of sex roles in modern Western societies, Dorothy Dinnerstein has suggested that the the sexual division of roles in the family, and the consequent fact that women monopolize early child-rearing, explain the identification of authority with male-dominated systems of rule. Dinnerstein argues that "our earliest and profoundest prototype of absolute power" occurs in infancy. This power is wielded virtually exclusively by the female sex through their monopolization of early child care, making later male domininion "an inexorable emotional necessity."[14] The power of the mother is experienced as absolute because it is she who both satisfies our deepest needs for comfort and security, and stirs our deepest fears of rejection and separation. It is the memory of the mother's body that reawakens a primordial desire that Freud called the "oceanic feeling," a desire to be in blissful union with the world, but which our existence as mortal, individual selves requires that we overcome. Both sexes, although with different consequences, then accept paternal authority as a model for ruling the world because, under prevailing social conditions, it provides sanctuary from maternal authority.[15]

In a related argument, Nancy Chodorow uses this paradigm to analyze the structuring of patterns of male and female personality characteristics. She argues that current patterns of child-rearing in Western industrial society—women's mothering occurs in the context of the isolated nuclear family—create specific personality types and structure gender-differentiated affective patterns. Nurturing activities become normatively female, and instrumental activities become normatively male. The consequence is that for women, intimacy and relation to others become part of the development of the female self. For men, the self is defined in isolation from others, with the consequence that intimacy is more fundamentally threatening to the male.[16]

Both of these accounts point to the importance of the meaning of the memory of the mother—the recognition of woman's body and gestures through the remembered fear of rejection—in the reading of the signs of authority. Why authority means rules may be connected to the sense of instability and discontinuity "most intimately related to our bodies and our everyday behavior."[17] But because this sense of instability is structured differentially for men and women, acceptance of the idea of

authority as rules may be more consonant with a male orientation to the world.

Recent feminist criticism has returned to the concept of gender differences to argue, from a nonessentialist stance, that the
history of women's experiences and women's voices about those
experiences leads to the development of alternative ways of
knowing and seeing.[18] If we are searching for a model that
moves away from defining authority exclusively as a form of
problem-solving, and toward a metaphor that emphasizes that
authority is a contextual, relational process of communication
and connection, then it may be that examining "female" experience will provide us with such an alternative. I would like to
consider the ways that the role of nurturing—a role not necessarily gender-defined, but one that has been associated historically with women—provides such a model.[19]

Carol Gilligan's work on women's moral development offers
some suggestive, though underdeveloped, hypotheses about how
to proceed. Commenting on her interpretation of the ways females reach decisions about complex moral dilemmas compared with males, and on the prevalence of images of relationship in girls' fantasies about dangerous situations, Gilligan
remarks that women appear to perceive the fracture of human
connections as violent, whereas men see connection itself as
threatening. Since women seem to tie the rupture of relationship to aggression, "then the activities of care, as their fantasies
suggest, are the activities that make the world safe, by avoiding
isolation and preventing aggression rather than by seeking rules
to limit its extent."[20] For men, rule-bound situations, with clear
boundaries and limits to aggressiveness, are safe: whereas for
women, it is precisely this inability to connect, or to affiliate,
that represents the dominance of aggression. If we now accept
the idea, as indicated earlier, that authority is opposed to power
and domination, then it would appear that what constitutes authority for women is exactly what is most feared by men: sustained connections, or what Freud called the altruistic urge for
union in relationship to others.[21]

Sophocles' *Antigone* can be read as a commentary on this ethic
of care as authority. Upon hearing of Antigone's willful defi-
ance of his edict forbidding the burial of Polyneices, Creon ex-

plains his condemnation of her to Haemon, his son: "The man the state has put in place must have obedient hearing to his least command when it is right, and even when it's not."[22] Haemon replies that the community speaks its discontent with Creon's judgment, though Creon's "presence frightens any common man from saying things [Creon] would not care to hear." Creon denies that he should be moved by the speech of his subjects or his son: "At my age I'm to school my mind by his? . . . This boy instructor is my master, then? . . . Is the town to tell me how I ought to rule? . . . Am I to rule by other mind than mine?"[23] But Haemon replies that "no city is the property of a single man," and warns that Creon wishes to speak but never wishes to hear.[24] Creon's insistence that his commands be heard is countered by Haemon's insistence that speech is communicative dialogue, not monologue. Antigone's actions speak compellingly to the community because they remain connected to the fabric of its life. Her being silenced by the authority of the state reminds us of what connections are lost in Creon's (male) view of authority: Antigone was burying the dead.

Contrary to the restricted understanding of authority as contingent on conflicting individual, and primarily, male, wills, authority is seen here as the construction of a meaningful world. Apart from the problem-solving that authority permits, its essence is the vitalizing of community itself. As Hannah Arendt reminds us, authority is derived, etymologically, from the verb *augere*, "to augment."[25] Authority adds meaning to human action by connecting that action to a realm of value and to justifications for action beyond criteria of efficiency or feasibility. If we define authority as expressing and enabling political action in community—interaction among equals—then authority would be represented as a horizontal rather than a vertical relationship and as male/female rather than primarily male.

This alternative view accepts authority as an essential feature of human social behavior because that behavior is a type of interaction that involves "speech, communication, and mutual understanding."[26] Since being in community is given ontological priority, then authority as a system of rules for securing private rights, structuring individual obligations, or protecting autonomy through reciprocal duties gives way to authority as a way of cohering and sustaining connectedness. Much of the fabric of communal connectedness is lost in the male-rule, instrumental model. In this female perspective, the quest for authority becomes the search for contexts of care that do not deteriorate into mechanisms of blind loyalty.

Gilligan notes that female caring traces a path of "deprivation followed by enhancement in which connection, though leading through separation, is in the end maintained or restored." The female self in connection with others "appears neither stranded in isolation screaming for help nor lost in fusion with the entire world as a whole, but bound in an indissoluble mode of relationship that is observably different but hard to describe."[27] Some myths contain the dramatic-poetic discourse on authority as the augmentation of community that is obscured in the rule-dominant mode. For example, this pattern emerges clearly in the Demeter-Persephone myth. Persephone, daughter of Demeter, while playing in the fields one day, admires the narcissus. As she picks it, the earth opens, and Persephone disappears into the underworld. Angered at the loss of her daughter, Demeter, goddess of agriculture, refuses to allow the fields to grow until she is returned. The earth lies fallow until Zeus agrees to release Persephone from his brother Hades' control. Once Persephone is reunited with Demeter, the fields again are productive. But Persephone is required, as part of the agreement between Zeus and Demeter, to return annually to the underworld. And so, in Greek myth, is the origin of the seasons explained.

In interpreting this myth, David McClelland argues that it suggests an alternate interpretation of power, and I would add, of authority. Whereas power is often conceptualized as the willful assertion of control over another—the power of taking— this "female" myth, which invokes "interdependence, building up resources, and giving," contains different understandings of the resources of power.[28] Demeter's authority seems to stand in a more literal relationship to the activity of augmenting that authority connoted originally. Her augmentation of the life of the world is born of the restoration, albeit on a constantly changing basis, of her intimate connection with her daughter.

What remains troubling about the idea of authority as an augmentation is that we are aware that every search for harmonious connectedness contains choices and, therefore, losses and limits. Antigone loses her life, Demeter loses her relationship to her daughter, and Persephone is limited by the requirement that she regularly return to the underworld. We perceive these limits as threats to the self and fear the authority that constructs them. In part this is because the dominant notion of autonomy is a disembodied one that abstracts human will and agency from the meaning of living as mortals in a world filled with those who are different from us. The refusal to consider the internal connection between authority and caring leads us to search for a spaceless and timeless order through rules, and paradoxically, to the embrace of domination and bondage to those authorities whom we want most to reject.[29]

The inability to reconcile authority with human agency is the result, in part, of a conception of the self in isolation from others as opposed to a self in connection with others. Authority does not have to be conceptualized in opposition to personal autonomy so long as autonomy does not deny the critical function of nurturance and its relation to the humanization of authority. Richard Sennett notes that the dominant forms of authority in our lives are destructive precisely because thay lack nurturance and compassion. These emotions are what enable us to "express a full awareness of one another," and, consequently, "to express the moral and human meaning of the institutions in which we live."[30] It is out of this emotive connectedness to others that genuine authority as an augmentation of the texture of daily life emerges.

But there may be reasons to fear the establishment of compassionate authority. In *On Revolution* Hannah Arendt argued that it was the substitution of compassion for the masses by authoritative decision-making that accounted for the destructiveness and violence of revolutionary authority. Virtue, Arendt contended, can be embodied in lasting institutions: compassion cannot. Virtue facilitates political action. It operates in the sphere of choice and knows the limits of human existence. Compassion precludes political action. It knows only force and violence. By overwhelming the political world with "the cares and worries which actually [belong] to the household" compassion makes a lawful civil society impossible. It substitutes power for authority, and will—the force of the multitude—for consent, or the considered opinion of several, particular interests.

If virtue is rational and its mode of expression is argumentative speech or persuasion, compassion speaks only the language of emotive gestures. Its presence in the political realm triggers the release of the "force of delirious rage."[31] To base authority on compassion makes the idea that violence is a legitimate form of conflict resolution compelling. To make compassion the foundation of authority would permit an "irresistible and anonymous stream of violence [to replace] the free and deliberate action of men."[32]

But is it possible to reconcile freedom and rational discourse with compassion, and still distinguish political authority from compulsion? What Arendt translates as the "barbarian vice of effeminancy" and rejects as a principle of authority may provide an important way to make authority more compatible with autonomy.

In Arendt's terms, human understanding is understanding the limitedness of human action in the world. It is living in a world in which one has to make choices and suffer the consequences. But authority seems to lift one beyond one's emotions, beyond "merely" private, "merely" personal feelings. Authority is embodied in the judge who orders the sentence of death despite sympathy for the accused. It is Arendt's interpretation of Captain Vere in Herman Melville's *Billy Budd* that best represents her view here. Arendt argues that Vere must condemn Budd, even though he knows that Budd is innocent in some larger sense of the term. Authority cannot be modified by compassion in this instance. To allow compassion to rule would be to allow unreflective immediate action to be substituted for the processes of persuasion, negotiation, and compromise. It would substitute faith for reason.[33]

Budd cannot defend himself. He lacks the capacity for predictive or argumentative speech. Compassion, says Arendt, "speaks only to the extent that it has to reply directly to the sheer expressionist sound and gesture through which suffering becomes audible and visible in the world."[34] And it is the very directness of the compassionate response, according to Arendt, that removes it from the realm of politics, and hence the realm of lasting institutions.

But Vere's response to Budd is not unmediated, as Arendt claims. Nor is his compassion for Budd the result merely of the "belief" in Budd's innocence. Both he and his officers know that Budd is innocent since Budd "purposed neither mutiny nor homicide."[35] Most importantly, Vere's response to Budd is mediated by his relationship to Budd as a father to a son. Although Arendt is correct that this sort of connection, born of compassion and caring, is particularized, it is not without its own rules of recognition. Vere's caring for Billy Budd provides him with the knowledge that the law he is required to apply is more barbaric than the act it thereby punishes. But the discourse of authority subjugates this knowledge through an imperious gaze that focuses attention on disembodied agents whose intentions are read by the effects of their acts. As an ironic commentary on Arendt's interpretation that following the rule of law secures the public space for rational, persuasive discourse, Vere declares that among his reasons for condemning Billy is that the people, "long molded by arbitrary discipline, have not the kind of intelligent responsiveness that might qualify them to comprehend and discriminate."[36] Finally, too, the death of Billy, while ostensibly carrying out the "measured forms" of politics, achieves no positive, nurturing, political value.

The importance of connecting compassion and authority is that it reminds us that the order authority imposes "does not correspond to the world in all its complexity."[37] Compassion can respond to the gesture of those who are inarticulate, thereby helping "that which is subordinate to find its own voice and, perhaps, to expand the space in which [the subordinate] can be for itself rather than only for the order."[38] In the compassionate view, Budd's last words are not mere gestures, as Arendt characterizes them. They, like Jesus' embrace of the Grand Inquisitor in *The Brothers Karamazov,* represent acts of resistance to repression, because, as Sennett suggests, they are a response outside the terms of repression.[39]

Without consideration of the meanings of words and gestures outside the realm of past dominant discourse, the logic of any theory of authority as the rational practice of freedom is dubious. Many voices speak to us from different perspectives. This does not make what they communicate "mere" gesture. The rational modes of speech taken to be constitutive of authority exclude certain critical human dimensions, voices, and "interests" from the public realm. Indeed, the structure of authority in the public realm is connected internally to this exclusion. These dimensions, voices, and interests cannot be translated simply into the language of dispassionate, discursive speech. Nevertheless, their expressiveness is essential to understanding the nuances of meaning, and the recognition of what is silenced, by the speech of political actors.

For example, Sara Ruddick describes the ways that the mother's interest in the growth and preservation of her child—an interest oriented toward the particularity of each child's person—leads her to a dramatically different orientation to the child's needs than that required by the culture's imperative of "acceptability." This imperative constrains the mother's attention to the child, a particularized attention with a more ambiguous, flexible set of rules, in favor of regimenting the child to fit the culture's desiderata. From the perspective of "maternal thinking," the raising of girls for self-abnegating roles in our culture, and the raising of boys for military service, is irrational. It violates the mother's interest in protecting the child. But the subordination of this interest in favor of the "rationality" of acceptability makes the mother's "knowledge" of her child's needs appear irrational.[40]

The dominant discourse on authority places strict limits on the publicly expressible, and limits critical reflection about the norms and values that structure "private" life, and which affect the melodies of public speech.[41] By rejecting the ambiguities that our feelings introduce, we reject a mode of compassionate authority that would remind us that the construction of an harmonious world is always an "ambiguous achievement: it excludes and denigrates that which does not fit into its confines."[42] Nevertheless, accepting the concept of compassionate authority does not permit one to use it as a cover for maudlin sentimentality. Nor does it permit one to so over-broaden the concept of authority as to render it meaningless. The difficult task of distinguishing authority in this looser sense from other types of political action remains. Compassion has the potential for humanizing authority. If women do not speak authoritatively, perhaps their hesitancy reveals the ambiguity, and the choices, behind all rule systems. By reminding us of this ambi-

guity, the voice and gesture of compassion shocks us into a
memory of what has been hidden by the ordered discourse of
authority.

<h1 style="text-align:center">NOTES</h1>

1. Initially this exclusion extended to the denial that even individual
   women could enter into the establishment of the "social contract."
   Even as liberalism was modified to include more and more persons, the exclusion of specific forms of "authorizing" remained
   gender-specific. See Teresa Brennan and Carole Pateman, "Mere
   Auxiliaries to the Commonwealth: Women and the Origins of
   Liberalism," *Political Studies* 27 (1978); and Irene Diamond and
   Nancy Hartsock, "Beyond Interests in Politics: A Comment on
   Virginia Sapiro's 'When Are Interests Interesting? The Problem
   of the Political Representation of Women,'" *American Political Sci-
   ence Review* 75 (1983): 191.
2. See Jean Bethke Elshtain, *Public Man/Private Woman* (Princeton:
   Princeton University Press, 1982); Dorothy Dinnerstein, *The Mer-
   maid and the Minotaur* (New York: Harper and Row, 1976); Nancy
   Chodorow, *The Reproduction of Mothering* (Berkeley: University of
   California Press, 1978) and Susan Okin, *Women in Western Political
   Thought* (Princeton: Princeton University Press, 1979).
3. See Michel Foucault, *Power/Knowledge: Selected Interviews and Other
   Writings, 1972–1977* (New York: Pantheon Books, 1980), espe-
   cially chapters 6 and 8. See also Ann Kaplan, "Is the Gaze Male?"
   in Ann Snitow et al. eds., *Powers of Desire: The Politics of Sexuality*
   (New York: Monthly Review Press, 1983), pp. 309–327.
4. See the general discussion of excuse and justification in law in
   George Fletcher, *Rethinking Criminal Law* (Boston: Little, Brown,
   1978), and "The Individualization of Excuse," *Southern California
   Law Review* 47 (1974): 1269–1304. See also my discussions of the
   implications of this for a theory of criminal responsibility in "The
   Irony of the Insanity Plea: A Theory of Relativity," *The Journal of
   Psychiatry and Law* (Fall 1982): 285–308.
5. Jessica Benjamin, "Master and Slave: The Fantasy of Erotic Domination," in Snitow, *Powers of Desire*, p. 295.
6. See Ivan Ilych's review of research on gendered speech in his *Gender* (New York: Pantheon Books, 1982), pp. 132–139.
7. I am not using the term "female" only in the biological sense. I
   mean to suggest that the social construction of femaleness has
   contributed to the reading of the meaning of female bodies, etc.,
   in ways that are hidden by the language of authority, and seem to
   be irrelevant to it.

8. R.S. Peters, "Authority," in Anthony Quinton, ed. *Political Philosophy* (Oxford: Oxford University Press, 1967); Richard B. Friedman, "On the Concept of Authority in Political Philosophy," in Richard Flathman, ed., *Concepts in Social and Political Philosophy* (New York: Macmillan, 1973); and R.F. Kahn, "A Note on the Concept of Authority," in Gehan Wijeyewardene, ed., *Leadership and Authority* (Singapore: University of Malaya Press, 1968).
9. Friedman, "On the Concept of Authority," p. 127.
10. Hannah Arendt is a theorist who dissents from the classification of authority as a subset of what Max Weber called imperative coordination. But the degree to which her model of authority succeeds in breaking out of the classification of authority as a type of hierarchical relationship will be examined below.
11. See Friedman, "On the Concept of Authority," p. 127.
12. Friedman, p. 134.
13. See Joseph Raz, *Practical Reasons and Norms* (London: Hutchinson, 1975) for an extreme formulation of the separation of moral judgments and the obligation to obey.
14. Dinnerstein, *The Mermaid and the Minotaur*, pp. 166, 177.
15. Dinnerstein, p. 176.
16. Chodorow, *The Reproduction of Mothering*, pp. 180–1.
17. Foucault, *Power/Knowledge*, p. 80.
18. See Evelyn Fox Keller, *Gender and Science* (Cambridge: Harvard University Press, 1985), Carol MacMillan, *Women, Reason, and Nature* (Princeton: Princeton University Press, 1982), and Sara Ruddick, "Maternal Thinking," in Joyce Trebilcot, ed., *Mothering: Essays in Feminist Theory* (Totowa, NJ: Rowman and Allenheld, 1984).
19. Jean Elshtain, "Antigone's Daughters," *democracy* 2 (1982): 51.
20. Carol Gilligan, *In A Different Voice* (Cambridge: Harvard University Press, 1982), p. 43.
21. At this juncture it must be reiterated that the apparently cavalier use of "women" and "men" in no way is meant to imply derivation from biology, or to ignore real differences for men and women of different races, classes, etc., as well as individual differences.
22. Sophocles, *Antigone* in Green and Lattimore, eds., *Greek Tragedies* (Chicago: University of Chicago Press, 1960), vol. I, p. 204.
23. *Antigone*, p. 206.
24. *Antigone*.
25. Hannah Arendt, "What Is Authority?" in Arendt, *Between Past and Future* (New York: Viking Press, 1961), p. 121.
26. Friedman, "On the Concept of Authority," pp. 98–9.
27. Gilligan, *In a Different Voice*, pp. 48, 47.
28. David McClelland, *Power: The Inner Experience*, (New York: Irvington, 1975), pp. 96–99.

29. See Sennett's discussion in *Authority* (New York: Vintage, 1981).
30. Sennett, p. 6.
31. Hannah Arendt, *On Revolution* (New York: Viking Press, 1963), pp. 86, 107.
32. Arendt, *On Revolution,* p. 109.
33. Arendt, *On Revolution,* p. 82.
34. Arendt, *On Revolution.*
35. Herman Melville, *Billy Budd and Other Tales* (New York: Signet, 1961), p. 70.
36. Melville, "Billy Budd," pp. 68–9.
37. William Connolly, "Modern Authority and Ambiguity" (Amherst: University of Massachusetts, unpublished manuscript, 1984), p. 21.
38. Connolly, p. 22.
39. Sennett, *Authority,* p. 198. See also my discussion of George Orwell's images of women in "Women, Compassion and Rationality: Rethinking the Power/Authority Distinction," *Papers in Comparative Studies* 4 (1985): 81–90.
40. Ruddick, "Maternal Thinking."
41. For an interesting discussion of the consequent reduction of the meaning of human communication see Oliver Sacks's exploration of the world of "idiots savants" in "The Twins," *The New York Review of Books* 32 (1985): 16–20.
42. Connolly, p. 18.

10

THE AUTHORITY OF ALTERNATIVES

KIM LANE SCHEPPELE and KAROL EDWARD SOŁTAN

RETHINKING AUTHORITY

When Charles I was beheaded by order of Parliament in 1649, both politics and political theory lost something important also. Sovereignty, so central to the practice and theory of politics, was executed with him, although it died a more lingering death. The political institutions of Britain were almost completely transformed in consequence; over time, a more democratic system of governance, a powerful parliament and a weak monarchy, replaced the old order.[1] In political theory, however, a mere adjective disguised the radical restructuring; *"popular* sovereignty" allowed the old ways of thinking to survive more forcefully than the monarchy itself. "In political thought and analysis," Michel Foucault observed, "we still have not cut off the head of the king."[2]

Nowhere is this deference to the still-whole Charles more apparent than in discussions of authority. Max Weber's three types of authority—rational, traditional, and charismatic—are all cen-

The authors' names are listed alphabetically. We are most grateful to Robert Axelrod, Richard Brandt, John Chamberlin, Michael Cohen, James Coleman, Richard Hall, Don Herzog and Roland Pennock for providing insightful comments in record time as this paper was being written. We would also like to thank Mark Brandon, Daniel Levine, Robert Powell and Joseph Vining for suggesting useful leads in early conversations about this subject.

tered in offices or persons who are obeyed,[3] although Weber was describing not only monarchical but also legal and bureaucratic forms of political control. In a recent article, Joseph Raz noted that "it is common to regard authority over persons as centrally involving a right to rule."[4] One might argue that the concern with *sources* of authority, identifying authority with the person from whom it flows, necessarily reveals a breakdown of the monarchy; when the king dies one has to figure out what authorizes someone else to step in to replace him. But the basic *structure* of thinking about the subject—that authority involves a hierarchical relationship between authority figure and subject, a relationship which gives one the right to give orders to the other and which creates obligations for the other to obey— still reflects the development of political thinking in the monarchical past.[5]

In this paper, we cut off the head of the king. We argue that the association of authority with obedience to authority figures is just one example of a more general phenomenon. Authority, in our view, is not simply the right of actor A to get actor B to carry out A's will voluntarily. Instead, authority is found when actor B finds compelling particular properties of A, when A may be a person, a solution to a puzzle, or, more generally, any alternative in a choice situation. Authority is constituted not by person A willing a particular state of affairs which is then carried out, but rather by person B being attracted to the state of affairs offered by alternative A and voluntarily choosing that option over others. When generalized this way, authority resides not only in persons or offices, but also in texts, rituals, types of explanation, justifications, reasons, or particular real or ideal social arrangements. Saying a law, a set of religious beliefs, a dictionary, a moral theory, or a particularly good argument has authority becomes less mysterious with our conception because one does not have to assume that these things have wills or preferences. We can say properties of these things attract us to select them, without having to assume that they are willing us to do so.

We argue that *positive authority* may be revealed empirically in the alternatives selected through collective choices made by political actors acting under a special set of conditions. When autonomous individuals are given an implicit or explicit choice among alternatives, the alternative chosen in a collective choice process possesses more authority than the alternatives not chosen. These positive choices may reveal *normative authority* to the extent that the attractive properties implicit in the alternative chosen are made explicit[6] and provide the motivation for the decision, to the extent that the actors choosing the alternatives are free from the influence of force or fraud and can make their decisions purely on the basis of the attractive properties the alternative possesses, and to the extent that this alternative would be chosen by an extensive and diverse set of political actors with different individual interests, thus ensuring that the alternative has wide approval not reducible to its appeal to narrow self-interest.

Looking at the authority of alternatives permits us simultaneously a more general and more unified view of a variety of different aspects of authority. In the rest of this chapter, we explicate and justify this more general view of authority and show how it provides a clearer alternative to the discussions of authority currently in use.

A COLLECTIVE CHOICE FRAMEWORK FOR THINKING ABOUT POSITIVE AUTHORITY

Our notion of positive authority can be made clearer by reference to models of collective choice.[7] Collective choice models begin by postulating a set of individuals, each having his or her own interests or preferences. These individuals also have different amounts of resources which, when used, are capable of influencing collective choice in much the same way that a field of individual forces of different strengths determines the final location of a moving object. The individuals' interests or preferences determine the direction in which the group decision is pulled, just as the individual force fields in physics determine the trajectory of a projectile.[8] The collective choice is the result of these forces. By a collective choice, we mean a decision that is collectively *made,* rather than an outcome that is arrived at through innumerable and uncoordinated independent decisions. A collectively made decision is characterized by a procedure that specifies the relationship between the individual decisions and the decision of a particular social group. The general model can be useful in understanding many types of situations, including the varieties of market which approximate what Friedrich von Hayek[9] has called a "spontaneous order" and the political structures which are the result of central design, characterized by Hayek as a "made order." Our interest in this chapter will be mostly in the latter. As Charles Lindblom[10] might characterize it, we are interested primarily in politics, not markets.

Two complications need to be introduced into this basic model to begin to understand the problem posed by the notion of authority. First, we must distinguish resources that belong to the actors who participate in the decision from resources that are attributes of alternatives among which the choice is to be made.[11] A resource, as we conceive of it, is anything that can influence a decision.[12] The resources that belong to individuals can be used to promote alternatives favored by those individuals, regardless of the attributes of those alternatives.[13] In an election, for example, individuals may use their personal resources, such as money and organizing skills, to help their favored candidate win. In a war, a state may use its arms and military personnel to achieve a victory. An outcome in a collective choice problem like an election or a war (where potentially conflicting individual interests are eventually combined in one result) may be, and often has been, seen entirely as a function of the different personal resources that the actors bring to bear in the competition among interests.

But resources also belong to the different alternatives among which the various interests are competing. The more resources a particular alternative has, the more likely it will be selected or will win in a battle of interests, no matter who favors it.[14] Fighting armies often divide the contested turf at a river and individuals bargaining over money tend to split the difference,[15] even when personal resources are quite unequal. The solutions of the river and an equal split have attributes which make them obvious choices. These solutions, which may be anomalies if only personal resources are considered, provide the basis for our discussion of authority. Authority exists in an alternative when autonomous individuals collectively choose it because of the resources it possesses.

The authority an alternative possesses, then, is a function of the strength of its resources. An alternative is not simply authoritative or not authoritative, but rather more or less authoritative depending on the resources which are possessed by that alternative. Decisions among alternatives that are made on some basis other than the alternative's resources do not reveal authority. For example, the decision to promote a friend in business simply because he is one's friend or the decision to steal a car simply because one would like to have it are not authority-revealing choices. Friendship, self-interest, or naked personal gain in these cases are not resources of the alternatives, but attributes of a particular actor. Choosing an alternative because someone else wants one to also reflects not the resources of the alternative selected, but rather the attributes of a particular social relationship and context. Not all choices, then, reveal authority. Only those choices that are based on the resources possessed by the alternatives do. The stronger the resources the alternative has, the more authority it has.

We will examine two types of resources possessed by alternatives that make them more likely to be the solution to collective choice problems: the obviousness of an alternative and the force of persuasive justifications which may be marshalled on its behalf.[16] An obvious alternative is more likely to be chosen because expectations converge on it and it is, as a result, easy to agree on. A persuasively justified alternative is also more likely to be chosen because individuals see and may be persuaded by the good reasons for choosing it. The more resources an alternative possesses, the more likely it will be chosen, and the more authority it reveals.[17]

A second complicating factor in the collective choice framework needs to be introduced to facilitate our discussion of authority. We must make more explicit the role of procedures in collective choice. A typical collective choice is a process that arrives at some conclusion using a more or less well-defined procedure, where the goal is usually to determine some substantive outcome. But collective choices are more properly seen as two-stage processes, where first a procedure for making the decision is chosen (explicitly or implicitly) and then a substantive decision is made.[18]

In the case of American government, for example, we would ordinarily say that the Constitutional Convention in Philadelphia made certain choices of procedures (for choosing leaders and for making laws, for example) and that these have been only infrequently modified by amendment or court interpretation. One might think that these collective choice procedures were chosen only once, leaving most current collective choices to decide only on substantive outcomes. Strictly speaking, however, this is not true. Every time Congress acts to create a statute, for example, it has to choose a procedure for enacting that law. Every time, a procedure *other* than the established one *could* be chosen. We rarely see deviations from the constitutionally established procedure because the established procedure has become obvious (that's just the way we do things) and because it has been persuasively justified (separation of powers minimizes the chance of tyranny; the Constitution creates a set of constraints on government that make possible the realization of particular ideals; without following this procedure, the Congress would not be creating an official law within a constitutional framework). But it is not impossible that some other alternative could be chosen, and occasionally debates over particular aspects of procedure (abolishing the Electoral College, for example) make the implicit choice of procedure explicit.

Most of the time there is not much point in stressing the (theoretical) possibility that well-established procedures are rechosen each time a decision is made using them. But it is useful to call attention to this fact if we are to understand authority. We need to remember that every time a collective choice is made *using* a procedure, a choice of procedure is implicitly made. Procedures are alternatives that may have authority in much the same way that substantive outcomes are alternatives that may have authority. The strength of the resources possessed by the procedure determines the degree of authoritativeness of that alternative.

This focus on procedures allows us to see another constraint on the ability of positive choices to reveal authority. Only those choices that are made on the basis of the resources the alternative possesses demonstrate the authority of the alternative, and even these choices demonstrate more authority to the extent that they are the products of collective choice rather than of purely personal choice. Collective choices necessarily respond more to the more general values revealed in an alternative's resources than does purely personal choice. Trivial personal decisions, like deciding on a brand of toothpaste, are less likely to reveal authority because the decisions are unlikely to incorporate any reference to the authoritative resources possessed by the particular choice; in fact, the particular alternative chosen may not have any of the resources that reveal authority in the first place. The sorts of choices likely to be made in a collective, public decision process are more likely to have the relevant resources and the collective choice process is more likely to bring them to the fore in decision making.

These two modifications of the traditional collective choice framework give us a coherent way of thinking about authority. Authority exists in an alternative when the alternative possesses resources that would make autonomous, rationally choosing individuals select that particular alternative on the basis of the resources it possesses in a collective choice process. These alternatives may be of two types: substantive and procedural. Both substantive and procedural alternatives may possess resources (like obviousness and justifiability) that make them more likely to be chosen than alternatives which possess less of these resources. The degree of authority of a particular alternative is a function of the strength of the resources it possesses.

ATTRIBUTES OF AUTHORITATIVE OUTCOMES

What makes particular solutions to collective choice problems compelling? Discussions of authority have generally assumed that the characteristics of persons and offices rather than the characteristics of the arrangements or outcomes produced by collective choices command deference and obedience. Some solutions to collective decision problems, however, may be adopted by a group not because there is a particular sort of leadership favoring it, but rather because of the attractiveness of the outcome independent of the source of the suggestion. The rule "first come, first served," for example, may be adopted to solve a queuing problem even when it is suggested as a solution by a five-year-old child. The solution "split the difference" may emerge as an outcome when forwarded by one of the bargaining parties even when the other bargaining party has grown deeply angry and suspicious of the suggester. The larger point is that the characteristics of the outcome itself may recommend the adoption of a particular choice even when the characteristics of the person forwarding the outcome would tend to operate in the opposite direction. In short, the attributes of an outcome may make that outcome authoritative. The authoritative alternative beckons us to choose it over other less compelling alternatives on the basis of the resources it possesses.

Anthropomorphizing alternatives (saying they beckon) is intended, with its metaphorical quality, to enable comparison with authoritative persons. Most discussions of authority emphasize that compliance with the wishes of an authority is a matter of will, not compulsion. People voluntarily choose authoritative alternatives, allowing them to lead. One chooses a doctor to consult about a medical problem, for example, because one believes that the doctor is most capable of choosing an authoritative solution to one's ailment. In much the same way, people are led to choose particular alternatives and voluntarily comply with the direction they provide because the alternatives are judged to be most authoritative. Following the alternative "first come, first served," people order their actions accordingly. They give up their independent, explicitly reasoned judgment, allowing themselves to be affected by the "attractive" or "magnetic" properties of the outcome, in much the same way as they give up their independent judgment when they see a doctor for a medical problem.[19] It is the authoritativeness of the alternative, like the authoritativeness of the person or office, to which we surrender our independent judgment, at least provisionally. We follow where the alternative beckons.

The nature of this beckoning needs to be explored. Just as with authority of persons and offices, the ways in which alternatives beckon are varied. Persons and alternatives may beckon as authority because they possess charisma or obviousness, appealing to our emotions and intuitions as their basis for support. Persons and alternatives may also be authoritative because the person's choices and the alternative's attractiveness may be supported by elaborated arguments, appealing to reason as the basis for support. The combination of intuitive and reasoned appeals, with both persons and alternatives, makes the person or alternative much more persuasive than he/she/it would be with only one source of support. Thus the charismatic, talented doctor has far more authority than the competent but nerdish doctor or the flashy but flawed one. So the "split the difference" alternative has more authority than a complicated but proportionately fairer solution (split the disputed amount according to the proportion of existing resources possessed by each of the parties so that the distribution at the end is more nearly equal) or an equally simple but less justifiable solution (give everything to Matilda). We will discuss each of these bases of authority in turn, first examining the intuitive appeals of alternatives in which the central property is their obviousness and then exploring the reasoned appeals of alternatives in which the central principle is their justifiability.

Obviousness as a Basis for Authority

Thomas Schelling once posed the following problem: suppose that you and a friend had arranged to meet at noon on Saturday somewhere in Manhattan, but you had neglected to determine where the meeting should take place.[20] Ideally, you would like to go and stand in a particular place where your friend would be most likely to show up. And your friend would like to pick the place where you would be most likely to go to wait for her. The circular, self-referential problem in which all the parties gain only through the convergence of mutual expectations is called a coordination game and the solution to a coordination game is perhaps the clearest example of an authoritative alternative.

Coordination games become trivial when there is some sort of communication or central leadership which can provide clues about the activities of others. But sometimes stable solutions may emerge in the absence of communication or leadership because the parties know enough about the array of choices and the relevant circumstances to select that solution which others, acting independently, would also choose. Residents of New Haven know when meeting someone else from New Haven that the place most likely to be the scene of a joint meeting in Manhattan is under the giant clock at Grand Central Station. The situation and the problem press a particular solution upon the decider in much the same way as an authoritative person or office can make authoritative suggestions, which are obeyed. In either case, authority, which compels the choice of some alternatives over others, is revealed when multiple independent individuals in a situation resembling a coordination game can choose the same alternative.

Obviousness, the intuitive appeal of a particular solution for a particular problem, may appear to be simply in the eye of the beholder, but the fact that coordination games do often have solutions (in other words, that individuals can choose the same answer when trying to coordinate their answers with others) indicates that there is something more going on here. The outcomes themselves must possess properties which make them obvious choices. These properties or resources enable particular outcomes to beckon us to surrender our judgment to them; that is, they are authoritative. These properties will be discussed in this section under the general headings of precedent, symmetry, uniqueness, simplicity, and prominence.

Precedent. One obvious choice for an obvious solution is to select the solution that was previously selected the last time the same problem arose. This is the basic idea that drives the common law, but its importance can be seen in many other contexts. A simple behavioral habit may come to be perceived as binding, since normative expectations can be created out of nonnormative but regular patterns. If one comes along each day in a car and gives a ride to a friend who plans to walk, even though the meeting is never formally arranged, the friend may feel he has a right to expect one's arrival the more the happy coincidence continues. Lateness one day may require an apology or at least an explanation, signs that a normative violation has occurred. Other things being equal, an alternative's obviousness is increased when it has been used before. This is one important factor in the authoritativeness of traditions.[21] Traditions matter in part because they *are* traditions, apart from their content.[22] A deeply conservative force in decision-making, precedent tends to preserve the status quo. Special reasons are required to alter existing arrangements that, because of their endurance, have become authoritative, the obvious choices.

Symmetry. Where the situation requires a distribution to be selected from among a set of alternative distributions, those distributions which are symmetric will by and large have more authoritative force than those which are not symmetric. Hermann Weyl noted that throughout the history of mathematics and the arts, symmetry has been a pervasive theme.[23] The prevalence of patterns in which the ability to map one image into another has featured prominently suggests that symmetry has a magnetic or attractive force. The solution "split the difference" or the alternative of turn-taking both possess this critical aspect of symmetry. The "eye for an eye" punishments in Islamic law can be understood at least in part by their symmetrical character.[24] Reciprocity, which seems close to a universal social norm,[25] derives some of its authoritative character from its translation of the principle of symmetry.

Uniqueness. Other things being equal, a solution that stands out as being conspicuously and uniquely different from all other solutions will beckon choice. Studies of the identification of criminal suspects have shown the eyewitnesses will be sure they have rightly identified the guilty one when they have chosen the one photograph in the set which looks different from the rest, rather than the one of the person who actually committed the crime.[26] The clock at Grand Central Station is selected as the preferred meeting site for New Haven residents in Manhattan, in part because it is the only one of its kind.[27] Uniqueness probably contributes to the authority of presidents and other single leaders, even though a legislature or other collective body may constrain the leader at every turn. Uniqueness focuses attention and makes its bearer more likely to be chosen as authoritative.

Simplicity. Simple outcomes are likely to be chosen in preference to more complicated ones, in part because simple outcomes are easier to grasp and easier to communicate. They also derive their authoritativeness by appearing to capture the essence of a phenomenon. The ideal in the natural sciences that simpler formulations are to be preferred to more complicated ones[28] reveals these properties. The U.S. tax code has been attacked for its complexity, even though some of the complexity is due to the attempt of the tax code authors to be fair or to encourage investment in publicly desirable projects. Complexity in this debate appears to be bad in itself, regardless of the reason for it. Simplicity attracts, other things being equal.

Prominence. Prominent alternatives are those alternatives that are evident against a socially constructed backdrop. A particular solution may appear prominent if everyone believes everyone else will choose it and, as a result, expectations converge on it. Circulating a rumor that "everyone" wants a particular option makes it more likely that the option will be selected, even if "everyone" did not in fact want the option when the rumor got started. The rumor creates expectations that become self-fulfilling prophecies. Similarly, the anniversary of a particularly important event may become prominent because the date stands apart from others as special, and expectations converge on that date as the time that something special will happen again. Prominence, created from the construction of expectations in particular social situations, can make an alternative appear obvious, and can compel the choice of that outcome over other potential choices. Prominence is different from the other attributes that make alternatives obvious because, while the others may have magnetic force across times and cultures, prominence is specific to particular cultures and moments. What makes something prominent depends on the particular background of expectations at the specific place and time. It may be possible for the individuals in that setting to see the obviousness of a particular outcome, but that obviousness may not be reducible to the more culturally invariant properties of precedent, uniqueness, symmetry, and simplicity. Prominence identifies the specific choices that appear obvious because of the unique background or history of a particular social group.[29]

These elements of obviousness attract choice, compelling us to choose alternatives that possess these attributes without necessarily reasoning through a separate justification. Obviousness rests on an appeal to intuition in much the same way that Weber's notion of charismatic authority appeals to the irrational.[30] But obviousness is different from charismatic authority as described by Weber because charismatic authority always sets itself against the routine, expected, and traditional, while obviousness draws its compelling character from the fact that individuals' expectations converge on solutions that possess it, reinforcing established patterns. In both cases, however, the appeal of obviousness or charisma can exist independently of a rational foundation and so can the authority generated by these means.

The more different elements of obviousness a particular outcome possesses, the more likely the outcome is to be chosen. Turn-taking, for example, may recommend itself because it is symmetrical, but it is also simple and unique. Deciding like cases alike has not only precedent on its side, but also symmetry and prominence. These solutions, selected almost automatically, possess authority because we are willing to choose them, not because they will us to obey. And we are willing to choose them precisely because they are obvious.

Justifiability as a Basis for Authority

"Sentence first, verdict afterwards," ordered the Red Queen at the trial of the defenseless Knave of Hearts accused of stealing the Red Queen's tarts. "Stuff and nonsense," cried Alice, obviously believing that the Queen's order, even with its royal origins, merited no particular deference.[31] The Red Queen clearly lost whatever authority she might have possessed as Alice came to learn that her commands, despite their occasional rhyme, had no reason.

The ability to give persuasive reasons for one's choices can be seen both as a cause of the decisions and as evidence of the authoritativeness of the decisions one has made. The ability of a particular person to consistently give persuasive reasons for her decisions may serve to make that person authoritative, as Friedrich notes.[32] But even in Friedrich's view, the persuasiveness of the reasons, not the person herself, provides the basis of authority. Alternatives for which persuasive justifications can be marshalled are more likely to be chosen than alternatives that have fewer or weaker justifications, and so the reasons can be seen as causes of the decision. John Kingdon reports that congressmen think through how they might explain particular stances to their constituents before they vote.[33] Explainable votes are cast; unexplainable votes are avoided when possible. Without the reasons to back up the choice, the alternative may not be selected.

The presence of reasons may not only motivate the actor to make a particular decision, but it may also provide evidence that the decision is itself authoritative. The more a decision can be persuasively justified, the more authoritative it is because the reasons will have a tendency to convince others to make the same choice. The Supreme Court in *Roe v. Wade*[34] was criticized by legal scholars not so much for the conclusion it reached, but for its departure from the conventions of justification that characterize authoritative Supreme Court decisions. Scholars who might have agreed with the result for other reasons felt the particular justifications that were given could not have persuaded those who felt differently.[35] As a result, the decision created a visible, organized group to fight the result. The reasons did not persuade; they alienated. The decision lacked authority to the extent that it did not lead others to reach the same conclusion from the justifications given.

In our view, what makes reasons *authoritative* reasons is their capacity to persuade.[36] But what *about* reasons makes them likely to achieve this result? Some of the signs that indicate that justifications are more likely to be authoritative are their reliability, robustness, and universality, as well as the tendency of the justifications to reduce arbitrariness. We will take each of these in turn.

Reliability. It is a sign that justifications are stronger, and hence more likely to serve as the reason for a particular decision, when they are reliable. Justifications are reliable when particular individuals, asked at different points to give reasons for a decision, find the same reasons convincing each time. Reliable justifications endure; they are not subject to the pressures of particular temporary circumstances. Judicial decisions must attempt to meet this standard of justification, for once cases have been decided, the reasons for decisions will come back to haunt judges in later cases. Judge Benjamin Cardozo, in *MacPherson v. Buick*[37] and *Palsgraf v. Long Island Railroad*[38] emphasized that foreseeability should be the basis for liability in negligence cases in tort, carving a particular sort of justification deep into the common law. Cardozo found the same reasons persuasive over and over again, giving his justifications a sort of consistency over time that probably helped his opinions become highly authoritative. In another example, the general lack of dissenting opinions in implied warranty cases in nineteenth-century New York might be attributed to the persistence over the century of a common justification for decisions in these cases, one that emphasized symmetry.[39] Justifications that remain reliable over time are more compelling than justifications that are called upon to account for single, particular, idiosyncratic decisions.

Robustness. It is a sign that justifications are stronger, and hence more likely to provide a basis for choice, when *different* individuals, especially individuals with very different interests, find themselves justifying their decisions in the same way when confronted with the same alternatives. Justifications that one would not use if one were in the other's place lack robustness. For example, suppose two people were trying to decide how to divide $100. Person A, absent special circumstances, cannot justify why she should get $75 of it because if she were Person B she would not find such an appeal convincing. Person B cannot claim $75 for the same reasons. When one puts oneself in the position of the other and the justifications fall apart, then one has nonrobust justifications.[40] We can see this is other contexts. Appeals to the fairness of a particular labor-management agreement are more likely to be accepted by others when these appeals come independently from both sides. An elected official's authority is stronger to the extent that voters from many different backgrounds justify their votes for the official in the same way. Court opinions are stronger to the extent that the reasons given for the judgments are the same both for all court members and in relevant cases across jurisdictions, and to the extent that the reasons given are accepted by the losing parties. Justifications that are used by a variety of people with different interests are more compelling as a basis for the choice of a particular alternative than justifications that do not have such widespread acceptance.

Universality. It is a sign that justifications are stronger, and hence more likely to provide the basis for choice, when they can be easily transferred across different social contexts, to the extent that they are universally persuasive. Wage and salary systems, providing sets of criteria that can be used to justify differential pay, are more authoritative to the extent that they can be transferred to a wide variety of different sorts of firms.[41] The decline in the hierarchical structure of the Catholic Church in Latin America following Vatican II provided a set of meanings and justifications for more egalitarian and less mystical institutions. These justifications could be transferred across institutional settings, providing a model for justification in making political institutions less mystical and more egalitarian in Venezuela and Colombia.[42] Justifications that can be transferred in this way show signs of being more authoritative than justifications that resist transfer. Generally, the more a particular reason is comprehensible and provides guidance in a wider variety of different social circumstances, the more evidence we have that the reason is compelling and that the choices which are implied by the reason will be selected as authoritative.

Reduction of arbitrariness. Justifications that make clear the capacity of an alternative to minimize arbitrariness will be more persuasive than those that do not and are more likely to serve as the rational basis for the choice of that particular alternative. Justifications for alternatives that appeal only to narrow self-interest or to the idosyncratic features of the particular choice situation do not have this arbitrariness-reducing quality. Unless the justifications suggest principles of criticism, standards against which future justifications can be judged, they do not reduce arbitrariness either.[43] For example, justifying a particular administrative decision by saying that the decision was what the administrator felt like at the time is unlikely to be perceived as reducing arbitrariness. The skepticism of small children at the "because I said so" justifications of parents reveals this principle also. The reduction of arbitrariness is quite close to a substantive standard for justifications, because certain sorts of reasons which avoid either appeals to self-interest of the decider or reference to particular idiosyncratic or irrelevant features of the choice situation are limited in substantive scope.

Justifiability of alternatives rests on an appeal to reason, just as Friedrich's concept of authority does.[44] But while Friedrich argues that authority springs from the assumed ability of authoritative persons to elaborate reasons for decisions, we have argued here that the authority resides in the alternatives rather than in the persons who can justify them. While the cleverness of particular people in discerning reasons may matter in justifying any particular decision, the ability of an alternative to generate reasons is more critical for assessing authority. The cleverest of people may find it hard to justify a particular alternative, while the least perceptive may be able to articulate general reasons why another alternative should be favored. The skills of the justifier are not the source of authority; rather the ability of justifications for the alternative to attract support is the real basis of authority. In both Friedrich's formulation and ours, the appeal to reason provides the source of authoritativeness. With the discussion of obviousness and charismatic authority in the section above, the discussion of persuasive justification gives authority both a rational and an intuitive basis.

If a particular alternative has both obviousness and justifiability working in its favor, it will be even more likely to be selected than if either is operating alone. Equality, on this view, not only is a reliable, robust, and universal principle that reduces arbitrariness, but it also has symmetry and simplicity operating on its behalf. If hunches based on obviousness can be backed up with good reasons, then choices for which is it possible to marshal both sorts of resources will have more authority than others which cannot.

ATTRIBUTES OF AUTHORITATIVE PROCEDURES

Authority of procedures is more closely related to traditional discussions of authority than authority of outcomes. Hierarchical authority, in which one or many persons allow another to decide for them, is the standard example of authority in most such discussions. Allowing someone to decide for you is, of course, a decision-making *procedure,* a procedure according to which the king, or chairperson, or president shall decide such issues. To allow someone to choose for you is to follow a procedure no less than if you allow a majority to choose for you, although, of course, the two procedures are quite different in other critical respects. The choice and use of a procedure in making collective choices is always present, even if not explicit.[45]

Some procedures are more likely to be chosen than others, just as some substantive outcomes are more likely to be chosen than others. Procedures, like outcomes, differ in the strength of the resources they possess and are chosen when they possess more strength than other possible alternatives. The bases of authority for outcomes and procedures are the same, as a number of examples suggest. Having precedents counts in an alternative's favor for both outcomes and procedures, and the status quo is more likely to win than other alternatives. Once a procedure has been used in a particular type of situation, it is far easier to agree to use it in the future. Thus, simple repetition of a pattern of behavior gives that pattern authority. The precedent may be very specific; for example, a particular chess club may have always used the Borda method of voting to make decisions. But it may also be very general; for example, in most (perhaps all) democratic cultures precedent strongly favors decisions by majority vote, whether in chess clubs or in parliaments. Someone organizing a new chess club may be influenced by a general cultural precedent in favor of making at least key decisions by majority vote. The cultural precedent favoring majority rule may be so strong that it blurs our perceptions of other attributes of majority voting that give it a claim to authoritativeness.[46]

But there are other considerations beside precedent that would favor majority voting. Majority rule is unique, since it requires the fewest consenting parties consistent with a guarantee of a unique decision (barring ties) in every case. If we allow a decision based on the will of a group smaller than the majority, then two such groups may decide differently, and we will have two inconsistent decisions instead of one. Majority rule is obvious because in the class of reasonable, simple, and roughly democratic decision rules, it requires the consent of the fewest people. There are also, of course, persuasive justifications in favor of majority rule.[47] But a great deal of the power and authority of majority rule in democratic countries is due to the rule's *obviousness* once the choice is restricted to plausibly democratic procedures.

A rule that would require unanimity is another potentially authoritative choice of decision procedure. Requiring unanimity may have precedent on its side in a number of different situations. It is also an obvious alternative and relatively easy to agree on, other things being equal, because it is conspicuously unique in requiring *everyone's* consent. It is simple and easy to grasp. Again, there are also persuasive justifications that can be marshaled in favor of the unanimity rule.[48] Still, the obviousness of unanimity is likely to be an even more important factor than persuasive arguments in choosing this procedure.

Relative to most other procedures, both majority rule and unanimity are the obvious ones to select. Which of them is more obvious in a particular situation will depend upon various situation-specific considerations. In either event, their simplicity commends their adoption over other more complex rules. Alternatives that follow precedent, that are in some way conspicuously unique or simple and easy to understand, or that exhibit symmetry or prominence, are more likely to be chosen than other alternatives, regardless of whether the alternative is a procedure or an outcome. Similarly, the susceptibility of an alternative, whether procedural or substantive, to persuasive justification determines its likelihood of being chosen.

A rather different perspective on the authority of procedures can be gained if we consider *why* the obvious procedure will be more likely to be chosen. Obvious procedures may be chosen because their choice saves on decision costs. If we assume that one important goal for collective decisions is to minimize decision costs,[49] then an alternative will have authority to the extent that it serves this goal, other things being equal. We can assume, then, that the strength of resources possessed by a procedure is, in part, a function of the extent to which choosing that procedure allows us to save on the costs of reaching decisions using that procedure.

There is some anecdotal evidence that alternatives that are simple, unique, symmetrical, prominent, and have precedent on their side (that is, *obvious* alternatives) are in fact *easier* to agree on. Precisely because they are easier to agree on, it is easier to coordinate expectations around them. There is also evidence that such alternatives are more *likely* to be agreed on than others. If minimizing decision costs were the main object in choosing procedures, then we would expect to find systematic evidence that the alternatives that are cheapest to use are also the most often selected.

If collective decisions minimize decision costs, then it must be the case that, no matter how obvious a procedure might otherwise be, it will be less likely to be chosen when it is expensive to *use*. Other things being equal, a procedure will be more authoritative the cheaper it is to use. This is, of course, one of the key factors working against the unanimity rule.[50] It is very costly to obtain unanimity, somewhat less costly to obtain a majority and least costly of all to obtain the consent of one person. If collective decisions only minimized the cost of the *use* of the procedure (that is, the cost of getting people to consent), then the procedures requiring the choice of one person (either *any* one person or a particular person, as in a system of hierarchical authority) would always be the most likely to be chosen. This is obviously not the case, however, Other costs must be considered as well.

Not all the costs of a decision procedure are incurred at the time a choice is made, just as not all the costs of highway transportation are incurred during the movement of cars and trucks. Roads and vehicles must be built and they must be maintained. The same is true with procedures. They, too, must be established and maintained before they can be used in making decisions, and this is certainly not costless to do.

It is easier to understand what it means to build and maintain a road than to establish and maintain a procedure. In our view, a procedure is established to the extent that it becomes authoritative—that is, to the extent that the resources it possesses gain in strength. The procedure may gain arguments in its favor or become easy to agree on because it has precedent in its favor. For example, the Constitutional Convention in Philadelphia in 1787 and the ratifying conventions in the various states established, among other things, a set of procedures for creating federal laws. These conventions established these procedures and provided arguments that could be used to justify persuasively the use of these procedures. Since then, the maintenance of these procedures has required thwarting the use of alternative procedures, policing for violations of the procedures, punishing actions that undermine them, and calling new justifications for them to the attention of others. These maintenance efforts are not limited to a single historical moment, but must continue throughout a procedure's life. The costs of establishment and of maintenance of a procedure must be added to the cost of using the procedure to understand fully its costs.

The contrast between hierarchical authority and exchange, two decision-making procedures commonly used in contemporary political economies, can be made clearer by considering the relative costs of establishing and maintaining the two procedures. If we compare decision-making costs by simply looking at the costs of using the procedure, without considering the establishment and maintenance costs, then the results will be fairly clear. Heirarchical authority, since it does not require bargaining, will be cheaper to use than exchange. But if we incorporate establishment and maintenance costs, the picture becomes more complicated. As Lindblom points out, the high costs incurred by authority are mainly maintenance costs, not costs of use.[51] By contrast, the costs of maintaining exchange systems are low, although their use costs are higher. Considering both the costs of establishment and maintenance as well as the costs of use, we find that hierarchical authority does not look nearly as attractive as it might have if only use costs were considered.[52]

Even if we consider all the relevant decision-making costs, however, we will surely not exhaust all possible bases of authority an outcome or a procedure can possess. Another important resource for an alternative lies in the persuasiveness of the arguments that show it to be better than other alternatives, or more nearly right than they are. An alternative is authoritative to the extent that it can be chosen at low cost (where obviousness is one indicator of low cost) *and* to the extent the resulting choice is of high quality (where the fact that an alternative can be persuasively justified is one indicator of high quality).

What counts as a procedure of high quality will depend in general on the standards of quality that are found persuasive in the setting within which the authority is established. A few general comments are nonetheless possible on the subject. There are at least two different *types* of argument for a procedure being better or more nearly right than another. It can be justified as a better means to some accepted end, or it can be seen as a better end in itself. A number of authors recently have urged us to consider more seriously procedures as ends in themselves, as embodiments of values (such as respect for persons) independent of the other uses they may have.[53]

Procedures are more commonly justified with instrumental arguments, as representing a better *means* to some particular end. Although these justifications will probably depend both on the ends being sought and on the culture in which the justification is being made, one recurring standard for evaluating

procedures is that they produce authoritative outcomes, outcomes that are obvious or have persuasive arguments in their
favor. Courts of law provide good examples of procedures whose
authority derives, at least in part, from this sort of instrumental
consideration. Legal procedures, and the principles of due process and procedural justice that back them up, are authoritative
in part because they enable courts to arrive at authoritative
conclusions. When courts decide questions of fact, good procedures make it likely that they get the facts right. When they
decide questions of law, good procedures make it likely that
these decisions either seem obvious in light of existing law, or
can be persuasively justified, or both. Such good procedures
will be authoritative to the extent that they are effective instruments, independent of how costly they are to use.

Legal procedures are perhaps the most developed procedures of collective choice that are in part designed as instruments to obtain authoritative outcomes.[54] But other examples
are not hard to find. If we think of science as a special kind of
process of collective choice, in which theories are alternatives,
it is clear that scientific methods can be conceived as analogous
to legal procedures. They too are authoritative, and they are
authoritative to the extent that they are successful in obtaining
authoritative outcomes. Some of the best-rehearsed arguments
for hierarchical authority in many situations are also of this instrumental form. The ship captain or the doctor maintains her
authority to the extent that allowing her to make decisions produces good results. This type of instrumental basis for the authority of procedures is, as these examples demonstrate, of great
social significance.

The authority of procedures, then, derives from the same
attributes that we discussed in assessing the authority of outcomes. But we have elaborated here the connection between
obviousness and low cost of using a procedure as well as the
connection between justifiability and high quality in the selection of authoritative outcomes. The ability of a procedure to
minimize decision costs and the ability of a procedure to ensure
authoritative outcomes indicate that the particular procedure
possesses more resources than other alternatives. And the more
resources a particular procedure has, the more likely it is to be
chosen, acquiring authority.

NORMATIVE AND POSITIVE AUTHORITY

A positive choice has more normative force to the extent that: (1) effective authority (the resources actually used in making the decision) equals potential authority (the resources that could be marshaled in making the choice); (2) the choice is made by individuals acting under conditions of maximum autonomy, making the strength of resources the alternative possesses the primary basis for choice; and (3) more individuals participate in the decision process (extensiveness) and more individuals with different personal interests favor the same choice (diversity), ensuring that the justifications for the choice are likely to be persuasive in a wide variety of contexts and over a diverse range of interests. Positive choices by social actors may develop normative force the more the choices can be described as having met these conditions.[55] We will take each of these conditions in turn.

Effective versus potential authority. The potential authority of an alternative is a function of the resources an alternative has, whether or not those resources serve as the basis for choice. Effective authority is a function of the resources that are actually used in making a choice. An alternative may have persuasive arguments in its favor, for example, but the arguments need not actually be used in justifying the choice. In fact, no one in the collective decision situation may be aware of the existence of these potentially persuasive arguments. In such a case, the potential authority of an alternative is greater than the effective authority. The example given above of majority rule as an authoritative procedure is also relevant here. It may be that majority rule is selected over and over again as a procedure for making collective choices, strictly on the basis of precedent. But those selecting it may not be aware of the properties of uniqueness, simplicity, and justifiability that it possesses. To the extent that those choosing the alternative are not aware of the potential sources of authority of a choice, the effective authority of the alternative is less than the potential authority.

The study of effective authority is mainly a descriptive study; it is a study of actual patterns of authority. The study of potential authority can be, by constrast, the beginnings both of a normative theory of authority and of a standard of criticism of existing patterns of authority. If a group decides to move away from majority rule to a plurality system, or decides to abolish elections altogether, one can point to the potential authority of the alternative of majority rule and the varied resources that operate in its favor. If the newly chosen alternative does not have as many authoritative resources as the one discarded, then one can criticize the move because there is a loss of potential authority. The less potential authority some alternative has, the less normative force it has as well.

Choice under the condition of maximum autonomy. Actors' choices have more normative force to the extent that the choice is made under conditions which guarantee the actor maximum autonomy. At a minimum, this means that the actor cannot have made the choice while being forced or defrauded. The actor must know the full range of available alternatives and must be able to acquire all of the relevant information about each alternative.[56] To the extent that actors' choices are made under these conditions, the choices are not only positively authoritative, but normatively authoritative.

Extensive participation and diverse interests. An alternative is more normatively authoritative to the extent that it is chosen by a wide range of actors with diverse interests. The closer the number of participants in the decision is to the total number of possible participants[57] and the more diverse interests are represented in making the collective choice, the more normatively authoritative such a choice will be. When an alternative is chosen by an extensive group with diverse interests, this is a signal that the alternative chosen is selected for the authoritative resources it possesses and not for the narrow self-interest it might serve.

The more the conditions in which positive choices are made approach the standards specified here, the more normatively authoritative these choices are. The reasons for this are not hard to see, and provide another bridge to more traditional thinking about authority in normative theory. To the extent that individuals are pressured or tricked into making choices they would not make under more ideal circumstances, their choices are suspect from a normative point of view. Our discussion of the conditions of maximum autonomy is intended to distinguish positive choices that reflect social pressure from positive choices that are responsive only to the attributes of alternatives that make them authoritative. The more a choice reflects only the attractive properties of the alternatives and does not incorporate other potentially distracting elements, the more normative authority the choice reveals.

Extensive participation and the representation of diverse interests in collective choice ensures that decision will not exclusively represent the narrow self-interest of a particular ruling individual or group. To the extent that individuals in the potential deciding population are systematically excluded from participation, the resulting decision is less normatively authoritative. To the extent that individuals with diverse individual interests agree on the same choice, the more normative force that choice has. If everyone in a culture shares the same standards for obviousness and justifiability, then this criterion for normative authority will be redundant, because all will respond to the same features of authoritative alternatives and extensiveness and diversity will simply produce more the same sort of judgment. But if there are substantial differences in a population over standards of justifiability or over the elements that make a particular alternative obvious, then alternatives that appeal only to certain segments of the population will be less authoritative than those that appeal to all.

Our other criterion, that the effective authority of an alternative come as close as possible to its potential authority, provides a standard for criticism of choices among alternatives. To the extent that the choice of an alternative is made with incomplete understanding of the attractive (or detractive) resources of that alternative, the choice reveals less normative authority. By pointing out the available resources that were not used for the alternative chosen, or the superior resources available to an alternative not selected, one can criticize existing patterns of authority and propose new ones. A normative theory is implied in the criteria of obviousness and justifiability, a theory that argues that the very attributes of alternatives that make them likely to be empirically chosen is, when fully understood and voluntarily selected by an extensive and diverse group of individuals, the essence of legitimate authority in a normative sense.

The Authoritativeness of the
Authority of Alternatives

We have recast the problem of authority so that it is revealed in collective choices made from a set of alternatives. Instead of viewing the paradigmatic case of authority as one where A (a person or occupant of an office) wills B to follow A and B voluntarily complies, we have argued that authority resides in the attractiveness to B of particular resources (like obviousness and justifiability) offered by A (an alternative). When B chooses a particular alternative because of the resources it possesses, that alternative may be said to possess positive authority. When B chooses a particular alternative under a special set of conditions that guarantee the autonomy of B, the representativeness of the selection process and the full use of A's potential resources, the alternative then possesses normative authority.

By generalizing the notion of authority in this way, we move toward a more coherent form of theorizing. The attractiveness of an alternative can be either intuitive or rational, but both may be present in the same alternative, reinforcing each other and increasing the alternative's likelihood of being selected. Decisions about outcomes and decisions about procedures are responsive to largely the same set of attractive forces, attractive forces that also account for the authority of persons and offices. Our theory provides both a set of hypotheses about how choices will be made and a standard of criticism against which actual choices may be judged. Positive choice may fall short of normative choice for reasons normally associated with the exercise of power (the infringement on autonomy or the arbitrary exclusion of potential deciders), but the conceptual transition from power to authority is a matter of degree.

We have tried to develop a coherent theory of authority. Obviously, however, the present chapter is just a beginning. We are painfully conscious of how much work of conceptual clarification, empirical research, and normative argument remains to be done.

Notes

1. We are indebted to Don Herzog for calling our attention to the relevance of these events for our chapter.

2. Michel Foucault, *The History of Sexuality* (New York: Vintage, 1980), pp. 88–89.

3. All three types are located in persons, although rational-legal authority derives its legitimacy from the "legally established, impersonal order." Max Weber, *The Theory of Social and Economic Organization* (New York: Free Press, 1964), p. 328.

4. Joseph Raz, "Authority and Justification," *Philosophy and Public Affairs* 14 (1985): 3–29 at p. 3.

5. Hannah Arendt's discussion of authority explicitly recognizes that authority is associated with particular historical forms, forms that have eroded in practice even as they are preserved in theory. Hannah Arendt, "What Was Authority?" in Carl Friedrich, ed., *NOMOS I: Authority*, (Cambridge: Harvard University Press, 1958), pp. 81–112.

6. The attractive properties possessed by an alternative may be made explicit either by the decision-maker or by others. For normative authority to exist, the decision-maker must be aware of these properties and base the choice of alternative on the extent to which the alternative possesses them.

7. Models of collective choice derive their key inspiration from the theory of the market in economics. Outside economics, the particular version of collective choice we are interested in (because it is built around a set of actors who possess resources capable of influencing collective decisions) has been developed in mathematical form by James Coleman, among others. See James S. Coleman, *The Mathematics of Collective Action* (Chicago: Aldine, 1973). More informal versions are common in political science, especially in the pluralist tradition. A useful survey is provided by Eric Nordlinger, *On the Autonomy of the Democratic State* (Cambridge: Harvard University Press, 1981).

8. This analogy to physics does not imply that we have a "billiard ball" view of human action, where only observable, tangible forces can cause behavior. Instead, we believe that reasons and justifications can act as "causes" of human action, that these reasons and justifications may be socially constructed (and so understanding the way individuals make meaning becomes central) and that a collective choice may represent some total of these persuasive "forces."

9. Friedrich A. von Hayek, *Law, Legislation and Liberty, Volume I: Rules and Order* (Chicago: University of Chicago Press, 1973).

10. Charles Lindblom, *Politics and Markets* (New York: Basic Books, 1977).

11. For a further development of this idea, see Karol Edward Soltan, "Rule of Law, Objective Standards and Pluralist Democracy," pa-

per read at the meetings of the Conference Group in Political Economy at the American Political Science Association, August 1985.

12. We use the term resource to denote a valuable attribute of a person or an alternative, which can be used but does not have to be used in making a decision. When a person possesses resources, she chooses whether or not to employ them; when an alternative possesses resources, the resources may or may not be used by the people invoking that alternative.

13. This does not mean that any alternative can be promoted through the deployment of any resource. Love may not be bought for money and negotiation may not be carried on by one powerful party.

14. The authority of an alternative may be formalized as a function of the probability of its being selected. The most authoritative alternative is the alternative with the greatest probability of being chosen. We are indebted to John Chamberlin for this formulation. This way of thinking about the problem allows us to see that even an alternative with a one-third probability of being chosen can be more authoritative than other alternatives, if it has a higher probability than these others. In this way, authoritativeness may be a relative phenomenon—alternatives can be more or less authoritative, depending on the set with which they are compared.

15. For these and other illuminating examples, see Thomas Schelling, *The Strategy of Conflict* (Cambridge: Harvard University Press, 1960).

16. Obviousness and justifiability are just two important sorts of resources that an alternative may have. There may be others, although we do not discuss them here.

17. Our view of the authority of alternatives borrows from the work of Thomas Schelling on bargaining and Kenneth Arrow on organizations, both stressing the importance of obviousness and the convergence of expectations. See Schelling, *Strategy of Conflict* and Kenneth Arrow, *The Limits of Organization* (New York: Norton, 1974). But our view also borrows from the more rationalist views of authority of Friedrich and Raz, and from related conceptions in legal theory that place emphasis on rationally persuasive justification as the basis of authority or as the core of the legal ideal. See Carl Friedrich, "Authority, Reason and Discretion" in Carl Friedrich, ed., *NOMOS I: Authority*, pp. 28–48 and Carl Friedrich, *Tradition and Authority* (New York: Praeger, 1972). See also Raz, "Authority and Justification." In legal theory, we draw on Philip Selznick, *Law, Society and Industrial Justice* (New York: Russell Sage, 1969).

18. For an elaboration of this view, see Karol Edward Sołtan, "Insti-

tutions and Common Sense," paper presented at the meetings of the Public Choice Society, March 1985. See also Bernard Grofman and Carole Uhlaner, "Metapreferences and the Reason for Stability in Social Choice: Thoughts on Broadening and Clarifying the Debate," *Theory and Decision* 19 (1985): 31–50.

19. This is an unusual sort of attraction. Only when the individuals involved are "seduced" by the authoritative resources an alternative possesses does this swooning reflect authority.

20. Schelling, *The Strategy of Conflict.*

21. Tradition, however, incorporates more than merely a reflected notion of precedent. Traditions matter not simply because they are obvious choices, but also because they may incorporate strong nonrational loyalties. Robert Axelrod has pointed out to us that tradition may matter so much in some settings that it may trump all of our other bases of authority. We suspect that this may be true when tradition incorporates elements both of obviousness and of justifiability.

22. Edward Shils, *Tradition* (Chicago: University of Chicago Press, 1984). See also Friedrich, *Tradition and Authority,* p. 13, where he notes that tradition and authority have been closely linked in the history of political theory.

23. Hermann Weyl, *Symmetry* (Princeton: Princeton University Press, 1954).

24. N.J. Coulson, "Islamic Law," in J. Duncan M. Derrett, ed., *An Introduction to Legal Systems* (New York: Praeger, 1968), pp. 54–79.

25. See Alvin Gouldner, "The Norm of Reciprocity," in *For Sociology* (New York: Basic Books, 1977), pp. 226–259; Marcel Mauss, *The Gift* (Glencoe, Ill.: Free Press, 1954) and Bronislaw Malinowski, *Crime and Custom in Savage Society* (London: Routledge and Kegan Paul, 1926).

26. Robert Buckhout, "Eyewitness Testimony," *Scientific American* 231 (1974): 3–11.

27. Schelling, *The Strategy of Conflict.*

28. Ernest Nagel, *The Structure of Science: Problems in the Logic of Scientific Explanation* (Indianapolis: Hackett, 1979), p. 190.

29. There may be some properties other than the ones discussed above which stand out against any cultural background. Johan Galtung and Mari Holmboe Ruge have argued from the literature in cognitive psychology that certain features of situations always stand out as obvious regardless of cultural context, like the moving object against a still background. The findings in cognitive psychology generally may be of some help in unpacking the rather large and unwieldy notion of obviousness. Johan Galtung and Mari

Holmboe Ruge, "The Structure of Foreign News," in Jeremy Tunstall, ed., *Media Sociology* (Urbana: University of Illinois Press, 1970), pp. 259–281.

30. Weber, *The Theory of Social and Economic Organization*, pp. 358–363.

31. Lewis Carroll, "Alice in Wonderland," in Marvin Gardner, ed., *The Annotated Alice* (New York: Bramhall House, 1960), p. 161.

32. Friedrich, "Authority, Reason and Discretion," and Friedrich, *Tradition and Authority.*

33. John Kingdon, *Congressmen's Voting Decisions*, 2d ed. (New York: Harper and Row, 1981), pp. 47–54.

34. 410 U.S. 113 (1973).

35. See, for example, Guido Calabresi, *Ideals, Beliefs, Attitudes and the Law.* (Syracuse: Syracuse University Press, 1985).

36. As we will explain below, reasons are more authoritative to the extent that they persuade people under a special set of conditions in which a diverse group of individuals can make rational choices and where all of the available resources possessed by each of the possible alternatives are mobilized. For a more detailed discussion of the preconditions of rational choice, see Kim Lane Scheppele, *Legal Secrets: Efficiency and Legality in the Common Law* (Chicago: University of Chicago Press, forthcoming). Simple persuasion, as was accomplished by Hitler, is not sufficient to establish normative correctness, however. For a more detailed account of the circumstances under which persuasion will be taken as evidence of normative correctness, see Karol Edward Sołtan, *A Causal Theory of Justice* (Berkeley: University of California Press, forthcoming.) Our normative requirements for authority will be outlined later in the chapter.

37. 217 N.Y. 382 (1916).

38. 248 N.Y. 339 (1928).

39. Scheppele, *Legal Secrets*, chapter 6, *"Caveat Emptor:* Law and the Economy in Nineteenth-Century New York State."

40. This property might also be called reflexivity, indicating more clearly how the justifications need to be tested against their capacity to be persuasive when forwarded from alternative points of view. We are indebted to James Coleman for pointing out the importance of this way of seeing the problem.

41. Sołtan, *A Causal Theory of Justice.*

42. Daniel H. Levine, *Religion and Politics in Latin America: The Catholic Church in Venezuela and Colombia* (Princeton: Princeton University Press, 1981).

43. The discussion of the reduction of arbitrariness in Selznick, *Law, Society and Industrial Justice* is helpful on this point.

44. Friedrich, "Authority, Reason and Discretion" and Friedrich, *Tradition and Authority*.

45. If a choice of procedures is always present in making any collective choice, then choices of procedures always imply more choices of procedures. This can quickly become an infinite regress. That we do not generally see these sorts of infinite regresses in collective life, however, indicates that something must stop the choice of procedures for choosing procedures for choosing procedures. We argue, although we cannot develop it further here, that one can eventually trace these potentially infinite chains back to an implicit choice of procedure that is not contested, an informal use of a procedure that does not raise debates, or a seizure of the means for choosing procedures by force that settles the question by forbidding challenges.

46. It may be that the power of precedent weighs so heavily in an alternative's favor that it outweighs other considerations. Plurality voting, which has precedent on its side but a seriously flawed social choice pedigree, may be chosen because precedent matters more than the ability to justify persuasively the choice through social choice theory. The more alternatives are chosen on the basis of *all* of their available resources, the more normatively authoritative they will be, however.

47. For justifications of majority rule see Brian Barry, "Is Democracy Special?" in Peter Laslett and James Fishkin, eds., *Philosophy, Politics and Society*, 5th series (New Haven: Yale University Press, 1979), pp. 155–196; Kenneth May, "A Set of Independent, Necessary and Sufficient Conditions for Simple Majority Decisions," *Econometrica* 20 (1952): 680–684 and Douglas Rae, "Decision Rules and Individual Values in Constitutional Choice," *American Political Science Review* 63 (1969): 40–56.

48. But see Douglas Rae, "The Limits of Consensual Decision," *American Political Science Review* 69 (1975): 1270–1294 for an argument against the unanimity rule.

49. There are, of course, other goals as well.

50. See, for example, the discussion in James Buchanan and Gordon Tullock, *The Calculus of Consent* (Ann Arbor: University of Michigan Press, 1962).

51. Lindblom, *Politics and Markets*.

52. Of course, there are other reasons hierarchical authority may not be attractive, which have little to do with decision costs.

53. See J.R. Lucas, *On Justice* (Oxford: Clarendon Press, 1980) and Robert Summers, "Evaluating and Improving Legal Processes—A Plea for 'Process Values,'" *Cornell Law Review* 60 (1974): 1–52.

54. Legal procedures also may gain authority from their even-hand-

edness (symmetry) as well as from their universality (law-like procedures may apply in a wide variety of contexts within a culture although not necessarily across vastly different cultures).

55. This is the same sort of move John Rawls develops in specifying a veil of ignorance behind which moral choices may be made. See John Rawls, *A Theory of Justice* (Cambridge: Harvard University Press, 1971). Of course, in any real-world situation, the conditions of choice are likely to stray far from the ideal. But positive choices may be taken as *evidence* of normative ideals the more they are made under circumstances like these.

56. These rather extensive information requirements are just one reason purely autonomous choices are rare. Also, they beg the question of how individuals autonomously choose to acquire information in the first place. A rational choice framework is not particularly useful for determining what an optimal amount or distribution of information might be. See Scheppele, *Legal Secrets,* for a discussion of the information conditions of an autonomous choice and the incompatibility of rational choice models with the determination of an ideal distribution of knowledge.

57. We are indebted to Rick Hall for pointing out the importance of this criterion.

11

DOES MIGHT MAKE RIGHT?

RUSSELL HARDIN

It is a commonplace that, as Thomas Jefferson says, "force cannot change right."[1] Nevertheless, we often suppose that what is is right for little reason other than that it is. We may be reinforced in this spurious deduction by the fact that its conclusion is very often correct: what is is right. Moreover, it is often true that it is right largely because it is what happens to be the case. At first blush this sounds like the quintessentially conservative claim that the status quo is good, even that it is the best state of affairs. Indeed, conservatism may gain much of its appeal from the fact that the status quo can justifiably be claimed prima facie to have a privileged moral position over various alternatives. It is the sometime merit of the moral priority of the status quo that I wish to discuss. In particular, I wish to show why might sometimes makes right. More accurately, I argue that might can contribute to the rightness of a state of affairs, that, for example, it can contribute to the moral authority of the law.

Thomas Hobbes is often supposed to hold that might makes right. Gregory Kavka argues that, for Hobbes, might does not create right, it merely creates propitious circumstances in which to abide by the right of nature.[2] There is another way to make sense of Hobbes's views. We may establish that an extant state of affairs is only contingently right, and that a substantially different state of affairs would be right if it were the state of affairs. This fits Hobbes's evident view that, although monarchy was the best form of government in his time, still, once the

201

revolution deposed the monarchy and brought in a different government, citizens owed that government obedience and they would have been wrong to try to fight to reinstall monarchy.[3]

It is relatively easy to establish that might can make right simply by giving an example. Once this premise is established, we may then explore the fuller implications of the larger claim. It will help us to understand many otherwise opaque notions, such as the greater force of minatory over hortatory moral norms, the perversity of the conflict between welfare and equality in any theory whose point is to commend meliorative action, and the obligation to obey the law.

The Prima Facie Plausibility of the Claim

In many contexts we are relatively indifferent between doing things one way and doing them some other way. In social contexts we are sometimes similarly indifferent between having everyone do something one way and having everyone do it another way. The typical example is that we do not really care in principle whether everyone drives on the left or on the right. But we do very much care in principle whether everyone drives according to the *same* convention. That we have established a convention of driving on the right, say, therefore makes driving on the right the morally right thing to do. It is morally right because it would only bring harm to do otherwise. This is an essentially utilitarian conclusion that any moral theorist, utilitarian or otherwise, must find compelling.

If we have reached our convention of driving on the right through the authoritarian imposition of a despicable tyrant, it may nevertheless be the right thing to do—now that we have the established convention. Hence, might may make right. It makes right in this case because there is no compelling moral reason to do other than follow the convention even if it was established by tyrannical imposition.

This is not to say that it was right for our tyrant to impose the driving-on-the-right convention. It may have been an outrageous and immoral imposition. For example, it may have been done by whim to counter a prior, well-established convention of driving on the left. The change may have been very costly, even deadly. But if to change back would itself be costly, perhaps deadly, with no offsetting benefits in the longer run, then we cannot readily justify upsetting the tyrannically imposed convention. We could give no compelling reason, no purpose for the reversal. The most frivolous, even destructive application of might has made right.

There are several ways in which one might argue that might makes right that I do not wish to address here. The boldest of these is that might simply makes right: the strong are entitled to what they can take. At one level this would seem to mean that a stronger individual not merely could but also should prevail over a weaker. When Jean-Jacques Rousseau declares flatly, "Let us agree . . . that might does not make right,"[4] it is presumably this position that he is rejecting, although his meanings cannot always be clearly read. It is also this position that Socrates seems to want to pin on Thrasymachus when in fact Thrasymachus argues that since it is the powerful who establish the law, the rules of what is just, they establish laws that serve their interest. Hence, "the just is nothing else than the advantage of the stronger." As though it were merely a definition or an equation rather than a causal relation, Socrates deviously inverts this claim: "You say that the advantage of the strongest is just."[5]

There is a level at which Thrasymachus's view seems more nearly honorable, less cynical than he means it. Many individuals may combine resources and energies to gain collective strength, and they may then prevail over others. We may often suppose that there is something right in joint efforts to establish political control either because we think the means of establishing control are right or because we think the results of establishing it are right. In these instances, it is not the use of might per se that makes right but either the prior rightness of the might or the particular rightness of the results of its exercise. I may use power to force you to do something you do not wish to do and I may be justified in doing so because I hold a particular role in a justifiable institution that requires my use of force. Or I may use force, perhaps in a strictly ad hoc way that is not grounded in any institutional role, to compel you to do what benefits someone else or to keep you from harming someone.

The last possibility here, that power may be justified when it is used to produce a good state of affairs, is at some remove similar to the capricious imposition of a new driving rule. The chief difference is that the imposed driving convention becomes right only later, not immediately in its establishment. If I force you to stop harming someone, I do good. If, as dictator, I capriciously change our driving convention, I do not do good. Yet the eventual good that results from our having the driving convention in force after my imposition is clearly the result of my use of power. Might has brought about what is now a good state of affairs.

CONVENTION AND RIGHT

The problem of collectively settling on a driving rule is an instance of a coordination game. A coordination game is defined by the following condition: there are generally two or more choices that, if made uniformly by everyone, yield more or less equally good outcomes, whereas other choices made by everyone or the failure of everyone to make the same choice would yield worse outcomes. The way to resolve this game successfully is to get everyone to coordinate on one of the two or more best joint outcomes. As David K. Lewis argues, we may sensibly understand the standard notion of convention as simply successful coordination on some one of the two or more best outcomes in a repeated coordination game.[6]

You and I face a two-person coordination game in Game 1. If we both choose strategy A or we both choose B, we each receive a benefit of 10; if one of us chooses A while the other chooses B, we each suffer a loss of −10. There is no conflict in this interaction—merely the opportunity for each of us to do better by coordinating with the other. If we face this game repeatedly, we may eventually settle on both always choosing A. In that case, we will have established a convention of choosing A. We may do this even without discussion or agreement—hence we speak of a convention rather than of a contract or agreement. The convention of driving on the right in many nations may have arisen in this spontaneous fashion, without need of legal coercion. On the other hand, as the recent experience of Sweden suggests, it may also have been organized by the power of the state: Sweden once followed the convention of driving

Game 1: Coordination

		You	
		A	B
I	A	10,10	−10,−10
	B	−10,−10	10,10

on the left but in 1967 recoordinated on the convention of driving on the right. Although one might resent intrusion by the state in such a matter, as some Swedes did in 1967,[7] one would be foolish and wrong to defy a driving convention it has successfully established.

What are the conditions under which a convention is right even if it has been established by force, even wrongful force? The minimal conditions are essentially utilitarian: that it not be beneficial to change the convention once it is established. Often this condition can be met under the least-demanding value theory: that in which interpersonal comparisons are not made and aggregate welfare is merely an ordinal function of individual welfares according to the Pareto criterion. If no one would be made better off by changing the convention but some would be made worse off, then the change is not justified. The American convention of driving on the right can plausibly be thought to meet this condition. There may be conventions that require compromising the interests of some to the benefit of others, so that changing these conventions would benefit some while harming others. To defend these against change would require interpersonal comparisons of at least a weak kind. The conventions of a system of law may commonly be compromises of this kind.

Note that the minimal, utilitarian condition above has two elements. First, there is the comparison of benefits under a convention and under an alternative. Second, there is the consideration of costs of making a change from the present convention to any alternative. The monetary costs of making the change from driving on the left to driving on the right in Sweden in 1967 were estimated at $120 million.[8] It was also feared that the change would result in traffic accidents causing deaths and injuries beyond the numbers to be expected by the continuation of the old convention during the first months of transition. The latter fear seems not to have been justified, perhaps because of the extra attention devoted to traffic control by authorities, the effect of mass advertising on drivers' attentiveness and care during the transition, and lower speed limits after the switch.[9]

Driving conventions are not the central matter of political theory. Their value here is their clarity in formulating the structure of a class of problems. The more urgent issues for authority and political theory concern the rightness of adhering to conventions that are not so neutral as the driving convention. John Austin attributes to Hobbes the view that the choice between monarchy, aristocracy, and democracy is itself just a matter of convention in the strategic sense above. That is to say, "which is the best of these three kinds of government, is not to be disputed there where any of them is already established."[10] Many have disputed this claim of Hobbes or its analogue in many contexts. In disputing it we would want to consider the costs of making a change and who bears them, the relative benefits of the new convention and who enjoys them, and the relative losses under the new convention and who suffers them. Austin, as would many others, thinks Hobbes exaggerated "the evils of rebellion and strife."[11]

WELFARE AND DISTRIBUTIVE JUSTICE

In contemporary political theory probably no issue is more pervasively discussed than the apparent division of theories into those concerned with welfare overall and those concerned with distributions. Utilitarianism and distributive justice are commonly thought to be incompatible in principle. While I think the incompatibility has been overstated and miscomprehended, I will not discuss the miscomprehension here. Rather, I wish to address the way in which might may affect our assessments of the rightness of seeking redistributions. The most influential modern contribution to political theory is John Rawls's *A Theory of Justice*,[12] which is posed in part as a counter to utilitarian theories of political order. Rawls presents us with an ideal theory of distributive justice, a theory that addresses the basic structure of society. According to this theory that structure is just that maximizes the wellbeing of the worst-off class in the society.

Much of moral and political theory seems to be directed, as Rawls's theory is, at the appraisal of particular states of affairs. It becomes action-guiding only when coupled with relevant causal theories, especially social scientific theories of the governance, design, and change of institutions. It is generally hard not to read it as nevertheless implicitly action-guiding without serious attention to causal theories. For example, one might read Rawls's theory of justice as straightforwardly critical of some particular form of government or ordering of society if one could imagine workable alternative arrangements that would produce a better state of affairs by the criterion of the difference principle. Yet it need not follow that it would be unjust to continue with the defective arrangements because there might be no way simply to move from the status quo to the superior alternative.

Suppose it were true, as seems plausible, that a revolution to change from an unjust to a more just structure of society will make the worst-off class even worse off during the generation of the change. Then Rawls's theory of justice, with its difference principle, cannot justify making the change, indeed, must weigh against it. Any change would be rather a move from the status quo to that state of affairs that includes the process of change and its result. But that state of affairs might, by the criterion of the difference principle, clearly be inferior to the status quo. Given a sufficiently strong value theory for the comparison of welfare across individuals, a utilitarian may well argue for revolutionary change even though the difference principle, considered over the dynamic period of change, would recommend against it.

We may recast this problem as one of justice between generations. Suppose we can move our society from an inferior set of institutions to a superior set but only at the expense of the current generation of that class whose welfare is to be increased by the change. Dogged continuation of the status quo may mean that the worst-off class for all future generations will be increasingly worse off than it would be if we changed our form of government now. But if we consider the actual state of affairs we achieve in making the change, it is one in which the worst-off class is even worse off for the generation of the transition than the worst-off class in the status quo. In a sense, these people must be exploited now in order to benefit their successors later. This is, of course, a variant of a traditional argument against revolution: ideally, the changes to be brought by revolution would be good but practically they are not worth the cost. This traditional argument is commonly put in vaguely utilitarian terms. The twist in the traditional (and traditionalists') argument is that on Rawls's theory we may object to revolutionary change because we are concerned with losses suffered by the worst-off class and not with losses suffered more generally. Yet even this highly restricted concern may block the argument for redistributive revolution. Interestingly, however, the Rawlsian concern may also block redistributive revolutions that a utilitarian would favor, because on the utilitarian account losses to a present generation of the worst off might be more than balanced by gains to future generations of the worst off and everyone else.

It is not merely some notion of overall welfare that conflicts with equality but the egalitarian concern with the welfare of the worst-off class in the long run that conflicts with equality within that class across generations. When it seems valid, this must be a far more distressing conclusion for egalitarians than is the usual concern of traditionalists. For example, suppose it were true, as is widely asserted, that blacks of the present and perhaps even near future generations in South Africa are better off under the current white supremacist regime than they would be under a black majority regime. The transition might entail loss of welfare and even a reduction in freedom for almost everyone in South Africa in the present and perhaps next generation. One could then morally support revolutionary change in South Africa only if one morally approved trading the welfare of some for that of others in a way that certain utilitarians might readily assent to but that many anti-utilitarians would object to.

Minatory and Hortatory Moral Norms

A long tradition holds that minatory norms are more urgent and forceful than hortatory norms. Between these lies, John Findlay says, "one of the deepest gulfs in morals."[13] Minatory norms typically include a "not," as in "Thou shalt not kill." Hortatory norms generally exhort positive actions, as in "Thou shalt love they neighbor as thyself." Of these two exemplars there can be little doubt that the former is more urgent than the latter in the sense that its violation would be of greater consequence. In another sense it may be that the latter is the more urgent: it takes little effort to impress most of us with the first norm, which we fully inculcate, but it seems almost impossible to impress many of us with the second norm, which we honor only weakly. Much of the reason for this second difference is that conventionally organized force can readily be brought to bear to back the former norm but not so easily to back the latter. Norms that are actively enforced are apt to become norms that are actively held.

Moral and political philosophers have often been concerned to explain the difference in the force of these kinds of norms. Gilbert Harman explains the difference with a functionalist argument.[14] He argues that everyone wants minatory norms to protect themselves against attack from others, while it is chiefly the poor who want hortatory norms to help those in need because it is the poor who want to induce the well off to help them. It is by conventional resolution of our coordination problem in securing the protection against harm that we establish the minatory norm. But since it is the well off who have most to lose if that norm is violated, there is an artificial connection between their interest and the interest of the poor in getting help on occasion. This artificial connection creates a second coordination problem that is then resolved by the convention that all follow the minatory norm if the well off also follow the hortatory norm. Because of their greater power, Harman argues, the well off get the greater benefit under this latter contract by convention.[15]

Bishop Berkeley argues that minatory norms are to be taken in an absolute sense whereas hortatory norms cannot be. Why? Because it is impossible that one can do all of the positive good things that one might do, either because they are mutually inconsistent or because one simply cannot do all of them simultaneously. On the other hand, it is clearly "consistent and possible that any man should, at the same time, abstain from all manner of positive actions whatsoever."[16]

One may propose an alternative crudely functionalist explanation that turns on considerations not unlike those of Berke-

ley. It is commonly true that individuals are in sufficient position to cause great harm but relatively seldom that they are in
a position to bring about comparably great good. For example,
almost anyone could commit murder any day. It is almost never
going to be the case that I can do a similarly great good. Similarly, it is much harder to build than it is to destroy. This is
true of property and also of good relations that depend on trust,
as in marriage or international relations. For an extreme example, the minatory norms against indiscretion in marital relations can be instantly overridden, while the effort to restore
a faith that is broken can take years. Similarly, ten minutes with
a Molotov cocktail can destroy what it would take thousands of
hours to build.

It is surely because of the scale of damage that can be done
in violations of many minatory norms that we enforce these
norms with the power of states, communal shaming, and even
ad hoc retributive violence. Yet, behind these protections often
lies a justification for specific norms that is little more than the
might of tradition or convention. I own a house and gain extraordinary benefits from it. Why? Because there is a powerful
state to enforce certain behaviors on the part of others with
respect to that particular house. We may justify the exercise of
state power for such purposes as protecting my property in
various ways. In political philosophy of the not distant past, the
justification was often based on so-called natural right or rights.
This kind of justification cannot withstand the ridicule of those
who point out that what is supposed to be a natural right in
one community should have no claim in some other. Even in
the best of hands, claims for natural rights seem little more
than rhetorical: they are an act of politics, not a justification for
it. That is perhaps why they have been most eloquently stated
by revolutionary leaders, such as Thomas Paine, Thomas Jefferson, and the French revolutionaries.

A compelling justification for certain political norms, such as
property rules, that is not inherently inconsistent has been given
by utilitarians. This justification turns on the fact that any such
norm may be selected from a larger set of many that would do
about as well for us. But, as in our driving convention, once we
have settled on one norm we may not be able to improve on
our state of affairs by radically altering it. This is, again, the

view of Hobbes cited above, that once we have either a monarchy, an aristocracy, or a democracy, we can do best by sticking with it. Once we have an institution for handling property or governance that works we may be able slowly to alter it marginally to achieve better results. As in most governments and in the Anglo-Saxon property regimes of the last few centuries such marginal changes over time may add up to radical changes. But the cost of making radical changes directly might typically be too great to be justified.

Because the claims for and against revolutionary change are fraught with difficult issues of assessing benefits and costs, one may doubt the validity of Hobbes's view on forms of governance and still recognize its force in other contexts. For a relatively trivial example, it has been claimed of many of the European cities destroyed in World War II that efforts to redesign them in better—more functional and more pleasing—ways ran aground on the difficulties of reassigning property rights to fit radically redesigned cities. Hence, cities such as Cologne still have awkward street placements that are inefficient in moving traffic and wasteful in the use of land. The destruction of virtually all buildings was not a sufficient first step toward more sensible city designs.[17] If we suppose that there were mutual gains to be made from redesigning Cologne, we must also suppose that there would have been reallocations of property rights that would have left everyone better off. The obstacle, of course, was that the transition would have involved massive administrative and legal efforts that would have hampered the change and that might well have soaked up all the supposed benefits from it for the next generation. The prior convention on the allocation of property rights plausibly dominated any superior convention once the latter had the costs of transition added into it to define it as a final state of affairs.

The Obligation to Obey the Law

If we put the two accounts above—of the claims of welfare and distributive justice and of the claims of minatory and hortatory norms—together, we get an implicit account of the obligation to obey the law in certain societies. In brief, on this account the authority of the law must rest on its service to us. An inherent difficulty in asserting that it serves us well is that it may serve us differentially well, so that the authority of law may itself be an issue in the conflict between welfare and distributive justice. A further, and in some ways more fundamental, difficulty is that we may wonder with respect to what alternative it serves us well, which is to say, better. Let us consider this more fundamental issue first. Through it we may then turn to the conflict between welfare and distributive justice.

A, perhaps the, chief value of a system of law is that, as Lon L. Fuller says,[18] it is facilitative. Legal protections enable us to seek our own well being, both on our own and in interaction with others. Law is not used extensively to get us to do specific things so much as to prohibit us from doing certain things. Law facilitates in three very general ways. First, it governs conflict. For example, it does not force you to create wealth; rather, it prohibits me from interfering with your enjoyment of what wealth you create. Second, it enables us to coordinate our actions to smooth the way for us to get past one another without too great mayhem. For example, law may be used to control traffic and to establish various standards. Finally, in a third general class of problems it enables us, through mutual coercion, to act in our joint interest. For example, law may be actively used to provide certain services. More than in the other classes of law one might contend that the use of law to provide services is rather more pro-active than facilitative. To some extent, this issue turns on whether one supposes that the provided services are what we the people want. If they are, then legal intervention seems to do little more than facilitate our desired collective action.

In all these classes of legal interventions, except possibly the third, the law seems chiefly minatory rather than hortatory. Even in the third class it will be minatory if it facilitates collective action by extracting resources or cooperation from the citizenry in order to provide them services. At last resort it is through sanctions that it operates, although if it works well its sanctions should seldom be brought to bear. That is to say, it works by force—by might. To say further than I am morally obligated under the law, rather than merely obliged, requires that the force of the law be right. Generally we wish to assert that a moral obligation to obey is a concomitant of a good system of law. It will be possible to do so if we can establish that a minatory law is sufficiently good at enhancing our lives.

If the value of law depends on how well it facilitates our achieving or maintaining valued outcomes, we cannot make serious claims about how good a particular system of law is except by comparison to alternatives. Our first tendency in making comparison may be to compare life under a given or ideal system to life without law in some supposed state of nature. Unfortunately, as in Hobbes's view above, almost any orderly system may seem better than no system at all, so that this minimal comparison commends almost any legal system. Suppose our system seems to pass this minimal test but that we can imagine a substantially different system that would be superior. As argued above, we cannot guide our actions by this comparison alone. Rather, we must further consider the costs of getting from our present system to the superior system.

Now suppose that the chief difference between our present system and a plausibly superior one is that ours works to the distinct disadvantage of some members of the polity and to the greater interest of others. If this is true, it is likely to be in part the result of deliberate action on the part of the more powerful. Recall the argument of Thrasymachus that it is the powerful who determine what in practice we consider to be just, which is likely to include the exploitation of the weak by the strong.

Bernard Williams chastises Thrasymachus for failing to see that power is no less a matter of convention than is justice: "Thrasymachus speaks as if political or social power were not itself a matter of convention, and that is a view barely adequate to the school playground."[19] It may be that Thrasymachus misses this point, but then this point misses its mark. Power can arise by convention and it can be maintained by convention in the strategic sense of David Hume and Lewis. For example, it is maintained when those of us subject to it continue to coordinate on the strategy of submission rather than jointly coordinate in moving to the strategy of rebellion. We are all generally better off if we all choose the one or the other of these two strategies than if only so few of us rebel that we and perhaps many bystanders are harshly put down. The power that is thus created by convention can then be used to create exploitative laws to extract resources from the weak or to keep them better

Game 2: Unequal Coordination

Class II

		A	B
Class I	A	10,5	-10,-10
	B	-10,-10	5,10

under control in order better to ensure that they do not eventually coordinate on rebellion. It is in this latter sense that Thrasymachus explains the source of law and in which we might say that it is conventional, meaning merely that it is what is rather than that, like power, it is strategically definable as a convention in the sense of Hume and Lewis. The power that Williams says is also a matter of convention is less easily manipulated than this.

The view of Thrasymachus is shared by many critics of contemporary societies and legal systems. Indeed, it has lately even been shared by a group of legal scholars, the so-called critical legal theorists. Suppose this view is correct, as to some extent it surely must be. Our situation may be roughly that of the perverse coordination problem in Game 2, in which one class of the society prefers that we coordinate at the (10,5) outcome while the other class prefers that we coordinate at the (5,10) outcome. Both classes may prefer that we coordinate at the one or the other of these rather than fail to coordinate. This is similar to the view of Hobbes. We may think some other form of government is better than what we have, but we would sooner coordinate on what we have than go through civil war.

Game 2 represents the structure of payoffs that Edna Ullmann-Margalit uses to define her "norms of partiality."[20] When we find ourselves in such a coordination game we are likely to resolve it by conventionally settling on one or the other of the two best outcomes. If we settle on the (10,5) outcome, class I dominates and "exploits" class II. Ullmann-Margalit supposes that class II will then develop a norm that it is somehow right that it be exploited. However this may be, it seems likely that any serious legal system has about it some of the character of the unequal outcomes of Game 2: it systematically benefits some at the expense of others as compared to some alternative system. Moreover, we may sensibly suppose, with Thrasymachus, that the benefits tend toward those who have greater power in running the system. And, with Williams, we may conclude that power derives from convention, but in the strategic sense that it derives from a coordination game that is played out repeatedly. The exploited class II cannot readily force recoordination on its preferred outcome. Indeed, its members may not even be able to coordinate among themselves on attempting to force class I to yield sway.

If this is so, then what finally is the authority of the law? If we who are relatively exploited understand the inequality of results under our laws, we may, as Williams suggests and as Ullmann-Margalit's norm would have us do, come to think the laws are just and that we should do less well than our supposed betters. Or we may nevertheless honor the laws, not quite as just, but as better than actionable alternatives. If indeed we have no better alternative than obedience within our realm of possibility, we may simply reckon that obedience is right because it is the best we can achieve. And this is the correct way to put the issue: obedience is right. This is not to say that our state of affairs is right on some abstract assessment but that for us the right action is to obey the law even though it is an unequal law. This is not substantially different from Hobbes's conclusion that we should stick with and be obedient to our present form of government rather than engage in the turmoil of civil war to change to a theoretically better form.[21]

CONCLUSION

Does might make right? The answer is: to some extent, yes. It is not the only consideration, but it is a consideration. This answer turns on utilitarian concerns when there seems not to be a reachable alternative to the situation that might has made or put us in. Contrary to Jefferson's claim, force can change right. It can produce a state of affairs that is then right in part just because it is the state of affairs. And it can change our assessment of what it is right to do simply because what it is right for us to do is partly a function of what we must do to overcome force.

It is conceivable on this understanding that both sides in certain conflicts are morally wrong. Part of the reason that each is morally wrong is that, given the expected actions of the other, it cannot expect to bring about improvements of the kind it claims to fight for. The might of each side may make the actions of the other wrong. We may think better of the supposed aims of either the revolutionaries or the government in, say, El Salvador and still judge the actions of both to be morally reprehensible because their available means cannot fit their ends. Here we may not wish to say that might is right but only that opposition to it is wrong. Suppose that the better state of affairs would be that in which those in power behaved better. Alas, if they cannot be expected to before helping to wreak grievous carnage, revolutionary efforts to bring about a supposedly better final state of affairs may be wrong. Hence, might can change right. It can make right and it can make wrong.

NOTES

1. Thomas Jefferson, letter to Major John Cartwright, June 5, 1824, in Saul K. Padover, ed., *The Complete Jefferson* (New York: Duell, Sloan and Pearce, 1943), p. 293.

2. Gregory Kavka, *Hobbesian Moral and Political Theory* (Princeton: Princeton University Press, forthcoming), chap. 9, §45.

3. Hobbes asserts, "That you will esteeme it better to enjoy your selves in the present state though perhaps not the best, then by waging Warre, indeavour to procure a reformation for other men in another age, your selves in the meane while either kill'd, or consumed with age. . . ." Thomas Hobbes, *De Cive*, ed. Howard Warrender (Oxford: Clarendon Press, 1983), "Preface," p. 36.

4. Jean-Jacques Rousseau, *On the Social Contract*, Roger D. Masters, ed., Judith R. Masters, trans. (New York: St. Martin's, 1978); book 1, chap. 3, p. 49.

5. Plato, *The Republic*, trans. G.M.A. Grube (Indianapolis: Hackett, 1974), Book 1, §338c, p. 12. Although Thrasymachus has used the term "just" in an utterly cynical way, Socrates goes on to treat his claim as though he were using it in the honored way Socrates does.

6. David K. Lewis, *Convention* (Cambridge: Harvard University Press, 1969).

7. *New York Times*, September 5, 1967.

8. Paul J.C. Friedlander, "H-Day Is Coming in Sweden," *New York Times*, August 20, 1967.

9. *New York Times*, November 12, 1967.

10. John Austin, *The Province of Jurisprudence Determined* (New York: Noonday, 1954), long footnote, p. 277.

11. Ibid.
12. John Rawls, *A Theory of Justice* (Cambridge: Harvard University Press, 1971).
13. John N. Findlay, "The Structure of the Kingdom of Ends," in Findlay, *Values and Intentions* (London: George Allen and Unwin, 1961), p. 425.
14. Gilbert Harman, *The Nature of Morality* (New York: Oxford University Press, 1977), pp. 110–112. That his argument is essentially functionalist is argued in Russell Hardin, "Rationality, Irrationality and Functionalist Explanation," *Social Science Information* 19 (1980): 760–763.
15. Harman, *Nature of Morality*, p. 111.
16. George Berkeley, "Passive Obedience," in *The Works of George Berkeley*, Alexander Campbell Fraser, ed. (Oxford: Clarendon Press, 1901), vol. 4, §26, p. 118.
17. This example may be overdetermined. Those who have lived in Philadelphia and Washington, D.C., two planned cities, may suppose that redesigning cities according to an overall plan would not be sensible even if there were no difficulties in reassigning property rights.
18. Lon L. Fuller, "Human Interaction and the Law," pp. 211–246, in his *The Principles of Social Order*, Kenneth I. Winston, ed. (Durham, N.C.: Duke University Press, 1981), pp. 231–233.
19. Bernard Williams, *Ethics and the Limits of Philosophy* (Cambridge: Harvard University Press, 1985), p. 30.
20. Edna Ullmann-Margalit, *The Emergence of Norms* (Oxford: Clarendon Press, 1977), pp. 162–164, 173–176.
21. There is a significant difference in the underlying moral arguments. Hobbes bases his conclusion on simple egoism; we may prefer to base ours on more nearly general concern, especially utilitarian concern for all.

PART II

CONTEXTS: CONSTITUTIONAL, ADMINISTRATIVE, AND NONGOVERNMENTAL

12

THE AUTHORITY OF TEXT,
TRADITION, AND REASON:
A THEORY OF CONSTITUTIONAL
"INTERPRETATION"

MICHAEL J. PERRY

We are apt to be misled . . . by the ideological uses to which
the concept of a tradition has been put by conservative political theorists. Characteristically such theorists have followed Burke in contrasting tradition with reason and the
stability of tradition with conflict. Both contrasts obfuscate.
For all reasoning takes place within the context of some
traditional mode of thought, transcending through criticism and invention the limitations of what had hitherto been
reasoned in that tradition; this is as true of modern physics
as of medieval logic. Moreover when a tradition is in good
order, it is always partially constituted by an argument about
the goods the pursuit of which gives to that tradition its
particular point and purpose. . . . Traditions, when vital,
embody continuities of conflict. Indeed when a tradition,
becomes Burkean, it is always dying or dead. . . . A living
tradition then is an argument precisely in part about the
goods which constitute that tradition. . . . [T]he virtue of
having an adequate sense of the traditions to which one belongs or which confront one . . . is not to be confused with
any form of conservative antiquarianism; I am not praising
those who choose the conventional conservative role of *lau-*

dator temporis acti. It is rather the case that an adequate sense
of tradition manifests itself in a grasp of those future possibilities which the past has made available to the present.
Living traditions, just because they constitute a not-yet-
completed narrative, confront a future whose determinate
and determinable character, so far as it possesses any, derives from the past.

—Alasdair MacIntyre[1]

On what basis or bases ought the judiciary—in particular the
federal judiciary, especially the Supreme Court—resolve federal constitutional issues? What justificatory role, if any, ought
to be played by: (a) the text of the Constitution; (b) the political
morality constitutionalized by those persons who proposed and
those who ratified the Constitution (to whom I shall refer collectively as the "ratifiers"); (c) precedent;[2] (d) the values of the
political community—the polity—whose Constitution it is; (e)
the judge's own values; etc.?

It is axiomatic in American political-legal culture that the text
of the Constitution ought to play a justificatory role in—is authoritative for—constitutional decisionmaking. However, there
is no axiomatic or canonical conception of the constitutional
text. What is the constitutional "text"? How ought we to understand, to conceive of, the "text": as (a) the verbal or linguistic
embodiment of the political morality constitutionalized by the
ratifiers; (b) particular marks on a page; (c) a symbol of some
sort; etc.? And, relatedly, what does it mean to "interpret" the
text?

In this chapter I defend a particular conception of constitutional text and interpretation—a conception implicit in many
of the Supreme Court's most important "individual rights" decisions of the modern period,[3] such as *Brown* v. *Board of Education,*[4] *Baker* v. *Carr,*[5] *Gideon* v. *Wainright,*[6] *New York Times Co.*
v. *Sullivan,*[7] the gender discrimination cases,[8] and *Roe* v. *Wade.*[9]
I begin by considering the authority of the constitutional text.

I

" '[A]uthority' is a relational concept. To say *x* is 'authority' is
always to say, at least implicitly, '*x* is authority *for y.*' "[10] Con-

sider, then, this claim: "The constitutional text is authoritative for constitutional decisionmaking." That is a descriptive claim, not a prescriptive one. The claim is not that the constitutional text *should be* authoritative, but that it *is*.

What is the nature of the authority of the constitutional text? As David Kelsey has admirably demonstrated in his study of the uses of scripture in recent theology, "there is no one, and certainly no one 'standard' or 'normative' meaning of 'authority.' "[11] What does it mean to say that the constitutional text is "authoritative" for constitutional decisionmaking?

It means that judges justify their constitutional decisions at least in part by reference to the constitutional text, and that they do so because they believe they should. Of course, to say that judges justify their constitutional decisions "by reference to" the constitutional text is not to say that all judges do the same thing with the text, or even that they all understand the term constitutional "text" in the same way.

The descriptive claim that the constitutional text is authoritative is correct. Judges do justify their constitutional decisions at least in part by reference to the constitutional text, and they do so because they believe they should.

But why do judges believe this? I return to this question later.

II

Henry Monaghan writes that "[t]he authoritative status of the written constitution is . . . an incontestable first principle for theorizing about American constitutional law."[12] I do not dispute this. I do want to challenge, however, Monaghan's conception of the constitutional text, by offering a better conception.

Monaghan's conception is a fairly common one—shared by, among others, Raoul Berger,[13] Robert Bork,[14] and William Rehnquist.[15] Monaghan writes:

A distinction is sometimes posited between textual analysis and original intent inquiry such that only the constitutional text and not "parol evidence" can be examined to ascertain constitutional meaning. But any such distinction seems to be entirely wrong. All law, the constitution not excepted, is a purposive ordering of norms. Textual language embodies one or more purposes, and the text may be understood and usefully applied only if its purposes are understood. No convincing reason appears why purpose may not be ascertained from any relevant source, including its "legislative history." . . . Although the intention of the ratifiers, not the Framers, is in principle decisive, the difficulties of ascertaining the intent of the ratifiers leaves little choice but to accept the intent of the Framers as a fair reflection of it. . . . [The constitutional] language constitutes the best evidence of original intentions.[16]

As this passage makes clear, Monaghan conceives of the constitutional text as the verbal or linguistic embodiment of the political morality the ratifiers understood the text to embody. His conception entails a conception of constitutional interpretation: to interpret the constitutional text is to search for the political-moral judgments understood by the ratifiers to be embodied there. I shall call his (and similar) conceptions(s) "originalist."[17] It is originalist in the sense that the various provisions of the constitutional text are understood to embody that which the ratifiers understood them to embody, namely, particular beliefs about how the polity—more precisely, the government of the polity (state governments as well as federal)—should conduct its affairs. For Monaghan, the *original*—the ratifiers'—understanding is authoritative.

One might make either of two basic sorts of challenge to the originalist conception of constitutional text and interpretation. First, one might contend that, for some reason, an originalist approach to constitutional adjudication is not a real option for judges. I am skeptical of these challenges.[18] Second, one might contend that even if originalism is a real option, there is a better one—that a nonoriginalist approach to constitutional adjudication is the preferred option for judges. Here I take this line. In particular I argue that the nonoriginalist conception of constitutional text and interpretation I am about to elaborate has more descriptive adequacy and normative appeal than the originalist conception. Moreover, I contend that the conception of judicial role that attends my nonoriginalist conception of constitutional text and interpretation is defensible, notwithstanding the principal opposing argument: the argument from democracy.

III

Any conception of constitutional text and interpretation that aspires to *descriptive adequacy* must account for two persistent features of judicial practice in modern individual-rights cases:

1. The importance attached, not merely in judicial practice but in American political-legal culture generally, to the "writtenness" of the Constitution: The text is accorded authoritative status. Even at its most "activist," the Supreme Court insists that it is interpreting the constitutional text.

2. The status of the original—that is, the ratifiers'—understanding: The original understanding of the various textual provisions is often not accorded authoritative status. However, it is almost invariably treated as relevant and influential.

Any conception of constitutional text and interpretation that aspires to *normative appeal* must address certain basic questions:

1. To what extent, if any, can or does the text (conceived in the particular way in question) determine or at least constrain the Court's choices?

2. If the text, thus conceived, is not an important constraint, are there others?

3. If the text is not an important constraint, what is the point of maintaining the textual focus? Is the Court's invariable reference to the text merely a self-protective formality?

4. Is the Court's frequent reference to the original understanding merely a self-protective formality?

5. Given the nonauthoritative status of the original understanding, what is the point, the function, of constitutional *amendment*?

The conception of constitutional text and interpretation I defend here accounts for the two features of judicial practice, and addresses the five questions set forth above.

IV

A particular conception of constitutional text (and interpretation) is, of course, a particular way of conceiving, of understanding, what the text is. In elaborating my understanding of the text, I rely on some striking, illuminating similarities between the constitutional text and religious texts.

Consider the connections among (1) a religious community, (2) the religious tradition in which the community is the present participant, and (3) the sacred text, or texts, of the tradition. The key notions are community, tradition, and sacred text. By community I mean, roughly, a group of persons united principally by their identification of themselves as the present bearers of, participants in, a tradition. By tradition, I mean a particular history or narrative, in which the central motif is an aspiration to a particular form of life, to certain projects, goals, ideals, and the central discourse (in the case of a living tradition) is an argument—in MacIntyre's terms, "an historically extended, socially embodied argument"[19]—about how that form of life is to be cultivated and revised.[20] By sacred text (or texts) I mean the text that, in the community and tradition in question, is seen to charter, to mandate, the form of life to which the community and tradition aspire, and thus the text that, for the community and tradition, symbolizes that mandate.

A religious tradition has ceased to live when, inter alia, the community that is its present bearer is no longer sensitive to the need to criticize and revise the community's form of life in the light of new experience and exigencies. In the hands of the fundamentalists, a religious tradition has ceased to live. David Tracy, a Catholic theologian at the University of Chicago, writes that:

> fundamentalist and authoritarian theologies, properly considered, are not theologies at all.
>
> Nor is this the case merely because such theologies will not take account of contemporary experience. More basically, these theologies are finally not interpretations of the tradition itself. They are but simple repetitions. The heart of any hermeneutical position is the recognition that all interpretation is a mediation of past and present, a translation carried on within the effective history of a tradition to retrieve its sometimes strange, sometimes familiar meanings. But the traditionalist's use of tradition betrays the enriching, even liberating notion of tradition. It is naive to

assume that a thinker is so autonomous as to be no longer
affected by the effects and influences of that tradition in
our very language, a presence carrying us along by providing our initial prejudgments and often unconscious presuppositions as to the nature of reality. It is equally naive,
and equally destructive of systematic theology's herme-
neutical task, to assume with the traditionalist and fundamentalist that so autonomous in one's heteronomous obedience is the theologian that one can be faithful to the
tradition to which one belongs by repeating its *tradita* rather
than critically translating its *traditio*.

The systematic theologian, on the contrary, must operate in a manner more faithful to the actual finitude and
historicity of every thinker in any cultural tradition. Indeed, the surest mark of contemporary systematic theology
is precisely a profound acceptance of finitude and historicity.[21]

Consider both the role of the sacred text, and the activity
of interpreting the text, in the life of a religious community
that is the steward of a living tradition. In such a community,
the sacred text is not—not simply, at any rate—a book of answers, but rather a principal symbol of, perhaps *the* principal
symbol of, and thus the focal occasion for recalling and heed-
ing, the aspirations of the tradition. In that sense, the sacred
text constantly *disturbs*—it serves a prophetic function in—the
life of the community. Indeed, it is in significant part in virtue
of its "writtenness" and thus its "permanence"[22] that a sacred
text is (in the life of a community that might prefer, from time
to time, to ignore it) irrepressible, disturbing, and prophetic.
And it is in significant part because of its comprehensiveness
and indeterminacy and thus its "excess of meaning"[23] that a
sacred text, as symbol, achieves its power to disturb from one
generation to the next and from one place to another, over the
lives of communities separated in time and space and with very
different experiences and questions.

How shall we understand the activity of interpretation of a
sacred text in the life of a religious community that is part of a
living tradition? The referent of a text understood as simply
the linguistic embodiment of past normative judgments is, in a

sense, "behind" the text. One must look behind the text, to the original meaning, if one is to understand the text. The referent of a sacred text, however, is not "behind," but "in front of."[24] One must respond to the incessant prophetic call of the text. One must recall and heed the aspirations the text symbolizes, and thereby create and give always provisional, always reformable meaning to the text.

Yet it is not simply a matter of creating and giving meaning to, rather than taking meaning from, the text. We are creatures as well as creators of tradition. How, and to what extent, is interpretive activity the activity of persons as *creatures* of tradition? How, and to what extent, is it the activity of persons as *creators* of tradition? What is taken from the text are the aspirations the text symbolizes and indeed embodies. What is given to the text are the community's answers as to how those aspirations are to be heeded and realized in the life of the community, in the light of *its* experience and exigencies. That is the sense in which "interpretation," as Tracy says, "is a mediation of past and present."[25] Meaning is given to the sacred text in the sense that later communities who enter into dialogic encounter with the text will find there the meanings earlier communities have created; they will find them there because in symbolizing the aspirations of the tradition, the sacred text inevitably resonates with the ways the tradition has (provisionally and reformably) responded to those aspirations. Of course, just as meaning is thus given to the sacred text, later communities must sometimes exorcise from the text what they come to conclude are, for them, unacceptable meanings given to it by earlier communities. Think, for example, of the different and even conflicting meanings various Christian communities have given, over the course of the tradition, to the story—the narrative, the metaphor—of the Resurrection.[26]

Thus, in the life of a religious community that is the steward of a living tradition, to interpret a sacred text is, in essence, *to interpret the tradition itself, to mediate the past of the tradition with its present.* And because such a community is cognizant of the imperfect and therefore reformable character of its tradition, it will take a critical attitude to the tradition. This attitude is "the route to liberation from the negative realities of a tradition."[27] To exercise stewardship over the tradition, to see that the tradition lives, requires that the community maintain this critical distance. Although the community must mine the tradition for whatever resources the tradition bears that are helpful in fulfilling the central aspirations of the tradition, the community must also, as steward of those aspirations, reject those aspects of the tradition—those "negative realities"—that come to be seen as subversive of the tradition's aspirations. (There is no denying "the brokenness and ambiguity of every tradition and one's own inevitably ambivalent relationship to it.")[28] Consider, for example, the critical efforts of feminist Christian theologians, like Rosemary Ruether,[29] to uncover the patriarchal aspects of their tradition and to establish—in terms of their tradition's central aspirations—the "sinful" (alienated and alienating) character of those aspects.[30]

V

Some commentators have recently explored the similarities between interpretation in law and interpretation in literature.[31] But the sacred text analogy is better than the literary text one. The relation between a political community (and tradition) and its foundational text is much more like the relation between a religious community (and tradition) and its sacred text than the relation between an "interpretive community" (to use Stanley Fish's term)[32] and whatever literary texts happen to engage it. An interpretive community doesn't often approach a literary text with questions as to what the central aspirations of its tradition are, or how to fulfill them. (Indeed, it doesn't seem that an interpretative community has a tradition or aspirations in anything like the sense religious and political communities have them.) But, of course, both religious and political communities approach their foundational texts with questions of just that sort. In that sense, its sacred text is normative for a religious community, and its foundational text for a political community, in a way that a literary text is not normative for an interpretive community.[33] (Sacred texts are typically seen less as the work of particular authors than as artifacts of the tradition, whereas literary texts are typically seen more as the work of particular authors—a difference that reflects the fact that sacred texts and foundational texts are normative in a way literary texts are not.)

It is more fruitful, then, as I hope this chapter illustrates, to explore similarities between interpretation in law and interpretation in religion than similarities between interpretation in law and interpretation in literature—at least, insofar as foundational (constitutional) law is concerned.

I must be careful here. My claim is *not* that all constitutional interpretation is analogous to all interpretation of sacred texts. There are, after all, different sorts of constitutional interpretation *and* different sorts of interpretation of sacred texts. It is a common misconception in the secular academic world that interpretation of sacred texts by members of religious communities always and everywhere presupposes that the texts are divinely inspired, if not divinely authored. This great difference between interpretation of sacred texts and constitutional interpretation is thought to overwhelm whatever similarities there might be between the two. However, while some interpretation of sacred texts makes theistic presuppositions, not all such interpretation does. For example, Buddhism is, in the main, nontheistic, and interpretation of the Buddhist sutras does not presuppose that they are divinely inspired. In my tradition, which is Roman Catholic, the work of "the best and the brightest" of contemporary scripture scholars and theologians makes no theistic presuppositions.[34] (This is not to deny that many of those scholars and theologians are theists. At least, many of them find God-talk meaningful.) I am analogizing constitutional interpretation of a certain sort (the sort operative in cases like *Brown* and *Roe*) to the sort of interpretation of sacred texts that presupposes no more than that the texts are human artifacts and repositories of human wisdom.

The Gospels, for example, and the Constitution—more precisely, aspects of the Gospels and aspects of the Constitution—function, in the sort of interpretation I am portraying, as symbols that are both commemorative and prophetic. They are commemorative in that in each case, the text is an occasion of and for remembering. Remembering what? The founding, constitutive aspirations of the religious or political tradition of which we, the religious or political community, are the present bearers, in which we, the present community, participate. They are prophetic in that in each case, the text is an occasion of and for responding. Responding to what? To the founding, constitutive aspirations of the tradition. "Interpretation" both of the

Gospels and of the Constitution consists then in remembering those founding, constitutive aspirations and responding to them.

My suggestion is not that the sorts of constitutional and scriptural interpretation in question are identical, merely analogous. There are, of course, differences as well as similarities.[35] In any event, this analogy is considerably more illuminating than that between constitutional and literary interpretation. At least, sacred texts like the Gospels are essentially and paradigmatically commemorative and prophetic. The same cannot be said about literary texts (that are not also sacred texts).

In the American experience the role of the constitutional text and the activity of interpreting the text have been very similar to the role of the sacred text and the activity of interpreting the text in the life of a religious community that is the steward of a living tradition. For the American polity, the constitutional text is not (simply) a book of answers to particular questions (e.g., what is the minimum age for President of the United States?). It is, rather, a principal symbol, perhaps *the* principal symbol, of the aspirations of the tradition. (Recall Alexander Bickel's observation that "[w]ith us the principal symbol of nationhood, of continuity, of unity and common purpose, is, of course, the Constitution, without particular reference to what it means in this or that application.")[36] In that sense, the constitutional text constantly disturbs—it serves a prophetic function in—the life of the polity. The referent of the constitutional text, conceived as an originalist like Monaghan conceives it, is "behind": one must look behind the text, to the original understanding, if one is to comprehend the text. The referent of the constitutional text conceived as the symbolization of the fundamental, constitutive aspirations of the political tradition, however, is not behind, but "in front of." The polity must respond to the incessant prophetic call of the text—must recall and heed the aspirations symbolized by the text—and thus create and give (always provisional, always reformable) meaning to the text, as well as take meaning from it.

I shall now elaborate this conception of constitutional text and interpretation by addressing those basic questions to which any conception that aspires to normative appeal must respond.

First, to what extent, if any, can or does the text, so conceived, determine or at least constrain the Court's choices?

Few if any theorists resist the claim that texts constrain interpretation. Of course, what one perceives to be a text, or what one conceives to be the nature—genre, say—of a text, is not itself determined by the text. No aspect of reality, including marks on a page, mediates itself for us. Nonetheless, communities—including religious, political, and literary communities—do have shared visions as to whether something is a text and what sort of text it is. Indeed, these visions are partly what makes a group of people a community. Within the context of those visions, within those communities, texts constrain interpretation. That is, the shared vision as to the "boundary" and "nature" of a text constrains the interpretive activity that goes on in relation to the text. The disagreement is not *whether* texts constrain interpretation, but how and to what extent? My concern is with the way in which, and the extent to which, foundational texts—whether religious or political—constrain interpretation.

As I conceive it, the constitutional text is a symbol of the aspirations of the political tradition (which is not to say that that's all it is), and, as such, it constrains in the way and to the extent the aspirations of the tradition constrain. There is no question that the aspirations of a tradition do constrain. They constrain just as language, culture, and other aspects of a tradition constrain. But, depending on the particular resources they bear, language, culture, and tradition can liberate too. They can free us to create. We use our language to revise our language. We use our culture to revise our culture. In the American political tradition, one of whose most important resources is its self-critical aspect, we use our tradition to revise, to reform and to re-present our tradition.[37]

It is not possible to specify with anything approaching precision the extent to which the aspirations of the American political tradition constrain (as well as liberate). The crucial point, for present purposes, is that although constraining, the constitutional text conceived as the symbolization of the aspirations of the tradition, is significantly *less* constraining than the text conceived as simply the linguistic embodiment of the various concrete political-moral judgments constitutionalized by the ratifiers.

This brings us to the second inquiry: Are there other, significant constraints on the Court's choices—constraints that can fill in and do the work the text-as-symbol cannot do?

Some commentators (most notably, perhaps, Owen Fiss[38] and Robert Bennett[39]) have argued that certain accepted norms of judicial behavior—such as the obligation to relate present choices to past choices (precedent)—serve as constraints. And no doubt they do. But how significant are such constraints? Not very, in my view. A decision either way in *Plessy* v. *Ferguson*,[40] *Lochner* v. *New York*,[41] *Brown* v. *Board of Education*,[42] and *Roe* v. *Wade*[43] would have fallen within the boundary marked out by the constraints in question.[44] In fact, just about any choice a majority of the Supreme Court is likely to want to make would probably fall within that boundary. The accepted canons of judicial behavior—even in conjunction with the constitutional text conceived as symbolic of the tradition's aspirations—are significantly less constraining than the constitutional text conceived in originalist terms.

Third, given that the text, as I conceive it, is not a significant constraint on the choices any majority of the Court is likely to want to make, what is the point of maintaining the textual focus? Is the Court's invariable reference to the text merely a self-protective formality? Is the text at best a peripheral feature of constitutional decisionmaking?

The text is not peripheral. As the American experience shows, it is in significant measure by virtue of its "writtenness" and thus its "permanence" that the constitutional text has been irrepressible, disturbing, and prophetic. (The importance of "writtenness" should not be underestimated. As Paul Ricoeur has emphasized, "it is with writing that the text acquires its semantic autonomy in relation to the speaker, the original audience and the discursive situation common to the interlocutors."[45]) And it is in significant measure because of its comprehensiveness and indeterminacy and thus its "excess of meaning" that the constitutional text, as symbol, has achieved its power to disturb from one generation of the polity to the next.[46] The constitutional text, like other foundational symbols for other human communities, serves a crucial function in the life of the polity. The text provides, not, as Stephen Munzer and James Nickel suggest, "a shared standard of argument"[47]— the relevant provisions of the text are too indeterminate for that—but a shared occasion for confronting and struggling with the not-to-be-forgotten aspirations of the tradition. The text is the focal occasion for mediating past and present. It makes about as much sense—which is to say, little if any—to suppose that the constitutional text, conceived as symbolic of the tradition's aspirations, is a peripheral and maybe even dispensable artifact as it does to suppose that for Christians the Gospels are dispensable.

Fourth, given the nonauthoritative status of the original understanding, the ratifiers' understanding, of particular textual provisions, is the Court's frequent reference to the original understanding merely a self-protective formality?

Of course not. The ratifiers and their polity were participants in the tradition too. In their day, they were the stewards of the tradition. The ways in which they shaped and responded to the aspirations of the tradition may well shed light on how we should shape and respond to them.[48] Why assume that we have nothing to learn from our past? The Court is right to consult the ratifiers' normative judgments.

But to consult their judgments is one thing, to accord them authoritative status something else. Alexander Bickel observed that: "[A]s time passes, fewer and fewer relevantly decisive choices are to be divined out of the tradition of our founding. Our problems have grown radically different from those known to the Framers, and we have had to make value choices that are effectively new, while maintaining continuity with tradition."[49]

Fifth, under the originalist conception of constitutional text and interpretation, the principal point of amending the text is to control the future with the original understanding of the text of the amendment. Under the conception I am elaborating, however, the original understanding is not authoritative. Only the text is authoritative. What, then, might be the principal point of amending the constitutional text?

Not every provision of the Constitution symbolizes an aspiration of the political tradition, nor need every amendment to the text do so. To say that key provisions of the constitutional text function as a foundational symbol in and for the political tradition is not to say that every provision does so or that that is the only function of the text. Some parts of the Constitution, after all, cannot plausibly be seen as doing much more than settling housekeeping matters, such as the minimum age for President.

Moreover, a polity that wants to curtail the opportunity for constitutional interpeters to give any meaning to an amendment other than the original meaning can try to do so by adding language to the Constitution so determinate that, as a practical matter, the amendment will bear little if any new meaning. Imagine how different constitutional doctrine regarding freedom of speech might have been had the First Amendment said simply, in relevant part, that "Congress shall not establish any system of prior restraint of publication."[50]

But, given my conception of constitutional text and interpretation, and putting aside both housekeeping amendments and amendments with very determinate language, what is the function of constitutional amendment?

Recall the dialogic and critical character of interpretation understood as mediation of past and present (discussed above in connection with interpretation of sacred texts). Constitutional amendment is a principal instrument with which the present can participate in that dialogic and critical encounter with the tradition, in that ongoing interpretation of the tradition, which is mediation of past and present. For example, it is one way the present can decisively reject an aspect of the tradition and establish, in its stead, a new aspiration more consonant with what the present sees as the central, constitutive aspirations of the tradition. Consider, in that regard, the Fourteenth Amendment, or the proposed Equal Rights Amendment. Constitutional amendment is also one way—a principal, dramatic way—the present can speak to the future; today's amendment will be a part of that which the future must mediate with its own present. In short, constitutional amendment is an important instrument with which the polity can exercise its stewardship over the living tradition.

VI

One might accept my conception of constitutional text and interpretation as appropriate for members of the polity and their political representatives, but reject it as illegitimate for the politically unaccountable judiciary. One might think it is one thing, and acceptable, for Congress, or the President, to give meaning to (certain provisions of) the constitution (as well as take meaning from it), as of course both Congress and the

President have sometimes done[51]—one might even think it acceptable for the Court to defer to the meanings given to the Constitution by Congress or the President, as of course the Court has sometimes done—but another thing altogether, and illegitimate, for the Court to give meaning to the Constitution in the course of opposing itself to politically accountable branches of government.[52]

So, why is it important for the Court, in constitutional cases involving issues of individual rights, to continue to do what in the main it has done in the modern period of American constitutional law (and earlier), namely, play the judicial role that attends the conception of constitutional text and interpretation I have elaborated, rather than the much more limited role entailed by the originalist conception? I have addressed that question elsewhere.[53] The struggle to re-present the political tradition by re-envisioning its aspirations constitutes, in essence, political-moral inquiry—a search for political-moral knowledge—a search for answers to the various questions as to how we, the polity, should live our public, collective life, our life in common. By virtue of its political insularity, the federal judiciary has the institutional capacity to engage in the pursuit of political-moral knowledge in a relatively disinterested manner that has sometimes seemed to be beyond the reach of the politically accountable branches of government, for many of whose members the cardinal value is "incumbency."

This is not to suggest that the President or Congress (or state legislatures) shouldn't also pursue political-moral knowledge. Nor is it to suggest that the persons who occupy the executive and legislative branches of government aren't also capable of moral leadership. My argument is simply that because of its political insularity, the federal judiciary is institutionally advantaged.

The judiciary is institutionally advantaged in yet another important respect. Bickel put the point well:

> [An]advantage that courts have is that questions of principle never carry the same aspect for them as they did for the legislature or the executive. Statutes, after all, deal typically with abstract or dimly foreseen problems. The courts are concerned with the flesh and blood of an actual case. This tends to modify, perhaps to lengthen, everyone's view.

It also provides an extremely salutary proving ground for all abstractions; it is conducive, in a phrase of Holmes, to thinking things, not words, and thus to the evolution of principle by a process that tests as it creates.[54]

However, is it democratic for the Court to play that role? What precisely is at issue here? One way of conceiving the question is misguided, namely: assuming that a particular conception of democracy, of how our overall governmental apparatus should be organized, is axiomatic for the American political tradition. That begs the question: the issue is *how* our overall governmental apparatus should be organized. No particular conception of democracy—no particular conception of what the judicial role in that governmental apparatus should be—is axiomatic for the tradition,[55] not even Robert Bork's "Madisonian" conception.[56] The tradition has never really settled, even provisionally, on what the judicial role should be. That issue— unlike, say, the issue of whether blacks, or women, or eighteen-year-olds, should be permitted to vote—is widely contested within the tradition.

The debate, properly understood, is precisely about what conception of democracy should prevail. One must argue for a particular conception. How do we conduct that argument—by reference to what considerations?

Certainly we cannot hope to defend a position on the matter by invoking, as Bork does, for example,[57] the conception of democracy—or, perhaps less anachronistically, the conception of the proper separation of powers—constitutionalized by the ratifiers. To invoke their conception when an essential aspect of the issue is what authority, in the present, the ratifiers' norms should be deemed to have, is to run around in a circle.[58]

Henry Monaghan has written that "[o]ur legal grundnorm has been that the body politic can *at a specific point in time* definitevly order relationships, and that such an ordering is binding on all organs of government until changed by amendment."[59] I disagree. If that were our "legal grundnorm," if that were (to use a Hartian terminology) the supreme criterion of legal validity in our rule of recognition, then a lot of our constitutional law would look very different. The supreme criterion of legal validity in our rule of recognition seems to be "decisions of the

Supreme Court interpreting the text of the Constitution." One can adopt what Hart calls an "external" standpoint and question the legitimacy of our rule of recognition, on the ground, for example, that decisions of the Court presupposing the conception of text/interpretation/judicial role I have elaborated are undemocratic. But, for better or worse, that is our rule of recognition—as is evidenced by the fact that many citizens and officials question the legitimacy of the Court's decision in *Roe v. Wade* in terms of democratic theory, but not legal validity.

Again, by reference to what sorts of considerations can we conduct an argument for or against a particular conception of judicial role? (Richard Kay has soundly observed, in Hartian terms, that "such discussion is not about the proper application of an accepted standard of legal validity, but about what that standard should be. We are therefore necessarily outside the realm of conventional legal discourse. Our [agreement] . . . in this context must have reference to nonlegal criteria, to our basic political, moral, or aesthetic conventions.")[60] How else but by reference to the ways in which a particular conception of judicial role comports with (or fails to comport with) the constitutive purposes and projects, the central aspirations, of the political tradition? A lot turns, therefore, on how one understands those aspirations.

One such aspiration, of course, is for governance that is both responsive and, because it is not always responsive, accountable to the polity. But representative government is plainly not the only constitutive aspiration of the American political tradition. The tradition has aspired to "liberty and justice for all" as well as to "popular sovereignty."

If justice can be known and achieved, is the judicial role that attends my conception of constitutional text and interpretation one way to achieve it? (I am not suggesting that it is the only way.) Consider contemporary constitutional doctrine regarding, for example, freedom of speech, freedom of religion, and racial and other sorts of equality. Imagine what public policy regarding these matters might well have been today had the Supreme Court not played what some call an "activist" role in the modern period.

"But," you say, "there's no guarantee the Court won't mess up in the future. It has in the past. Remember *Dred Scott* and

Lochner."[61] Or, depending on your point of view: "Look at *Roe v. Wade.*" Certainly the Court is a fallible institution: it has made mistakes, and surely will again. But, in the modern period, on balance, the Court's record in the service of individual rights is admirable. An argument that the Court hasn't done enough in the modern period to secure "liberty and justice for all" hardly supports the conclusion that it ought not to do anything.

(Why focus on "the modern period"—the period, roughly, since *Brown* v. *Board of Education?* Because what the Court has done in the past generation is certainly more indicative of what we have reason to speculate it will do "in our own time," if it continues to play the judicial role in question, than what the Court did several generations ago.)

But what about the other constitutive aspiration of the American political tradition—the aspiration to representative government? Obviously a more constrained role is a better way of keeping faith with that aspiration. There is, however, that other constitutive aspiration—to justice. My suggestion is that what the tradition is likely to gain in terms of justice, in consequence of a judicial role of a sort the Court often has played in the modern period, more than offsets what the tradition is likely to lose in terms of "responsiveness" and "accountability."

What is the tradition likely to lose? Certainly the polity cannot exercise the comparatively direct and immediate political control (through its elected representatives) over the constitutional decisions of the Court that it can exercise over the Court's nonconstitutional decisions. But American history leaves little doubt that when a serious tension develops between the direction in which the Court is leading and the direction in which the polity is determined to move, the polity, not the Court, will prevail.[62] The various mechanisms of political control or influence over the Court have proven adequate in that regard.

Constitutional decisionmaking by the Court is responsive to the polity—not immediately, but it is responsive. Still, immediacy counts for something, and time can be lost. (Time is not always lost. In the course of the dialectical interplay between Court and polity I have discussed elsewhere,[63] the polity may eventually come to see it as a good thing that it did not get its way. When that happens, time is not lost. But sometimes, as in the case of child labor legislation, time has been lost.)[64] The significance one attaches to that occasional loss depends mainly on the significance one attaches to the gain, in terms of justice. A black person is more likely to attach greater significance to the gain, in the modern period, than a white person. Whose point of view is more likely distorted?

Does all this seem inconclusive? It *is* inconclusive, but for the critics of judicial "activism" no less than for its partisans. One's decision to accept or reject any given conception of judicial role, including the originalist conception, is always contingent, speculative, provisional and therefore revisable. The decision is contingent because it is rooted partly in one's sense and vision of justice. The decision is speculative because it is grounded partly on a prediction of future governmental, judicial and nonjudicial, behavior on the basis of past behavior.[65] And the decision is provisional and therefore revisable because one's sense and vision of justice may change, or one's predictions may prove wrong, or both.

Except for the true believers, constitutional theory is, alas, an inconclusive enterprise. How could it be otherwise?

VII

It is not surprising that debate in constitutional theory seems interminable. Any argument for or against a particular conception of judicial role is, in the nature of things, contingent, speculative, provisional and therefore revisable. That's why reasonable people have disagreed and will continue to disagree about judicial role. This is not to say that *every* argument offered is reasonable. For example, referring the question of the Supreme Court's proper role to the ratifiers is conspicuously circular. My point is simply that when all the bad arguments have been identified and discarded, disagreement will remain. The most we can hope to do is understand where and why we disagree. That is, we must try to identify, first, the various issues we face on the way to the ultimate issue of what conception of text/interpretation/judicial role to support; and, second, the various presuppositions and assumptions we make in resolving those issues and, so, the ultimate issue in our different ways.

The ultimate issue—of the Court's proper role in constitutional cases—and our disagreement about it are not merely theoretical, however. The issue is political. Obviously a lot depends on what conception of the Court's proper role is institutionalized in American politics at any given time. Who gets to decide what the practical resolution of the issue shall be at any given time? Who gets to decide what conception of judicial role shall be institutionalized?

In American political-legal culture, the answer to that question seems not to be controversial. The Supreme Court gets to decide (or a majority of it, at any rate). This is not to deny that the elected representatives of the polity can influence the Court's decision, most significantly, perhaps, by means of the appointments power.[66] But, after all is said and done, the Court gets to decide. Why? Because in American political-legal culture, we accept the Court's constitutional decisions as legally valid however much we might protest their legitimacy. The supreme criterion of our rule of recognition seems to be decisions of the Court interpreting the Constitution. Thus, we accept as well whatever conception of judicial role is implicit in those decisions (however much we might protest the legitimacy of a given conception).

Why do we do that? Why are we so compliant? Why are we content to let the Court decide what conception of judicial role shall be institutionalized in American politics? Two general reasons come to mind. The first is that we seem to be quite wary about lodging that power—in effect, the power to treat some decisions of the Court interpreting the Constitution as *not* legally valid—anywhere else in government. Not that we don't think there are risks in lodging that power in the Court. It's just that there are greater risks—or so we seem to think—in lodging it anywhere else. "As a counter-majoritarian institution the Court is relatively benign. Unlike military juntas, revolutionary vanguards and 'temporary' party elites the Court has neither purse nor sword. It can neither kill us nor cure us without our own active political collaboration."[67]

The second reason is that, after all the sound and fury attending particular controversial decisions of the Supreme Court has died down, we seem to be—that is, those members of the polity politically empowered to make trouble for the Court were they inclined to do so, seem to be—generally content with what the modern Court has done in the modern period. An observation by H.L.A. Hart is instructive:

> The truth may be that, when courts settle previously unenvisaged questions concerning the most fundamental constitutional rules, they *get* their authority to decide them accepted after the questions have arisen and the decision has been given. Here all that succeeds is success. It is conceivable that the constitutional question at issue may divide society too fundamentally to permit of its disposition by a judicial decision. The issues in South Africa concerning the entrenched clauses of the South Africa Act, 1909, at one time threatened to be too divisive for legal settlement. But where less vital social issues are concerned, a very surprising piece of judicial law-making concerning the very sources of law may be calmly "swallowed". Where this is so, it will often in *retrospect* be said, and may genuinely appear, that there always was an "inherent" power in the courts to do what they have done. Yet this may be a pious fiction, if the only evidence for it is the success of what has been done.[68]

VIII

At the beginning of this chapter, in considering the descriptive claim that "the constitutional text is authoritative for constitutional decisionmaking," I raised the question of the truth of the prescriptive claim that "judges should justify their constitutional decisions by reference to (inter alia) the constitutional text." It is now time to return to that question.

The way one answers it depends, of course, on how the constitutional "text" is specified. I have defended a conception according to which the text is, in part and whatever else it might be, the symbolization of the aspirations of the American political tradition. In these terms, the question becomes whether judges should justify their constitutional decisions by reference to the text-as-symbol. And I have argued, in effect, that they should. That is, I have argued that the textual focus is not peripheral, that that focus ought not to be abandoned but maintained. Again, the text-as-symbol—as commemorative, prophetic symbol—has served us well as a focal occasion for remembering and then responding to the central, constitutive aspirations of the tradition. Because judges should maintain the textual focus, and in that sense justify their decisions by reference to the text, it is not merely the case that the text is authoritative for constitutional decisionmaking. The text-as-symbol should be authoritative.

Thus, I understand the "authority" of the constitutional text functionally—that is, as (in part at least) a function of the role the text plays in the life of the American political community. The text ought to be authoritative not simply "in virtue of any inherent property [it] may have, such as being inerrant or inspired" or written by the framers or approved by the ratifiers, but also "in virtue of a function [it] fill[s] in the life of the . . . community."[69]

I wish those who understand the constitutional text in different terms would give us their reasons for thinking that the text understood in their terms should be authoritative. For example, I wish those who understand the text to be the linguistic embodiment of the ratifiers' particular normative judgments would tell us why the text thus understood should be authoritative. It won't do, of course, to say that the text thus understood should be authoritative because the ratifiers wanted it that way. To say that would be to beg the question, which is precisely whether the ratifiers' judgments should be authoritative. We can't refer that question to the ratifiers. What else, then, might be said? That the text understood in originalist terms should be authoritative for constitutional decisionmaking, because understanding it any other way falls prey to the argument from democracy? I have already explained that often proponents of the argument from democracy erroneously presuppose that there is an axiomatic conception of democracy.

But, of course, to say that the text-as-symbol should be authoritative for constitutional decisionmaking is not to say that the text thus conceived can do analytic work in constitutional adjudication. Justification in constitutional decisionmaking, where the text-as-symbol is the operative conception, is like justification in moral and political argument generally, namely, a matter of reason-giving that presupposes a context of shared beliefs.

In the title of this chapter, I refer to the authority, not merely of the text, but also of tradition and reason. All are authoritative for constitutional decisionmaking. That is, judicial justification of constitutional decisions, most evidently in cases like *Brown* and *Roe*, consists of reason-giving that presupposes a context of shared beliefs, in particular shared aspirations.

Moreover, tradition and reason, rather than the ratifiers' specific normative judgments, should be authoritative for constitutional decisionmaking. Judicial justification of constitutional decisions should not consist of taking the ratifiers' judgments as the alpha and omega of constitutionality. Rather, it should consist of reason-giving that presupposes a context of shared aspirations. If persons in their capacity as government officials should participate in the search for political-moral knowledge, then, in American government, the judiciary too should participate, because it is in an institutionally advantaged position to do so.

IX

But what precisely is this "reason-giving" I refer to? In what respects is the activity of practical reasoning in political-moral discourse alike, and in what respects unalike, the activity of practical reasoning in constitutional-legal discourse? What precisely does practical reasoning consist of? What moves does it comprise? Can constitutional decisions, understood as a species of political-moral judgments, bear the predicate "rationally" acceptable or unacceptable? Is there any such thing as political-moral *knowledge*? And is there an "American political tradition"—a "context of shared beliefs and aspirations"—or is that the sheerest fantasy?

I don't propose to answer all those questions here, although, by way of sketching an intellectual agenda for constitutional theory, I do want to say something about them.

How is a court to deal with constitutional questions understood as questions of political morality? How are any of us—judge, lawyer, citizen—to deal with them? Political-moral philosophy, after all, is in a state of serious disarray, as Alasdair MacIntyre has argued.[70]

Many different and competing conceptions of justice clamor

for our attention: for example, utilitarian,[71] contractarian,[72] libertarian,[73] and naturalist.[74] Each conception confronts serious problems (even if adherents of particular conceptions aren't always quick to see them). How are we to adjudicate among competing conceptions of justice? Indeed, can we? Some contend that conceptions of justice are merely matters of taste, and that de gustibus non est disputandum. Are they right? Others contend that conceptions of justice are merely matters of local (cultural) convention. Are they right?

Those of us who see constitutional questions—particularly constitutional questions regarding human rights—as questions of justice and of political morality, and who want the judiciary to see them that way too, must confront the serious disarray of political-moral philosophy. We must address the problem of moral knowledge: Is there moral knowledge? What does it consist of? How is it achieved? We must make that problem a central part of our intellectual agenda.

In addressing the problem—indeed, the possibility—of moral knowledge, MacIntyre has suggested that moral reasoning—*practical* reasoning—can operate only within the context of a particular sort of community and tradition:

[The decay of moral reasoning] is unsurprising in a society whose world view . . . obscures the connection between the possibility of moral reasoning and the existence of a certain type of tradition-bearing community. Any particular piece of practical reason has force only for those who both have desires and dispositions ordered to some good and recognize that good as furthered by doing what that piece of practical reason bids. Only within a community with shared beliefs about goods and shared dispositions educated in accordance with those beliefs, both rooted in shared practices, can practical reason-giving be an ordered, teachable activity with standards of success and failure. Such a community is rational only if the moral theory articulated in its institutionalized reason-giving is the best theory to emerge so far in its history. The best theory so far is that which transcends the limitations of the previous best theory by providing the best explanation of that previous theory's failures and incoherences (as judged by the

standards of that previous theory) and showing how to escape them.[75]

If MacIntyre is right, as I suspect he is, then in addressing
the problem of moral knowledge—of moral reasoning, of which
constitutional interpretation, as I have portrayed it, is merely
one version—we must be careful to clarify what is meant by
"tradition," a notion on which I have placed heavy reliance in
this chapter, and which is easily misunderstood. My understanding of "tradition" follows MacIntyre's. As I said earlier, by
tradition I mean a particular historical narrative, in which the
central aspiration is to a particular form of life, to certain projects, goals, ideals. In the case of a living tradition, the central
discourse is "an historically extended, socially embodied argument" about how the form of life to which the community—
the present bearers of and participants in the tradition—aspires, is to be cultivated and revised.

Thus, a central feature of a living tradition is an argument
among those persons, past as well as present, who identify
themselves as members of an historically extended community,
as to how they should organize and live their life in common,
given the particular beliefs and aspirations they share in their
capacity as self-identified members of that community. A tradition, then, connotes not consensus, but dissensus and consensus. A tradition is constituted in part by an argument as to how
that which is shared should be understood and socially embodied.

In my sense of the term, tradition presupposes community.
As the foregoing comments suggest, a necessary condition of
membership in a community (as I am using the term) is self-
identification as a member of it. Self-identification is not always
a sufficient condition; often there are other conditions, such as
baptism or citizenship.

We can achieve a better understanding of the relevant sense
of "community" if we compare it to "family." Just as one can
live amid a family without identifying oneself as a member of
that family, one can live amid a community without identifying
oneself as a member. Doubtless many citizens live amid the
American political community who do not identify themselves
as members of that community, who do not see themselves as

sharing that web of beliefs and aspirations in terms of which membership is the community is defined.

Of course, it is not always or even usually possible to indicate precisely what beliefs and aspirations are a necessary condition for membership in a community. For example, it is not possible to specify precisely what beliefs and aspirations one must share to be a member of the Roman Catholic community. But that doesn't alter the fact that there is a Catholic community, and that some persons are members of it and others are not. As Stanley Hauerwas has written, "[a] community is a group of persons who share a history [some if only by "adopting" that history] and whose common set of interpretations about that history provide the basis for common actions. These interpretations may be quite diverse and controversial even within the community, but are sufficient to provide individual members with the sense that they are more alike than unalike."[76]

Just as one can leave a family, in the sense of renouncing one's membership in it, one can leave a community. And just as one can return to, or join (even create), a family, one can return to, or join, a community, in the sense of again identifying oneself, or of beginning to identify oneself, as a member. The city in which I live, Chicago, is full of people who have not merely immigrated to the United States and become American citizens, but who have self-consciously joined the American political community by embracing its aspirations.

As with a family, one need not be physically amid other members of a community to identify oneself a member. And also as with families, membership in one community does not preclude membership in others. Indeed, we are all typically members of several communities. I am not a member merely of the Catholic religious community, or of the American political community, or of the Northwestern academic community, but of all these communities (and more). As a member of these various communities, I share particular beliefs and aspirations with certain other persons (although, again, it is not always possible to indicate precisely what they are), and I am engaged in ongoing (interminable!) argument with them as to how various of our shared beliefs and aspirations should be understood and embodied.

The fact of dissensus among Americans, even deep and widespread dissensus, does not mean that the notion of an American political community (and tradition) is a fantasy, any more than the fact that there is a very deep and widespread dissensus among Catholics means that the notion of a Catholic religious community and tradition is a fantasy. That Catholics are engaged in ongoing arguments with one another about the bearing of the Gospel ideal of *agape* on such matters as nuclear deterrence, patriarchal church structures, and capitalist economic structures, does not mean that there is no Catholic religious community of which to identify oneself a member. And that Americans are engaged in an ongoing argument with one another about the bearing of various of their political-constitutional ideals on a variety of matters (racism, sexism, abortion, etc.) does not mean that there is no American political community of which to identify oneself a member.

The relationship between tradition—understood as in part a historically extended and socially embodied argument—and practical reasoning, including constitutional interpretation, is a very complex one. We do not understand it very well. Which is to say, we do not understand very well the bearing of the past—*our* past—on the present—*our* present. Until we understand the relation between tradition and practical reasoning much better than we do—indeed, until we understand the nature of practical reasoning much better than we do—we will not understand constitutional interpretation very well either. To understand precisely how both tradition and reason (as well as the constitutional text) are authoritative for constitutional decisionmaking, and also why they should be authoritative, we must understand better than we do the nature of the activity of practical reasoning and, especially, the ways in which we use the past to transcend the past.[77]

NOTES

1. Alasdair MacIntyre, *After Virtue,* pp. 206–207 (South Bend, Ind.: University of Notre Dame Press, 1981).
2. For one view of the role of precedent in constitutional adjudication, see Monaghan, "Taking Supreme Court Opinions Seriously," 39 *Maryland L. Rev.* 1 (1979).
3. I take the modern period of American constitutional law to be the period since *Brown* v. *Board of Education,* 347 U.S. 483 (1954).

4. *Brown* v. *Board of Education*. If *Brown* seems a problematic example, then substitute *Bolling* v. *Sharpe*, 347 U.S. 497 (1954), the companion case to *Brown*.

5. *Baker* v. *Carr*, 369 U.S. 186 (1962).

6. *Gideon* v. *Wainwright*, 372 U.S. 335 (1962).

7. *New York Times Co.* v. *Sullivan*, 376 U.S. 254 (1964).

8. See, e.g., *Mississippi University for Women* v. *Hogan*, 458 U.S. 718 (1982).

9. *Roe* v. *Wade*, 410 U.S. 113 (1973). This is *not* to say that the conception in question is implicit *only* in (some) individual-rights decisions of the modern period or, indeed, only in individual-rights decisions. In this chapter, however, I am interested principally in the Court's seminal individual-rights decisions of the modern period, such as *Brown* and *Roe*.

10. David Kelsey, *The Uses of Scripture in Recent Theology* (Philadelphia: Fortress Press, 1975), p. 153.

11. Kelsey, *The Uses of Scripture*, pp. 1–2.

12. Henry Monaghan, "Our Perfect Constitution," 56 *N.Y.U.L. Rev.* 353, 383 (1981).

13. See Raoul Berger, *Government by Judiciary* (Cambridge: Harvard University Press, 1977); Raoul Berger, *Death Penalties* (Cambridge: Harvard University Press, 1982).

14. See Robert Bork, "Neutral Principles and Some First Amendment Problems," 47 *Indiana L. J.* 1 (1971); Robert Bork, "The Impossibility of Finding Welfare Rights in the Constitution," 1979 *Washington U. L. Q.* 695.

15. See William Rehnquist, "The Notion of a Living Constitution," 54 *Texas L. Rev.* 693 (1976). Not that there are no differences among Monaghan, Berger, Bork, and Rehnquist. For present purposes, however, the differences are less important than the similarities.

16. Monaghan, "Our Perfect Constitution," note 12, at 374–75 and note 130, at 377.

17. On the "originalist/nonoriginalist" distinction, see Paul Brest, "The Misconceived Quest for the Original Understanding," 60 *B. U. L. Rev.* 204 (1980).

18. Sanford Levinson makes such a challenge. See Levinson, "Law as Literature," 60 *Texas L. Rev.* 373 (1982). However, the challenge doesn't work. See Gerard Graff, " 'Keep off the Grass,' 'Drop Dead,' and Other Indeterminacies: A Response to Sanford Levinson," 60 *Texas L. Rev.* 405 (1982). For another example of such a challenge, see Mark Tushnet, "Following the Rules Laid Down: A Critique of Interpretivism and Neutral Principles," 96 *Harvard L. Rev.* 781 (1983). Tushnet's basic claim is that an originalist ("interpretivist") approach to constitutional adjudication is an available option only

on the basis of certain assumptions that contradict originalism's "liberal" (in the sense of "individualist") political-philosophical premises. The fundamental problem with Tushnet's challenge is his assertion that originalism's premises are liberal. Originalism is much more plausibly understood to rest on Burkean conservative premises. Tushnet's suggestion that a conservative (or other communitarian) political philosophy has no need for a constitutional theory—and that, therefore, originalist constitutional theory cannot plausibly be understood to rest on Burkean conservative premises—is simply wrong. In a political community with a constitution and a judiciary charged with enforcing it, even a conservative (or other communitarian) political philosophy must offer a constitutional theory—that is, a theory of what judges may and may not do in enforcing the constitution.

19. MacIntyre, *After Virtue*, p. 207. Cf. S. Hauerwas, *A Community of Character* (South Bend, Ind.: University of Notre Dame Press, 1981), p. 63: "Scripture is not meant to be a problem solver. It rather describes the process whereby the community we call the church is initiated by certain texts into . . . the 'vivid and lively pattern of argument and controversy' characteristic of biblical traditions."

20. On the notion of "a form of life," see Lawrence Hinman, "Can a Form of Life be Wrong?" 58 *Phil.* 339 (1983).

21. David Tracy, *The Analogical Imagination* (Los Angeles: Crossroads Pub., 1981), pp. 99–100.

22. Tracy, *Analogical Imagination*, p. 154.

23. Ibid.

24. Tracy, pp. 112, 122–24. See also P. Ricoeur, *Hermeneutics and the Human Sciences*, pp. 143–44, J. Thompson, ed. (Cambridge: Cambridge University Press, 1981).

25. Tracy, *Analogical Imagination*, p. 99.

26. See Thomas Sheehan, "The Dream of Karl Rahner," *N.Y. Rev.*, February 4, 1982, at 13, 14; Sheehan, "Revolution in the Church," *N.Y. Rev.*, June 14, 1984, at 35.

27. Tracy, *Analogical Imagination*, p. 100.

28. Tracy, p. 105.

29. Rosemary Ruether, *Sexism and God Talk* (Boston: Beacon Press, 1983); Ruether, "Of One Humanity," *Sojourners*, January, 1984, at 17. See also S. Heschel, ed., *On Being A Jewish Feminist: A Reader* (New York: Schocken Books, 1983).

30. Cf. Roy Larson, "Bishops Tackle Touchy Subject: Dialogue on Women's Role in Church Puts Committee in a Dilemma," *Chicago Sun-Times*, November 13, 1983.

31. See, e.g., Ronald Dworkin, "Law as Interpretation," 60 *Texas L. Rev.* 527 (1982).

32. Stanley Fish, *Is There a Text in this Class?: The Authority of Interpretive Communities* (Cambridge: Harvard University Press, 1980). For an interesting comment on Fish's views, see T. Eagleton, *Literary Theory* (Minneapolis: University of Minnesota Press, 1983), pp. 86–88.

33. See H.-G. Gadamer, *Truth and Method* (Los Angeles: Crossroads Pub., 1975), p. 275.

34. See Sheehan, "Revolution in the Church."

35. But see note 33 above.

36. Alexander Bickel, *The Least Dangerous Branch* (Indianapolis: Bobbs-Merrill, 1962), p. 31. See Richard Saphire, "Making Noninterpretivism Respectable: Michael J. Perry's Contributions to Constitutional Theory," 81 *Michigan L. Rev.* 782, 794–95 (1983).

37. See note 75 below and accompanying text.

38. Owen Fiss, "Objectivity and Interpretation," 34 *Stanford L. Rev.* 739 (1982).

39. See Robert Bennett, "Objectivity in Constitutional Law," 132 *U. Pa. L. Rev.* 445 (1984).

40. *Plessy v. Ferguson,* 163 U.S. 537 (1896).

41. *Lochner v. New York,* 198 U.S. 45 (1905).

42. *Brown v. Board of Education,* 347 U.S. 483 (1954).

43. *Roe v Wade,* 410 U.S. 113 (1973).

44. See Fiss, "Objectivity and Interpretation," 748: *"Brown v. Board of Education* and *Plessy v. Ferguson,* one condemning segregation, the other approving it, may both be objective and thus legitimate exercises of the judicial power, though only one is correct."

45. Ricoeur, *Hermeneutics and the Human Sciences,* pp. 37, 139–40.

46. Owen Fiss, "Objectivity and Interpretation," p. 743; see also K. Burke, *A Grammar of Motives* (Berkeley: University of California Press, 1969), pp. 366–67.

47. Munzer and Nickel, "Does the Constitution Mean What It Always Meant?" 77 *Columbia L. Rev.* 1029, 1059 (1977).

48. Richard Saphire, "Judicial Review in the Name of the Constitution," 8 *U. Dayton L. Rev.* 745, 790–91 (1983).

49. Bickel, *Least Dangerous Branch,* p. 39. See also Saphire, "Judicial Review in the Name of the Constitution," p. 792.

50. See Charles Curtis, "A Better Theory of Legal Interpretation," 3 *Vanderbilt L. Rev.* 407, 425 (1950).

51. For an interesting discussion of how Congress has given meaning to the equal protection clause, and the President to the treaty clause, see Munzer and Nickel, "Does the Constitution Mean What It Always Meant?" pp. 1047–50.

52. See M. Perry, *The Constitution, the Courts, and Human Rights* (New Haven: Yale University Press, 1982), pp. 33–35.

252   MICHAEL J. PERRY

53. Perry, pp. 100–01.
54. Bickel, *Least Dangerous Branch*, p. 26. See also P. Bator, P. Mishkin, D. Shapiro, and H. Wechsler, *Hart & Wechsler's The Federal Courts and the Federal System* 2d ed. (Mineola, N.Y.: Foundation Press, 1973), p. 82.
55. See Denvir, book review of *The Constitution, the Courts, and Human Rights* by M. Perry (1982), 44 *Ohio St. L.J.* 139, 144 and n. 43 (1983); Saphire, "Making Noninterpretivism Respectable," pp. 797, 798.
56. See Robert Bork, "Neutral Principles and Some First Amendment Problems," 47 *Indiana L. J.* 1, 2 (1971).
57. Ibid., pp. 8, 14, 17–18.
58. See Robert Cover, book review of *Government by Judiciary* by Raoul Berger (1977), *New Republic*, Jan. 14, 1978, pp. 26, 27.
59. Monaghan, "Our Perfect Constitution," p. 376.
60. Richard Kay, "Preconstitutional Rules," 42 *Ohio St. L. J.* 187, 193 (1981).
61. See, e.g., Rehnquist, "Notion of a Living Constitution," pp. 701–04.
62. The *locus classicus* of this argument is, of course, Robert Dahl, "Decision-Making in a Democracy: The Supreme Court as National Policy-Maker," 6 *J. Pub. L.* 279 (1937), reprinted in *Judicial Review and the Supreme Court*, L. Levy, ed. (New York: Harper & Row, 1967), p. 105.
63. See Dahl, "Decision-Making in a Democracy," pp. 111–14. For an interesting study of the dialectical interplay between judiciary and legislature in the State of New York between 1870 and 1920, see Janet Lindgren, "Beyond Cases: Reconsidering Judicial Review," 1983 *Wisconsin L. Rev.* 583.
64. See *Hammer* v. *Dagenhart*, 247 U.S. 251 (1918), overruled, *United States* v. *Darby*, 312 U.S. 100 (1941).
65. See Lawrence Alexander, "Painting Without the Numbers: Noninterpretive Judicial Review," 8 *U. Dayton L. Rev.* 447, 459–60, 462 (1983).
66. See Groves Rees, "Questions for Supreme Court Nominees at Confirmation Hearings: Excluding the Constitution," 17 *Georgia L. Rev.* 913 (1983).
67. Cover, book review, p. 28.
68. H.L.A. Hart, *The Concept of Law* (Oxford: Oxford University Press, 1961), pp. 149–50.
69. Kelsey, *The Uses of Scripture,* pp. 30, 47.
70. See A. MacIntyre, *After Virtue,* esp. pp. 6–10.
71. See, e.g., R. Hare, *Moral Thinking* (Oxford: Oxford University Press, 1981); Brandt, "The Problems of Contemporary Utilitarianism:

Real and Alleged," in *Ethical Theory*, N. Bowie, ed. (1983), p. 81.

72. John Rawls's work is contractarian, of course. See J. Rawls, *A Theory of Justice* (Cambridge: Harvard University Press, 1971); J. Rawls, "Kantian Constructivism in Moral Theory," 77 *J. Phil.* 515 (1980). See also Scanlon, "Contractualism and Utilitarianism," in *Utilitarianism and Beyond* (A. Sen and B. Williams, eds. (1981), p. 103.

73. See, e.g., R. Nozick, *Anarchy, State and Utopia* (New York: Harper & Row, 1974).

74. See, e.g., J. Finnis, *Natural Law and Natural Rights* (Oxford: Oxford University Press, 1980); J. Finnis, *Fundamentals of Ethics* (Washington, D.C.: Georgetown University Press, 1983).

75. Alasdair MacIntyre, "Moral Arguments and Social Contexts," 80 *J. Phil.* 590, 591 (1983).

76. S. Hauerwas, *Community of Character*, p. 60.

77. After this essay was completed, Jaroslav Pelikan's *The Vindication of Tradition* (New Haven: Yale University Press, 1984) was published. Pelikan's discussion, in particular his effort to analogize the development of the Judeo-Christian tradition to the development of the American-Constitutional tradition (see pp. 58–61), both supports and supplements my discussion.

A longer version of this essay was published as part of a symposium on "Interpretation" in the *Southern California Law Review* 58 (1985), numbers 1 and 2.

13

IN THE SHADOW OF ORIGINALISM:
A COMMENT ON PERRY

AUSTIN SARAT

My thesis, to put it simply, is that discussion of the authority of the text in constitutional decision-making is haunted by the specter of what Michael Perry calls "originalism," namely the view that constitutional interpretation must be guided by the intentions, or desired meanings, of those who authored or ratified the Constitution. So long as we are content to argue about the desirability of originalism we will be trapped by a discourse that inhibits our understanding of the ways in which the Constitution, or any text, can and cannot be said to be authoritative. Perry's chapter illustrates the problems of struggling against originalism on conceptual terrain largely occupied by it. It illustrates the difficulty of leaving originalism in place, or of acknowledging its plausibility, and, at the same time, trying to evolve a better way of understanding the Constitution. To get beyond originalism it is necessary to take on the difficult task of demonstrating that it is conceptually incoherent as well as operationally implausible. Failing to do so means that we cannot provide an adequate account of the authority of the text in constitutional law.

The set of issues to which Michael Perry addresses himself in his chapter can perhaps be framed by quoting from his book, *The Constitution, the Courts and Human Rights.*[1] There Perry states that, "in most constitutional cases, involving human rights, questions are adjudicated as to which no value judgment plau-

254

sibly attributable to the framers is determinative."[2] In this volume he takes this as a starting point and discusses whether in the absence of such determination the Constitution can be said to be authoritative. The descriptive proposition that the Constitution is authoritative is, in Perry's view, something of a non-problem. Judges, he tells us, "justify their constitutional decisions at least in part by reference to the constitutional text, and . . . they do so because they believe they should."[3] The more difficult problem, in his view, is finding a proper ground for explaining the basis of the authority of the text, for arguing that it should be authoritative. Yet, as I will argue, Perry's own analysis calls into question the very descriptive proposition he seems to think is so unproblematic.

Perry takes as his point of departure the idea that the Constitution is "the verbal or linguistic embodiment of the political morality constitutionalized by the ratifiers/framers."[4] This "originalist" conception locates both meaning and authority in the words and thoughts, the explanations and justifications, of those who "authored" the text. For originalists the interpretive task involves a "search" for the political-moral judgments understood by the ratifiers to be embodied there,[5] a search that begins with the words of the Constitution and asks how those words were commonly used or understood by the framers. This search, of necessity, goes beyond the words of the text and requires the interpreter to read what was said about those words as the document was drafted, redrafted, agreed to and ratified. Authority, for the originialist, resides in meanings and intentions that pre-exist and rest outside of the preferences, norms, or desires of the interpreter. Originalism, as Perry uses the term, requires the reader to leave himself behind, to bind himself to the task of seeing the Constitution through the eyes of its authors. The promise of originalism is to restrict judicial discretion, to honor the rule of law, and to protect the integrity of the democratic process from unwarranted judicial intervention.

Perry recognizes two strategic responses to originalism. The first, the one he chooses, is to try to produce a better conception of the Constitution, one that fulfills important political functions better than originalism. This strategy acknowledges, at least implicitly, the adequacy of originalism. It aims for a superior conception. The second strategy involves questioning the theoretical adequacy of the originalist position, an attempt to uncover its fatal flaws. Perry does not "contend that the originalist conception is flawed." Indeed, he expresses skepticism about such contentions.[6] Here I would like to provoke Perry's skepticism by illustrating some of the flaws in the originalist position and arguing that they distort all responses to it and all attempts to produce a better conception. Perry's decision to be tolerant of originalism is unfortunate.

Originalism is defective in three ways, the last of which is most serious. First, we might ask if originalism can provide a sustainable identification of the framers, a useable method for identifying their intentions or a plausible notion of authorial intentionality. The answer to all three inquires is no. Equally plausible arguments could be made that we ought to attend to the participants at the Convention, to the primary spokesmen for the Constitution at the time of ratification, to those who participated in the ratification process or to the vast silent majority in whose name the document was written. Even if we could agree on whom to place in the authorial position, originalism doesn't, and can't, tell us what ought to count as evidence of intention because whoever is counted as author didn't tell us. Moreover, the very concept of authorial intention requires greater specificity than originalism ever provides. Here I agree with James Boyd White when he says, "Intention can, after all, be stated with generality or particularity, as a matter of motive or a matter of aim; and we are always subject to conflicts in our intentions, many of which are . . . unconscious and out of our control. To try to follow the intention of the writer seems an inherently unstable procedure, leading to a radical conceptual collapse."[7]

Originalism fails precisely because the reference to intention does not itself produce answers to questions of meaning in the constitutional text that are clearer and more definitive than those provided by other interpretive approaches. Our ability to understand the original meaning or the original intent of the Constitution is, in fact, no greater than our ability to resolve, without resort to original intent, the legal and political problems for which we seek guidance from the Constitution.[8] Because the determination of the original meaning or the intent of the framers spawns as much controversy as whether, for example, states should be able to restrict abortion, originalism fails in its quest to limit judicial discretion in the name of majoritarianism.[9]

Yet the most serious flaws with originalism lie elsewhere. There are, it might be argued, two different strands of originalist thinking. The first, what I call its weak version, acknowledges that there are indeed difficulties and ambiguities in reading original intent or meaning. In this version originalists accept the inevitability of interpretive activity, of the effort to understand as well as apply binding norms in constitutional controversies. They insist, however, that the norms to be interpreted must be those found in the text itself or in the intentions of the framers. They insist ". . . that the Constitution must not be seen as licensing courts to articulate and apply contemporary norms not demonstrably expressed or implied by the framers."[10] The weak originalist acknowledges that there may be a plurality of meanings contained in the original understandings; they argue, however, that a good interpretation is one that plausibly could have been accepted by the framers.

Originalism, in its second or strong version, is noninterpretive. It seeks to transform interpretation into a mechanical task, to objectify meaning and to establish the independence of the text and the subservience of the reader. It requires a conception of the authority of the text that is linked to rigid textual determinism. This means that, in any case, judges should be able to find one right reading of the Constitution. Yet we know that the Constitution, and indeed all texts, embody and encode ambiguity, uncertainty, incompleteness, and contradiction. These, however, do not stand as indicators of imperfection but rather as necessary and inevitable parts of the process of turning thought into written expression.

Given such ambiguity, uncertainty, incompleteness, and contradiction, authorial position is dislodged but not displaced. As Stanley Fish points out, "Any text, whatever its conditions of production, is capable of being appropriated by any number of persons and read in relation to concerns the speaker could not have foreseen. Indeed it is a standard strategy in literary criticism to detach a text from what might have seemed to be its severely limiting original situation and turn it into the kind of text that speaks to all men in all circumstances."[11] The author and his intentions are not ignored, but neither are they accorded primacy. Texts are not owned by their authors. Indeed, authors assume the position of participants in a discourse about textual meaning and significance. Texts invite and provoke interpretive disputes; authors provide no final resolution.[12] Legal texts in general, and the Constitution in particular, are no exception although they, perhaps somewhat more than other texts, are invested in the effort to manage the terms on which such disputes occur.

It is very important that Perry is unwilling to acknowledge that legal texts can or should be read like literary texts. In so doing he acknowledges that the authority of the law, that is, its coercive force, must *severely* limit the range of acceptable interpretive positions. In contrast, much of the current vogue in literary theory seeks to open up the text, to pluralize its meaning, to reveal ambiguity, complexity, and unintended irony, and, in so doing, to recognize and realize its richness as literature. The purpose of judging is to stabilize, to legitimate an order to legality which, in turn, might provide some order to society. Thus, as Robert Cover argues, judging is "jurispathic."[13] Originalism, by assuming the existence of fixed meanings independent of judicial preference, provides the interpretive stability that the literary metaphor would dislodge.

The point is not that texts cannot and do not constrain interpretation. Perry is quite clear that they do and here I have no quarrel. All texts, not just legal texts, give guidance, guidance that narrows the range of interpretation. What is at issue is the pull of originalism's desire to limit *severely* or to eliminate plural interpretive possibilities. If judicial decision-makers or readers of literature are unchanged by the text it is irrelevant. All texts shape the imagination and influence readers. Perry, in his rejection of the literary metaphor, seems to want to go further in limiting textually guided interpretive activity than would be seen as appropriate had he more fully explored the literary metaphor.[14] Perry is reluctant to embrace the more radical textual indeterminacy that that exploration might have invited.[15]

Originalism casts a dark shadow over the judicial enterprise by suggesting that to reject it is to look into the abyss, to open the door for nihilism. But this is, of course, a trick.[16] Texts shape their readers just as surely as they are constituted by them.

Readers can't escape the texts they read. Interpretation can't occur if the text is rendered a nullity. There is a genuine mutuality between text and reader, an interdependence, a relation based on indeterminacy. Neither objectification nor nihilism provides a plausible way to describe the interpretive universe. Perry's strength is that he wants to recognize the false nature of that choice. Yet his own rendering of the logic of constitutional interpretation shows how much he still is affected by the originalist desire, the desire for some separation of text and reader.

While Perry acknowledges that "the constitutional text is not (simply) a book of answers to particular questions,"[17] his language suggests that the text has meaning prior to the interpretive act. "That which is taken from the text," he argues, "are the aspirations the text symbolizes and indeed embodies. That which is given to the text are the community's answers as to how those aspirations are to be heeded, realized, in the life of the community, in the light of *its* experience and exigencies."[18] If we take seriously the words "taken from" we are reinscribed in the world of textual independence, in a world that places meanings, now called aspirations, ahead of interpretive acts.

Perry, like the rest of us, is tainted by false oppositions derived from originalism. For him the problem of originalism is political, not conceptual. For all we know, originalism may, in his view, have a powerful conceptual claim. Perry rejects it because it serves to limit the ability of judges to vindicate individual rights, and because it threatens judicial activism in the name of justice.

Perry wants to find a way of defending the human rights decisions of the last two decades. He rejects originalism, not out of a conviction about its fatal flaws, but rather because it undermines the legitimacy of those decisions. Perry asserts, without argument, that there is no real distinction between legal discourse, on the one hand, and political or moral discourse on the other. While I am deeply sympathetic to that claim, I find it odd that Perry does not undertake to prove that the human rights decisions are the results of good interpretations or are good because of their impact. Having staked a claim for political-moral discourse, Perry backs away from it at critical points. Indeed I find myself imagining that Perry could live very well with the methodology of originalism, a methodology that I find indefensible, if only the framers had more clearly embraced his idea of justice.

Perry's defense of activist decisions from *Brown* to *Roe* rests, in important ways, on a defense of the authority of the Supreme Court. If, as he asserts, constitutional interpretation is simply one kind of political-moral discourse, then why should it be lodged, as Perry believes it should, exclusively with the Supreme Court? His answer has two steps. First is the argument that the Court has superior capacity to engage in this discourse because it is insulated from politics and, as a result, has a capacity to be "relatively disinterested"[19] that is superior to that of the other branches. Why "disinterested" as opposed to "interested" interpretive activity is to be preferred is not clear. Indeed, it is not clear what disinterested means in this context or if a disinterested reading of *Brown* or *Roe* would reveal them to be the product of disinterested inquiry. Perry advocates a political, yet nonpartisan, forum for constitutional interpretation, but is unable, or unwilling, to explore whether, or why, that forum would produce interpretations that more clearly accord with the aspirations of the traditions of our political community than readings of the Constitution that were more openly partisan. Or perhaps Perry would want to entertain that interpretive activity itself, no matter where it is located, might require limits on partisanship.

The second step in his defense of the Court involves the argument that justice as well as representativeness is crucial to our tradition.[20] The pursuit of justice is, in his view, properly placed in the hands of the Supreme Court. How do we know this? We do because ". . . in the modern period, on balance, the Court's record in the service of individual rights is admirable."[21] Here Perry slips into the kind of consequentialism that requires him to suggest why that record is admirable, a task he fails to take up. While I am no more eager than Perry to side with those who attack the Court, I worry that his defense is a self-fulfilling prophecy. Perhaps the alleged incapacity of the people to engage, in a disinterested fashion, in constitutional inquiry is itself the product of the decision to remove that responsibility from them.[22] Perhaps our human rights will never be fully secure until we have the responsibility for securing them.

Like Perry, I see great continuity between legal and political-moral discourse. Unlike him, I am not convinced that one can simultaneously establish that continuity and confidently defend the legitimacy of the Supreme Court without resorting to some version of an original understanding of the separation of powers.

Once again the logic of Perry's argument drives back to originalism. The ways in which he gets caught up in the originalist position, in its world of oppositions, is revealed in his book as well as in his contribution to this volume. In his book he distinguishes two positions on the authority of the text in constitutional law. One, which he labels interpretive review, arises when the Supreme Court "ascertains the constitutionality of a given policy choice by reference to one of the value judgments of which the Constitution consists—that is, by reference to a value judgment embodied . . . either in some particular provision of the text of the Constitution or in the overall structure of government ordained by the Constitution."[23] The other, noninterpretive review, involves "the determination of constitutionality by reference to a value judgment other than one constitutionalized by the framers. Such review is 'noninterpretive' because the Court reaches decision without really interpreting any provision of the constitutional text."[24] In noninterpretive review the "source of judgment is the judge's own values."[25] Perry thus describes an interpretive universe that includes both textual determination and textual irrelevance, a world in which the values of the judge are either extinguished or are independent, in which the reader neither constitutes the text, in the case of interpretive review, nor is constituted by it, in the case of noninterpretive review. This is, of course, exactly the universe that originalism describes. Perry defines the possibilities as any originalist would have them. In so doing he severely limits his ability to state a position on meaning and authority in constitutional interpretation that doesn't depend on originalist assumptions.

Yet the Perry of this volume of *NOMOS* is not exactly the Perry of his own book. The language of interpretivism and noninterpretivism disappears. In its stead Perry describes the Constitution as providing the "symbol for the aspirations of the tradition" that binds the American political community. The

Constitution doesn't incorporate particular value judgments; it stands as a symbol of aspirations. How does this redescription help him come to terms with the problem of textual authority in constitutional interpretation? How does it help provide a basis for understanding the Constitution that is superior to originalism? At one level it seems to allow Perry to escape the earlier opposition of textual determinism and readerly independence. Now we are told, quite without argument, that "The descriptive claim that the constitutional text is authoritative is accurate. Judges do justify their constitutional decisions at least in part by reference to the constitutional text. . . ."[26] If we take the word justify seriously, that is, if we read it to mean that judges derive reasons to decide cases from the text, and if this occurs even in the cases that Perry himself holds as the criterion against which his argument might be tested, *Brown* v. *Board* and *Roe* v. *Wade,* then noninterpretivism seems to be put to rest. Judicial activism can sit comfortably with a gentle, modified textualism.

Things are not, I fear, quite so easy for Perry. At several places in his chapter in this volume he comes very close to repudiating his descriptive claim about the authority of the text even as he attempts to do originalism one better in providing a normative basis for textual authority. While much of Perry's chapter is devoted to an explication of that normative basis, namely the idea of Constitution as symbol for the aspirations of the tradition, little time is spent exploring what we mean by authority when we use it to link text and interpretation. Authority, we are told, implies a relation between text and reader. So far, so good, but the nature of that authority is never adequately explained.[27] As nearly as I can tell, when Perry talks about the authority of the text he thinks about the extent to which the relation is one of determination "or at least" constraint. The Constitution is authoritative to the extent that it serves to "constrain the Court's choices."

Yet constraint is not unproblematic as a way of thinking about authority. It implies that the Constitution is authoritative only to the extent that it prevents judges from imposing any interpretation they wish. It implies, or requires, that we imagine an interpretive act unconstrained by the text, derived from some source that is not given meaning by the Constitution. Here Perry continues to think in terms of the oppositions that, at least in his endorsement of the descriptive claim to textual authority, he seems to want to avoid. He does not inquire into the ways our concept of textual authority is, of necessity, transformed, or, to use a word that Perry used in another context, disrupted, by the rejection of the distinction between interpretivism and noninterpretivism, determination and independence.

Perry is, however, quite aware that something happens to authority when this move is made. At several places he suggests that when the Constitution is seen as a symbol of aspirations interpretation must be "always-provisional, always-reformable."[28] Moreover, he suggests that ". . . the constitutional text, conceived as the symbolization of the aspirations of the tradition, is significantly *less* constraining than the text conceived of as simply the linguistic embodiment of the various concrete political-moral judgments constitutionalized by the ratifiers."[29] Authority, understood as constraint, is weakened; extraneous; readings become conceivable; plurality of view is invited. But the language remains the language of constraint. It is that language which, inspired as it is by the originalist oppositions, must be scrutinized if we are to find a way of talking about the authority of the text that is true to the descriptive claim he validates. Originalist assumptions demand that we acknowledge the possibility that the text could be without authority, a possibility that Perry wants to deny.

The Constitution, like any text, exerts its authority by shaping the way its readers see and imagine its world. Precisely because the way judges construct problems and understand cases is always within the constitutive power of the text, the text is authoritative. Precisely because the tradition that gives meaning to the Constitution is a force in giving meaning to the world in which judges live and work, and is, in turn, shaped and reshaped by them, the Constitution is authoritative. The relation between text and reader is one of mutually constitutive generative necessity. The text is, as Perry recognizes, inescapable, but not just or primarily as a boundary against readings that exist outside of it. It is inescapable in giving meaning to the very act of reading just as it has no meaning until it is read.

But even as I fault Perry for failing to allow his own conceptions of authority to be disrupted, I would like to suggest that his argument may serve to disrupt, in spite of its efforts to the contrary, its own descriptive claim. To say, as Perry does, that the Constitution is a "symbol" for aspirations is to say that its authority must rest with the capacity of symbols to constrain (if we are to continue to use Perry's language) interpretation. The Constitution could be said to be authoritative only if that capacity were independent and different from the constraining power of the traditions or of the aspirations that Perry argues it symbolizes. Yet, as I read him, he does not make the case for the independent constraining power of the symbolization of the tradition of which he speaks.

Surely some starts are made. Early on Perry notes the importance of the "writtenness of the Constitution."[30] Yet this idea is not developed. How writtenness, whether text or symbol, independently constrains remains unanalyzed. But more than the absence of argument is in play here. At the same time, we are being told that it is the text, presumably the text as symbol, that constrains, Perry suggests that the Constitution only "constrains in the way and to the extent the aspirations of the tradition constrain."[31] Here it seems as if the authority of the text, understood as Perry understands it, is largely, if not entirely, derivative, and, in that sense, unable to generate independent force.

Beyond this, Perry suggests that the Constitution may impose no constraint at all—that it may have no authority. As Perry puts it, in an earlier version of this chapter, ". . . significant parts of the text do *not* rule out any answer a majority of the Court is likely to want to give. Thus one should not make too much of the extent to which the text is more constraining than no text would be. If the constitutional text is a canvas, then, in many of what are for us its most important provisions, the text comes close to being not a bounded canvas . . . but an unbounded one."[32] We seem to be brought perilously close to the rediscovery of noninterpretive judging, to the point where, in his book, Perry argues that not only does the Constitution not constrain but that "there is no single, predominant American tradition—none so determinate, at any rate, as to be of much help in resolving the particular human rights conflicts that have come before the Court. . . ."[33] Indeterminacy of the text is compounded by the indeterminacy of the tradition from which Perry now argues the Constitution derives its constraining power.

All of this is presented to validate the descriptive claim that the text is authoritative in constitutional decisionmaking.

We come back, in the end, to the question of why Perry, and most of those who have written about constitutionalism, would be attracted to the question of whether the text ought to be authoritative in constitutional decisionmaking. The answer lies, I think, in the continuing pull of originalism. For many of those who write about the Constitution, originalism, while undesirable because of its tendency to produce conservative decisions, seems less threatening than does its opposite. We fear judges gone wild, using their power to ride roughshod over us. We fear judicial tyranny. We need, however, to rethink the way in which we see the problem of text and interpretation in constitutional law, to incorporate perspectives that would free us from the false opposition of textual determinacy and readerly independence.[34] Perhaps when that task is accomplished we can speak more meaningfully about the ways texts constitute, and are constituted by, their readers, the ways texts have authority over readers and readers have authority over texts. Judges, like all the rest of us, "are always and already thinking within the norms, standards, definitions, routines, understood goals, etc. that both define and are defined . . ." by their situation, their context.[35] The Constitution can never be other than authoritative even where its influence can't be found in plain language or original intention. Only by rejecting originalism at its core will we be able to get on with the task, which Perry himself embraces, of providing an adequate account of *how* textual authority operates in constitutional decisionmaking.

NOTES

1. Michael Perry, *The Constitution, the Courts and Human Rights* (New Haven: Yale University Press, 1982).
2. Ibid., p. 75.
3. Michael Perry, "The Authority of Text, Tradition, and Reason," part I, this volume.
4. Ibid., part II.
5. Ibid.
6. Ibid., part III.
7. James Boyd White, "Law as Literature," *Texas Law Review* 60 (1982): 419.

8. See Paul Brest, "The Misconceived Quest for the Original Under-standing," *Boston University Law Review* 60 (1980): 204. See also H. Jefferson Powell, "The Original Understanding of Original Intent," *Harvard Law Review* 98 (1985): 885.
9. This line of argument was suggested to me by Larry Wiseman.
10. Thomas Grey, "Do We Have an Unwritten Constitution?" *Stanford Law Review* 27 (1975): 706, n. 9.
11. Stanley Fish, "Interpretation and the Pluralist Vision," *Texas Law Review* 60 (1982): 503.
12. See Stanley Fish, *Is There a Text in This Class?* (Cambridge: Harvard University Press, 1980) and Jonathan Culler, *On Deconstruction* (Ithaca: Cornell University Press, 1982).
13. Robert Cover, "Nomos and Narrative," *Harvard Law Review* 97 (1983): 4.
14. See Ronald Dworkin, "Law as Interpretation," *Texas Law Review* 60 (1982): 527, and Sanford Levinson, "Law as Literature," *Texas Law Review* 60 (1982): 373.
15. Radical indeterminacy is explored by Mark Tushnet, "Legal Scholarship: Its Causes and Cures," *Yale Law Journal* 86 (1977): 1165 and "Critical Legal Studies and Constitutional Law," *Stanford Law Review* 36 (1984): 623.
16. See William Singer, "The Player and the Cards," *Yale Law Journal* 94 (1984): 1.
17. Perry, "The Authority of the Text," part V.
18. Ibid.
19. Ibid., part VI.
20. Ibid.
21. Ibid.
22. See Henry Steele Commager, *Majority Rule and Minority Rights* (Gloucester, MA: Peter Smith, 1943).
23. Perry, *The Constitution, the Courts and Human Rights*, p. 10.
24. Ibid., p. 11.
25. Ibid., p. 123.
26. Perry, "The Authority of the Text," part I.
27. Ibid.
28. Ibid., part V.
29. Ibid.
30. Ibid., part III.
31. Ibid., part V.
32. This version was presented at the annual meeting of the Association of Legal and Political Philosophy, September, 1984.
33. Perry, *The Constitution, the Courts and Human Rights*, p. 93.
34. See Stanley Fish, "Fish on Fiss," *Stanford Law Review*, 36 (1984).
35. Ibid.

14

SACRED TEXTS AND AUTHORITY IN CONSTITUTIONAL INTERPRETATION

MARTIN P. GOLDING

In an article published in 1934, "The Constitution as an Institution," Karl N. Llewellyn, like other legal realists, sought to expose the sham of what he called the "orthodox theory" of the Constitution.[1] The first among the ideas Llewellyn identified as elements of this theory is

> the notion that the primary source of information as to what our Constitution comes to, is the language of a certain Document of 1789, together with a severely select coterie of additional paragraphs called Amendments. Is this not extraordinary? The Document was framed to start a governmental experiment for an agricultural, seaboard folk of some three millions. Yet it is supposed to control and describe our Constitution after a century and a half of operation; it is conceived to give basic information about the government of a nation, a hundred and thirty millions strong, whose population and advanced industrial civilization have spread across the continent.

He ridiculed the notion that the Constitution could be interpreted in terms of its "original intent;" rather, it has required constant remodelling. "If no such remodelling had been achieved," he said, "it hardly needs argument that either Document or theory would have been junked these many years."

Llewellyn distinguished between the Document or Text, always with capital letters, and the "going Constitution," which is an institution, that is, a certain "set of ways of living and doing." The reconstruction of constitutional theory, he held, would have to come "without reference to the Document."

What then is the role of the text, according to Llewellyn? "There is," he said,

> in a word, one reason and one reason only, for turning to the Text. A 'written constitution' is a system of unwritten practices in which the Document in question, by virtue of men's attitudes, has *a little influence. Where it makes no difference which way the decision goes,* the Text—in the absence of countervailing practice—is an excellent traffic-light. Aside from such cases, any Text of fifty years is an Old Man of the Sea. For the rest, the Constitution is an institution. And 1933 has come—and gone [emphasis in original].

"Yet," Llewellyn concluded his article, "the year insists on being 1934. Theory that can face fact, including that fact, is what we need."

Almost any reader of Michael J. Perry's penetrating chapter in this volume will be struck, as I am, by the parallel between it and Llewellyn's article, now more than fifty years old. Both reject "originalism" as a theory of constitutional interpretation; both call for a "better conception" of the Constitution; and both want a theory that is "descriptively adequate," to use Perry's words. Yet important differences exist between them. Llewellyn's article exudes the adventurous aura of the legal realist's social science orientation, an orientation that would rescue a benighted orthodoxy from the cave in which it was locked. A theory that can face fact would not look to the text of the Constitution for "basic information" about the government of the nation; rather, the Constitution is a "set of ways of living and doing." One is hard put, however, to find in Llewellyn's article a *normative* theory that could guide the Supreme Court in the resolution of constitutional issues. And the pertinence of moral and political philosophy to the development of a theory is not explicitly recognized. In any case, the "Document" itself would not figure in the development of the sort of theory Llewellyn envisions.

Perry's chapter, on the other hand, represents a more recent brand of American jurisprudence, one that draws upon the resources of the humanities, e.g., theology and literary theory, as much as, and often rather than, the social sciences. It mandates a strong role for moral and political philosophy in the reconstruction of constitutional theory. If Perry regards his theory as incomplete, it is because he is still searching for moral-political knowledge and an adequate account of practical reasoning. While the legal realists sought to demythologize the Constitution, Perry would instead sacralize the "Document."[2] He offers a theory that has "normative appeal," as well as descriptive adequacy. This is his sacred-text conception of our written constitution, which he uses to defend "nonoriginalist" constitutional interpretation—that is, interpretation that appeals to values and aspirations other than those constitutionalized by the framers or ratifiers.

In this discussion I first wish to examine a few facets of Perry's thesis that the sacred-text conception of our Constitution and its nonoriginalist interpretation provide a better conception than originalism. One interesting feature of Perry's position is that the sacred-text conception is the basis of his endorsement of nonoriginalism, or at least his version of it. For it is this conception that permits and perhaps mandates a "prophetic role" for what used to be called the Nine Old Men and, in fact, the entire federal judiciary. But nonoriginalism has not always been held to rest on the sacred-text idea, nor does it need to. For plainly, theorists have maintained a normative nonoriginalist thesis (read: judicial activism) without also accepting a sacred-text view. In a paradoxical way, originalists have also acknowledged nonoriginalism. The air of paradox is of course dispelled when it is realized that originalism is a normative doctrine, to which originalists have appealed in condemning so-regarded nonoriginalist, mossback, or radical decisions of the Court. For these reasons it is important to take a close look at Perry's conception of a sacred text. Other conceptions are possible. I shall also examine the understanding of tradition that he invokes.

Perry insists that any conception of "text" must be argued for. The second thing I wish to do, therefore, is examine Perry's own positive argument for his sacred-text conception of the Constitution and the nonoriginalism that it entails, and also his rebuttal of counter-arguments. I shall show that his positive argument is not successful in establishing "normative appeal" for nonoriginalism. The negative side of his exposition, on the other hand, will be found to raise a rather interesting and important question, namely, the question of the authority of law and its continuity over time. I propose to discuss this issue within the context of an examination of Perry's views.

I shall assume that the term "sacred text" refers to a written document, although a story told in a nonliterate society could have that status. Perry writes: "By a sacred text (or texts) I mean the text that, in the community and tradition in question, is seen to charter, to mandate, the form of life to which the community and tradition aspire, and thus the text that, for the community and tradition *symbolizes* that mandate" (p. 226). The key terms in this definition are "community," "tradition," and "form of life," each of which, as Perry would admit, designates a rather complex notion. A religious text, of course, can be studied by scholars who have no commitment to the community that is or was the bearer of the text; it can be studied by people for whom the text is not sacred. A community in Perry's sense does involve committed individuals, and their commitment is to the values and goods that are constitutive of their tradition and to the text that is symbolic of those goods. When the tradition is a "living tradition," in Alasdair MacIntyre's terms, the tradition is an historically extended, socially embodied argument about those goods, that is, an argument about how those goods are to be realized, given contemporary needs and opportunities. Interpretation of the text, therefore, is conceived by Perry as a "mediation of past and present." The text-as-symbol provides occasions for remembering and responding to the community's constitutive aspirations. It is this conception of a sacred text that, according to Perry, provides a "better conception" of our written constitution than that of originalism. Perry is of course not maintaining that the Ten Amendments were given by God to George Washington on Mount Vernon, but rather that a close analogy exists between a sacred text and the Constitution so conceived.

Perry's conception of "sacred text" has some interesting features. Consider, first, his application of the sacred-text idea to the Constitution. He evidently thinks that this conception entails nonoriginalism, that is, interpretation that may go beyond the values constitutionalized by the ratifiers or framers. But what would the analogue of this be with respect to a sacred text? Nonoriginalist interpretation here would be interpretation that goes beyond the values that are sacralized in the document. Perry's view of sacred-text interpretation is in fact even more extreme. He allows that a later generation of the bearers of a sacred text may even "exorcize" from it meanings they find unwelcome. This surely is a strange view or, perhaps better said, a rather weak conception of a sacred text. An interpretive theory that allows the "exorcizing" of meanings might arguably be regarded as undermining the sacred status of the text. And nonoriginalist interpretation, going beyond the values sacralized, would come very close to accomplishing the same result. It seems to me that originalist interpretation has a better fit with according sacred status than nonoriginalism, and—what is extremely important—I see no need to identify originalism with literalism. Moreover, it is hard to see how nonoriginalism can count at all as a theory of textual interpretation. "Noninterpretivism," the word that Perry has used previously, would seem to be more appropriate. In any event, we can see how attenuated is Perry's notion of maintaining a "textual focus" for the Constitution. His reconstruction of constitutional law theory is perilously close to being, in Llewellyn's terms, "without reference to the Document."

But here caution is called for. It is important to distinguish between a descriptive and a normative sacred-text conception as well as between a normative and a descriptive theory of interpretation. Perry's version of sacred text cum nonoriginalism may in fact be accurate in describing how a sacred text was treated in a particular community although the community itself held to a normative originalist theory of interpretation. This proposition might be true of our written constitution; descriptively speaking the idea of "sacred text" may provide a "better conception" of the Constitution. Perry, however, seems at some places to want to rest the case for his normative nonoriginalism on the descriptive accuracy of the sacred-text conception as applied to the Constitution. I see no logical connection between them. (I shall have more to say about this aspect of his argument later.)

One suggestive note in the sacred text idea is that it is useful in explaining why a community takes a given text to be a source for resolving questions of practice—not independently, of course, from a theory or tradition of interpretation. A sacred text is not just an object of veneration, nor is it merely symbolic in the way in which a flag is. In these respects, therefore, a sacred text is not unlike sorts of authoritative texts, e.g., the bylaws of a club or university, that are not invested with sanctity. It is because sacred and other authoritative texts are used to resolve issues of practice that their "writtenness" is extremely important. No doubt, a sacred text has a deeper significance for the people bound to it than special-purpose documents. But in all these cases, sacred and nonsacred, it surely is too extreme to say, as Perry does in his discussion of amendments, that it is the *text* that is authoritative, as if a text were mere chicken scratches on a piece of parchment; only a text invested with meaning can be authoritative if it is supposed to be relevant to practice. Perry is right that the meaning need not be the original understanding of the words. But I think it plausible to hold that a conscious nonoriginalist interpretation of a text is indistinguishable from deliberate misinterpretation. Anyway, a useful theory of interpretation, especially one that is supposed to have "normative appeal," should also supply a way of identifying misinterpretations.

Perry quite rightly puts great emphasis on the idea of tradition, but his analysis has a curious though explainable feature. Because he wants to dissassociate himself from any sort of traditionalism, he underplays the importance of traditions or continuous practices and conventions. Even though, however, we should not identify a community's tradition with a mere set of traditions (for tradition is a more complex and flexible idea than that of *a* tradition), the former is inconceivable without the latter. Only through continuously maintained conventions, especially of language and relative fixity of meaning, can a community make sense of its past and its sacred texts.

Now communal traditions and social conventions have an important characteristic. Although they can change over time, no way exists deliberately to change them. No one legislates tradition and convention. In this respect, law, except in a regime of customary or divine law, is distinguishable from tradition and convention. But this consideration requires qualification. Although no one individual can "enact" the abolition or alteration of a tradition, a person claiming divine authority, a prophet, may well be able to do so. Prophecy of this sort, however, should be distinguished from interpretation or reinterpretation of the bearing of a tradition or a sacred text. It is hardly surprising that Perry thinks, though somewhat reservedly as far as the term goes, that the courts should exercise a prophetic role. This is what nonoriginalism amounts to in a system that provides for deliberate alteration of fundamental law.

In a way, Perry may be said to seek to escape the conclusion that nonoriginalism is not a theory of textual interpretation at all by his resort to Paul Ricoeur's distinction between the referent that is "behind" a text and what is in "front" of it. Every text has a referent, and for originalism, says Perry, the referent of the Constitution, the intention of the framers, is behind; for the sacred-text conception the referent is in front. So nonoriginalism is textual interpretation after all. I don't think that Ricoeur helps Perry very much.

It is important to see that Ricoeur introduces this distinction because he is concerned with the problem of objectivity in interpretation, particularly the interpretation of poetic works that use metaphorical language, though the theory he develops is meant to apply to actions as well as written texts, and of course not just to sacred texts or written constitutions.[3] Many late–nineteenth-century philosophers had sharply separated *Naturwissenschaft* and *Erklären,* on the one side, from *Geisteswissenschaft* and *Verstehen,* on the other, the former being "objective" and the latter "subjective." Ricoeur's theory is an attempt to bridge the gap between the two, between explanation and understanding, by rejecting the psychologistic trap that requires a projection of the reader's into the writer's self in order to understand a poetic work. According to Ricoeur a literary work is *about* something. It creates a world of its own and has "semantic autonomy." The reader's problem is that of "appropriating" that world by "merging" his world with the world of the text. In this act of appropriation, what the text says is not irrelevant to Ricoeur.

I find Ricoeur's notion of appropriation somewhat obscure, but in any case the behind–front distinction, insofar as I un-

derstand it, is fully compatible with originalism. A refined originalist in fact might use Ricoeur's distinction in elucidating his
own position, for originalism is not subjectivistic romanticism.
The framers of the copyright and patents provision of the Constitution (Art. I, Sec. 8.8) of course did not have in their heads
the telegraph or transistor, but originalism is not so crude as to
exclude these inventions from the meaning of the provision.
Nor is the world of the framers so remote from us as that of
the authors of ancient poetry that it cannot be recaptured.[4]
Originalist interpretation, defined as interpretation of the language of the Constitution in accord with values constitutionalized by the ratifiers or framers, is also "in front" of the text.
The problem of originalism is not its referent but rather what
it is going to do with any entrenched constitutional law and
doctrine that has gone beyond what originalism would have allowed and that is now part of the legal tradition.

I earlier pointed out that sacred texts and authoritative texts
are employed to resolve disputed matters of practice. Although
Perry does not discuss texts of the latter kind, one would suppose that he would admit the appropriateness of originalism in
their case. Such interpretation of course does not exclude reliance on traditions. Nor does it seem circular to appeal to the
original understanding of the ratifiers of the text that it ought
to be interpreted originalistically, in case someone wanted to
introduce a new kind of interpretation. On the other hand it
does seem question-begging to try to establish that a given text
is sacred by appealing to a statement to that effect in the text
itself. We shall consider the issue of circularity in the discussion
of Perry's rebuttal of counter-arguments to his view.

What, then, is distinctive about sacred texts? It does not follow from the concept of a sacred text that they must be interpreted nonoriginalistically. Nevertheless, it might plausibly be
maintained, given the history of the treatment of sacred texts
in the communities that held them, e.g., Holy Scripture, that
nonoriginalistic interpretation has been the general rule. And
this for a good reason: since a sacred text enshrines the fundamental values of a community, in contrast to other kinds of
authoritative texts, the only way for a text to survive as sacred
and yet undergo adaptive application is for it to be interpreted
nonoriginalistically. Still, this sort of interpretation always must

be presented as if it were originalistic, as for instance the recovery of the "true meaning" of the text or tradition, lest it be regarded as willful misinterpretation. Perry notes that this is how the Court in effect has frequently described its own interpretive activity, i.e., as "behind" the text. But it is still a big step from conceiving the Constitution as sacred, and as therefore having an affinity for nonoriginalism, to licensing conscious nonoriginalism. What is at stake is the legitimacy of nonoriginalism, its normative appeal, as Perry calls it.

Now in our discussion of tradition one important point has thus far been left out, namely, the idea of a "living tradition."[5] Perry evidently holds that a community whose tradition is living will interpret its sacred text or fundamental law nonoriginalistically, that is, in accordance with values that are, partly at least, other than those initially sacralized or constitutionalized. Perry follows Alasdair MacIntyre's definition. "[W]hen a tradition is in good order," MacIntyre writes, "it is always partially constituted by an argument about the goods the pursuit of which gives the tradition its particular point and purpose. . . . A living tradition then is an historically extended, socially embodied argument, and an argument precisely in part about the goods which constitute that tradition."[6]

In a sense, this approach can be viewed as an attempt to steer a middle course between Burkeanism and Jeffersonianism, between upholding the wisdom, and thus the authority, of traditions and the rejection of all tradition in the name of universal moral truths. It recognizes, on the one hand, that moral discourse and reasoning can operate only within a tradition, and that a community can be critical of its traditions, on the other. A community that has a living tradition shares in a common set of interpretations about its history and traditions, and yet these interpretations are diverse and controversial; a living tradition involves both consensus and dissensus. So while the upholders of tradition were correct in dismissing universal, self-evident moral truths and the "a priori road" in politics, they were incorrect in thinking that what Bentham called the "Chinese Argument" works, that something is right merely because our ancestors thought so.

The idea of "living tradition" probably is one of the more debated and debatable parts of MacIntyre's theory; it looks as though he wants to have his cake and eat it too. Moreover, it may make moral reasoning more rather than less problematic. Perry himself admits that the relation of tradition to practical reasoning is not understood very well. We have no clear way of telling whether a tradition is living or in disarray (the American political tradition?) or moribund. Calling a tradition living or dead may be special pleading. I think that the notion of living tradition is difficult (it is an instance of the ancient metaphysical problems of how something that changes retains its self-identity and of how the Many can also be One), fruitful, and important, but I cannot discuss it independently here. Our main question is whether a community that has a living tradition, which *arguendo* we may take our polity to have, is committed to interpreting its written constitution nonoriginalistically, especially if that document provides a procedure for amendment in order to change its fundamental law or constitutionalize new values, as does ours. It seems to me that it is not committed to nonoriginalism.

It is important not to conflate, as Perry seems to do, constitutional amendment and the dialogic and critical character, to use his terms, of the debate that properly goes on in the political arena over the goods affirmed by the tradition. To be sure, constitutional amendment is, as Perry says, "one way the present can decisively reject an aspect of the tradition and establish, in its stead, a new aspiration more consonant with what the present sees as the central, constitutive aspirations of the tradition." The crucial word here is "decisively," which Perry, however, seems to ignore. For although an amendment is a product of a debate that went on in the community, that debate has no official termination point and no official and decisive outcomes, by its very nature as part of a living tradition. An amendment, on the other hand, is the official result of an official process. An amendment in fact might not be absorbed into the prevailing practice of a large segment of the polity—the Prohibition Amendment is the obvious case. An amendment can also be decisively repealed; aspirations cannot, though they can dissolve over time. Because Perry underplays these significant differences and rather views constitutional amendment in terms of its function in the present's ongoing interpretation of tradition, his "living tradition" idea inclines him, mistakenly, to think that provision for amendment is no serious obstacle for nonoriginalism. But provision for amendment would be an obstacle for nonoriginalist interpretation even of a genuine sacred text, let alone the Constitution of the United States.

Behind this conflation, it seems to me, is a more serious confusion, a confusion encouraged by the expansive use of one of the most loosely used words in contemporary philosophical, literary, and legal circles: "interpretation." Because the word is used so broadly, Perry is able to regard amendment as just another instance of "ongoing interpretation of the tradition," especially since it is a living tradition, even when an amendment "decisively" rejects a traditional value. But furthermore, and more importantly, because of this broad use Perry is encouraged virtually to identify the ongoing interpretation of the tradition by the community, which presumably can and often will be nonoriginalist interpretation, and the interpretation of constitutional text by the judiciary. If both are instances of "interpretation," it is easy to think that the same sort of thing goes on in both cases.

Perhaps it does. According to its definition, a living tradition is in part an "argument" about the goods that constitute that tradition and, one supposes, thus is an interpretation of the tradition. Although I am not too clear on what this means, let us grant that such interpretation at least involves giving an argument, a moral argument of some kind. But so does the interpretation of constitutional language in cases in which a court is deciding questions of law, especially the "open-ended" clauses that are of interest to Perry, "equal protection," "due process," etc. Further, these arguments often rest on values other than those constitutionalized by the ratifiers. This is an old idea, much emphasized by the legal realists for instance, though they tended to think of these decisions exclusively as policy decisions. Perry's contribution, his "better conception," is that the sacred-text view explains why these nonoriginalist kinds of argument are made. For the reasons I have given, I do not find Perry's account altogether convincing. It seems possible to be a normative originalist and yet accept the sacred-text conception or be a descriptive nonoriginalist and yet reject the sacred-text conception.[7]

Perry also holds that his theory of interpretation, specifically nonoriginalism, has "normative appeal." While nonoriginalism can be detached from the sacred-text conception, I suspect that he wants the aura of sanctity that attaches to the Constitution, when conceived as sacred, to confer an aura of normativity on nonoriginalism. At any rate, we must consider how Perry sees the connection between the descriptive adequacy that he claims for nonoriginalism and the normative appeal that he claims for it. I shall argue that Perry is a realist in the last analysis and that he is unable to establish his case.

Perry begins by considering two questions that he says must be answered if nonoriginalism is to have normative appeal: Does the constitutional text as he conceives it constrain judicial choices and, if not, does anything else significantly constrain them? His answers, no in both cases, are not very encouraging. Neither can the text do analytical work in decisionmaking nor do the canons of judicial behavior constrain. All we have are the not very powerful constraints of the living tradition. On Perry's view the Court could come to (almost?) any decision it wants and the decision would still be valid. As he says in his parenthetical comment on the outcome in *Blaisdell,* the Minnesota Mortgage Moratorium Case, the decision is not "extra" or "contra," it is simply "constitutional." On his view, of course, any decision of the Court would be constitutionally valid.

Why does all this seem so unencouraging and unlikely to promote the normative appeal of nonoriginalism? Because the role that normative nonoriginalism prescribes for the Court is not a *judicial* role; it is rather a legislative role of a far-reaching sort. More particularly, it licenses the incremental, because reversible by later decision, amendment of the Constitution through judicial lawmaking. Perry is not arguing, as some have, that lawmaking would occur even under originalism, so that we may as well go all the way and allow nonoriginalistic interpretation. He admits that originalism prescribes a much more constrained role for the Court. Originalism allows only that degree of lawmaking that is inevitable in the performance of the judicial function, and it is mainly for this reason that originalists have maintained that their view is more consistent with popular democracy. And although Perry maintains that no particular conception of democracy is axiomatic, I think he is prepared to concede the last point.

To all this Perry has a ready response in two parts: first, that no particular conception of judicial role is axiomatic and, second, that the role that has been institutionalized comports with the tradition. The first point, it seems to me, is rather misleading. While the role of the Supreme Court has been rather controversial, and in that sense not axiomatic, we can, as legal anthropologists, distinguish between a body that performs a judicial role and a body that performs a legislative role. The distinction may be a matter of degree, but it is important nonetheless.

Perry's second point is crucial to his argument. He maintains that the role that has been institutionalized for, and by, the modern Court is one of constitutional decisionmaking through nonoriginalistic interpretation, particularly in the area of individual rights. At one level of argument—though this is not the whole of it, as we shall see in a moment—Perry seems to want to move from the descriptive claim that nonoriginalism has been institutionalized to the claim that it has normative appeal. It is here that his realism begins to show itself although his style is different from the realism of the 1920s and 1930s. Quite in character with legal realism, though the realists tended to avoid any explicit discussion of the matter,[8] Perry's account of "legal validity" leaves no room for any notion of judicial error, or of correctness for that matter. All of the Court's decisions are, as we noted, simply "constitutional." While originalism has a theory of judicial error, the *fact* of judicial error is an embarrassment to it.

According to Perry, the supreme criterion of legal validity in our rule of recognition is "decisions of the Supreme Court in interpreting the text of the Constitution." This assertion should be contrasted, I think, with a rather different candidate for supreme criterion, namely, that all decisions of the Court made in accordance with the Constitution are valid. On the latter view, the text of the Constitution presumably is an objective standard for determining the validity of decisions, while Perry's position comes perilously close to the old saw that the Constitution means whatever a majority of the Court says it means. Or as Chief Justice Hughes famously and more elegantly put it: "We are under a Constitution but the Constitution is what the judges say it is."

Now Perry puts great weight on the alleged fact of "acceptance." His candidate is the supreme criterion because we, the
American polity, accept the decisions of the Supreme Court.
And since the modern Court interprets the Constitution nonoriginalistically, he seems to be arguing, nonoriginalism has
normative appeal. This is how I understand the relation, for
Perry, between the descriptive account and the normative claim.
But this part of his argument can be questioned. First, it does
not follow from the fact that the Court's decisions are accepted
that any particular theory of interpretation is accepted. It is of
course true, with a few outstanding exceptions, that decisions
of the Court have not led to violence in the streets, but in this
sense contrary decisions probably also would have been accepted. Perry may have another sense in mind, however. It is
that "we" have generally been satisfied with the decision of the
court, as shown by the fact that, except for the Income Tax
Amendment in 1913, we haven't overturned them by amending the Constitution, leaving aside overturning nonconstitutional decisions by legislation. This fact, however, is subject to
different and more complex explanations. And the difficulty of
amending the Constitution needs no mention.

In any case, Perry's argument seems to me to be a red her-
ring. The dispute between him and the originalist is not, as he
takes it in one of his references to Henry Monaghan, over what
our supreme criterion of validity is in Perry's realist sense of
"valid." It is rather over just the question that Perry admits can
be asked of any decision but which he there puts aside, namely
the issue of legitimacy or, as he otherwise puts it, authority.
Originalists, of course, accept the legitimacy of the court's role
as the arbiter of constitutionality, because that is how they understand the Constitution. What they are concerned with is the
legitimacy of particular decisions made in performance of this
role or, in other words, the criteria or standards for making
such decisions. They insist that only originalist interpretation,
interpretation in accordance with values constitutionalized by
the framers or ratifiers, legitimates decisions.

Before I consider this issue, I want briefly to take up another
level of argument for the normative appeal of nonoriginalism,
in which I think Perry is on better ground. Here he argues that
the nonoriginalist decisions of the modern Court have not only

been accepted but they also comport with the tradition's aspiration to "liberty and justice for all." Sometimes he leaves out the "liberty" part. This is on better ground because it is a practical-moral argument for nonoriginalism. Yet this argument is said by Perry to be "inconclusive." The Court's record is mixed, subject to interpretation, and highly controversial. Still, he claims, we are on the whole better off as a result of these decisions, because of their creation of new rights, than we would have been without them. Let Perry's claim be granted. The question remains, however, whether the promotion of these aspirations by nonoriginalism, to the extent that the mentioned values were not constitutionalized by the framers or ratifiers, is permissible for the Court as interpreter of the Constitution. It should be noted in passing that the phrase "liberty and justice for all" is not in the Constitution but rather in the Pledge of Allegiance to the Flag (a sacred text?), which first appeared in an 1892 issue of *Youth's Companion,* a magazine. See, however, the Preamble.

Perry is of course aware that the issue is that of legitimacy, for according to his adversaries a nonoriginalist court would be arrogating to itself powers that it constitutionally does not have. He formulates the issue in terms of authority: Which understanding of the Constitution, originalist of nonoriginalist, should be authoritative? In addition to the positive arguments for normative nonoriginalism we have already considered, Perry attempts to rebut two counter-arguments, the arguments from democracy and from contract.

Very briefly put, the argument from democracy claims that the judicial role that nonoriginalism prescribes for the Court, and federal courts generally, violates democratic representative government, because it allows electorally unaccountable agencies to impose on the electorally accountable norms other than those constitutionalized by the ratifiers. In a nutshell, Perry's response is that no conception of judicial role or of democracy is axiomatic for the tradition, and he also offers the positive arguments for nonoriginalism we examined above. He adds the significant point that it would be question-begging for his opponents to appeal to the conception of democracy constitutionalized by the ratifiers, for the issue precisely is what authority, in the present, the ratifiers' norms should be deemed to have.

A similar point is invoked in response to the argument from contract. This argument views the Constitution as a sort of social contract about the structure of government and its claims that nonoriginalist interpretation breaches the Constitution so conceived. But this argument, says Perry, also begs the question against him because it presupposes the originalist conception of the text. And, we may add, even if, or even though, the ratifiers or framers had the understanding that the Constitution should be interpreted originalistically, in accordance with the values they constitutionalized, why should we be bound by that understanding?

Perry has here raised a fundamental problem in the philosophy of American law, so fundamental that we may be excused if we bypass some of the details of his exposition. For Perry, the question of the authority of the Constitution as binding basic law is always an *open question*. He is in effect asking why we, the present generation, should be bound by a document that was ratified in 1789, however that document was conceived. At stake is the continuing authority of our constitutional law and, perhaps, of any law, at an even lower level. Perry's question goes not only to the "open-ended" clauses but also to the "housekeeping" provisions, which he is prepared to interpret originalistically.[9]

A parallel problem arises for any contract theory of society or government for which the original contract is construed as a historical, e.g., John Selden's, rather than a hypothetical event, e.g., Thomas Hobbes's. And so also for the U.S. Constitution, a written contract of government as it were, adopted at a particular point in historical time. Underlying Perry's open questions about whether the text should be interpreted originalistically or nonoriginalistically and whether this or that conception of democracy should prevail is the more fundamental open question as to whether the Constitution binds us at all today, a fundamental question since all the powers of government, including those of the courts, derive from it.

But how far is this openness really the case? Are all the questions we have put here really open questions? The situation of the argument might be compared with the proposal Jefferson made in 1789 that the Constitution should automatically expire no later than thirty-four years after its ratification, thirty-four years being the average remaining life expectancy of persons already twenty-one years of age. Jefferson regarded a permanent, even if amendable, constitution as incompatible with the right of each generation to determine its own constitutional preferences.[10] If this incompatibility obtains, as indeed it might, is there a way of skirting around it?

These questions obviously are too large for consideration here. We must confine ourselves to the issue as it applies to interpretation of the Constitution by the Court and Perry's claim that arguments for originalism are circular. A general remark, however, is in order. We noted in our earlier reference to Jefferson that proponents of the importance of tradition stand in opposition to his universal-truths conception of moral-political reasoning. Thus MacIntyre, for instance, insists that moral reasoning can operate only within a tradition, and Perry goes along with him. What this implies is that moral and political debate, even in a living tradition, does not take place in a moral no-man's-land; rather it presupposes a context of shared values in which not all questions are up for grabs or open at the same time. In this context some practical disagreements are settled by direct appeal to the traditions of the community. But the question why follow tradition must be *disallowed*. When this question is asked, the tradition is showing signs of disintegration. It would be circular to appeal to tradition to answer it. Disagreement as to what the traditions are also is a manifestation of disintegration. For the proponent of tradition, the solution to disintegration is not the invocation of universal moral truths but rather recovery of tradition.

Now it can be argued, if we follow this line, that for the bearers of certain roles in the community there also are disallowed questions about how the role is to be performed. Here the issue is not whether anyone should have such-and-such a role at all but what in broader or narrower terms a role-bearer is committed to. From this perspective no role is so plastic that it is always an open question as to how it should be performed.

This is true of the judiciary. It is an overstatement on Perry's part that the tradition has never decided what the judicial role should be. At any rate, the Court, in deciding questions of constitutional law, is required by its role to refer all these questions to the language of the Document of 1789 and its Amendments.

It is *that* constitution that it interprets and not some other. If the Constitution had a provision that mandated originalistic interpretation, that would, I think, settle the matter against Perry, though I am not suggesting that there would be no disputes over what originalism requires in a particular case. Such disputes in fact are an embarrassment for originalism. But of course the Constitution contains no such provision. I strongly doubt, though, that we would be very happy with a provision that licensed nonoriginalist interpretation, which Perry in effect is arguing for. The written constitution is supposed to be constraining for the Court as well as other branches of government.

Perry and proponents of other theories of interpretation have a useful test for determining how far they would like to see their position adopted. It has been suggested by Professor William Van Alstyne.[11] Take the particular constitutional clause under consideration and read into it your preferred meaning as if it were written in the text: is that how you want the text to stand, as the text to which the court is now committed? In many instances, certainly, the theorist will be rather hesitant in answering affirmatively. I suspect that Perry would rather leave the document as it is than have nonoriginalist interpretations become the "Written Word."

Is the American polity committed to the language of the Constitution in the way that the courts are? This is a difficult question. Plainly, Perry is right in suggesting that the Constitution is not just a special-purpose authoritative text like the bylaws of a club and to be interpreted in like fashion. If this is an open question for the present generation, Perry's answer to it involves a sort of Hobbesian recognition theory of authority: the Constitution is binding because we recognize it as binding. To this he adds his own twist: this generation is committed to the Constitution as a sacred text because it accepts the decisions of a court that treats it as a sacred text. In this chapter I have tried to show that this complex of interesting ideas is highly problematic.

NOTES

1. Karl N. Llewellyn, "The Constitution as an Institution," *Columbia Law Review* 34 (1934): 1–40.

2. Are these approaches any more than not-so-hidden agendas? Llewellyn wrote in the depths of the Great Depression, when the Supreme Court invalidated social and economic legislation on constitutional grounds. Perry, however, is writing after the Great Rights Explosion, effectuated by means of constitutional interpretation, which he now sees as threatened.

3. Paul Ricoeur, "The Model of the Text: Meaningful Action Considered as a Text," *Source Research* 38 (1971): 529–62.

4. Perry himself admits that "originalism is a real option" in an appendix with that title to his article as published in *Southern California Law Review* 58 (1985).

5. "The terms 'living tradition,' 'living Gospel' made their appearance with the Catholic adversaries of the Reformation, who also made abundant use of the theme of the Gospel written, not with ink, but in the heart, to indicate a norm of belief in opposition to the *verbum scriptum* which the Protestants wanted to make the exclusive term of reference." Yves M.-J. Congar, *Traditions and Tradition* (New York: Macmillan, 1967), p. 190.

6. Alasdair MacIntyre, *After Virtue* (South Bend: University of Notre Dame Press, 1981), p. 206.

7. In the discussion of Perry's paper at the 1984 meeting of the American Society of Political and Legal Philosophy, Stanley Benn suggested that constitutional interpretation might be compared with interpretation in music: it is possible to have two or more good yet different interpretations of the same composition. I cannot discuss this interesting suggestion here. See, generally, the entry on Performing Practice in *The New Grove Dictionary of Music and Musicians* (1980).

8. A good example is Felix Cohen. See my article, "Realism and Functionalism in the Legal Thought of Felix S. Cohen," *Cornell Law Review* 66 (1981): 1032–1057.

9. It is interesting to note that a problem of this order arises for other legal systems and has been discussed by writers in quite different traditions. Thus, Isaac Arama (c. 1420–1494), a Spanish rabbinic jurist and Bible commentator, considers the problem in the context of Deuteronomy 29, 13–14: "Neither with you only do I make this covenant and this oath, but with him that standeth here with us this day before the Lord our God, and also with him that is not here with us this day." How can "this covenant and this oath," Arama asks, a covenant and oath that binds the children of Israel to the observance of the law, devolve on future generations, the descendants of the original parties to the compact (*Akedat Yitzhak*, sec. 99)? This issue is described by Don Isaac Abravanel, Arama's younger contemporary, as one over which "the sages of

our generation in the Kingdom of Aragon marshalled in battle"
(Bible commentary, on Deut. 29).

10. See *The Life and Selected Writings of Thomas Jefferson*, A. Koch and
    W. Peden, eds. (New York: Modern Library, 1972), p. 492.

11. William Van Alstyne, "Notes on a Bicentennial Constitution: Part
    I, Processes of Change," *Univ. of Illinois Law Rev.* vol. 1984, 933–
    58.

15

THE JUSTIFICATION OF ADMINISTRATIVE AUTHORITY

MICHAEL D. BAYLES

The purpose of this chapter is to examine the justification of administrative authority for what it reveals about justification of political authority, the nature of authority, and the relations between executive and epistemic authority. By "administrative authority" I mean primarily delegated government authority, especially that delegated by legislatures. One reason for this focus is that courts and others have rather extensively considered the matter. Another is the importance of governmental administrative agencies, which are responsible for the vast bulk of the day-to-day operation of government and are the main locus of contact between government and citizens. Although many elements of this analysis can be applied to other delegated authorities, no attempt is made to do so.

The first section considers the traditional hierarchical justification of administrative authority. On this model, if Z has authority to A and properly delegates some of this authority to X, then X's authority is justified so long as X does not exceed the scope of Z's grant. Because it does not eliminate capricious and arbitrary use of authority, the model at best provides a necessary, but certainly not a sufficient, condition to justify X's authority. The second section examines additional conditions for the justifiability of administrative authority. It concentrates on the procedures X follows in exercising the delegated authority. One conclusion is that justifiable administrative authority cannot be sharply distinguished from justifiable epistemic authority. Another is that to the extent justification of administrative authority depends on procedural considerations, it is direct and independent of delegation.

Before taking up these analyses, some general assumptions about what authority is and how it is justified need to be stated; space does not permit their defense. Richard De George has recently presented a general model of authority. X is an authority for Y if X stands in a relation of superiority to Y with respect to some realm, R.[1] This model allows further specifications to distinguish different types of authority. De George distinguishes between executive and nonexecutive authority; executive authorities have "the right or power to act for or on someone else" and nonexecutive authorities lack this right or power.[2] Epistemic authorities are one type of nonexecutive authority. An epistemic authority exists in a field of knowledge; the authority is grounded on X knowing more than Y about the field or at least Y taking X to know more. Executive authority includes both the authority to command and that to perform certain acts. Governmental administrative authority usually includes both kinds.

This account of executive authority lends itself to formulating power-conferring rules for executive authorities. A general form of a rule conferring executive authority is as follows: Person X, with qualifications Q, may perform act A, according to procedures P, on or for persons Y, in realm R, for goals or purposes G.[3] The use of such a rule for analysis need not fall afoul of Joseph Raz's points that rules are not necessary for authority and do not elucidate the nature of authority itself; it is compatible with Raz's analysis of authority as involving second-order exclusionary or preemptive reasons.[4] Such rules merely present the elements that are involved when X has executive authority.

Authority is justified if those persons affected by it have good reason to accept it.[5] They need not be aware of these reasons or in fact accept the authority. Thus, X can be a justifiable authority for Y even if Y does not accept X's authority. Conversely, X's authority might not be justified even if those subject to it accept it.

One can distinguish between indirect and direct justifications of authority. Indirect justifications depend on the justifiability of another authority, whereas direct justifications do not. An indirect justification of X as an epistemic authority in nuclear physics would be that X has a Ph.D. in the field from a reputable university. Here the justification depends on the authority of the members of the physics department in certifying X. A direct justification depends on evidence of X's knowledge of nuclear physics. For executive authority, the distinction between indirect and direct justifications is similar to, but not the same as, the distinction between internal and external justifications. Internal justifications are from within a system of authority.[6] They are always indirect. One might justify the actions of a corporate treasurer by reference to the corporation's bylaws and actions of its board; the treasurer's authority thus depends on other authority. External justifications rest on elements other than the rules and authorities of a corporation; for example, appeal might be made to ethical principles. Not all external justifications are direct; some are indirect; for example, the doctrine of the divine right of kings attempts to justify political authority indirectly by the authority of God. Ultimately, there must either be direct justification of authority, no completely justified authority, or an infinite regress.

TRADITIONAL HIERARCHICAL JUSTIFICATION

The prevailing concept of administrative authority is hierarchical. De George asserts, "A hierarchical model is implied in the delegation of authority."[7] One can think of the usual organization chart with the board or chief executive officer of a corporation at the top and various persons in a branching tree below. The same model applies to government, with the legislature or legislature and chief executive at the top.[8] Alternatively, at the top one might have delegation from the people to the constitution and from the constitution to the chief executive and legislature, but the structure is the same. Insofar as the model is hierarchical, justification of authority at the lower levels primarily depends on the justifiability of the higher authority and of the delegation.

Traditional conditions for, or limits to, the justifiability of delegations are few. De George contends that delegation is justifiable to the extent it helps the delegator achieve the ends of his or her authority.[9] However, a person cannot delegate all of his or her authority, because that would imply that the person chosen for the job does not perform it. Furthermore, a system will usually place limits on delegation; some powers or rights cannot be delegated. With these minimal limits, delegated authority is justified if the authority of the delegator is justified.

In the United States, growth of administrative agencies, especially in the federal government, increased greatly during the 1930s as the government acted to bring the country out of the Great Depression. The chief advantages of administrative agencies over the legislature or judiciary are flexibility, speed, and expertise.[10] One can roughly distinguish two types of agencies—regulatory and benefactory. Most of the standard alphabet agencies—ICC, FCC, SEC, and so on—are regulatory; that is, they are designed to control certain types or aspects of commerce and industry. Benefactory agencies, such as the Social Security Administration or the National Endowment for the Humanities, provide funds and resources to individuals or organizations.

Courts have traditionally used the hierarchical model in adjudicating the legitimacy of administrative authority, although developments during the last few decades have indicated at least a partial change in models. The traditional legal doctrines have been the rule of law, separation of powers, and nondelegation of legislative powers.[11] The nondelegation doctrine has been central. Congress cannot delegate legislative power, because the Constitution assigns it to Congress alone.[12] Legislative power is delegated when no standards or intelligible principles are stated defining the realm in, and basis on, which the administrative authority is to operate.[13]

The hierarchical model and its nondelegation doctrine have not significantly restricted the legal validity of administrative authority. The Supreme Court has used it to declare congressional delegations of authority unconstitutional in only two or three cases.[14] The cases involved New Deal legislation and significantly motivated President Roosevelt's court-packing plan. Since then and even before, extremely vague standards, such as regulating in the public interest, have satisfied the requirements. Although the nondelegation doctrine has more vitality when criminal penalties or individual rights are involved and in state courts, overall it provides slight hindrance to the internal or indirect justification of administrative authority.

One might conclude that administrative authority is indeed justified so long as the delegator's authority is justified and the minimal limits to delegation are met. However, courts, governments, and scholars have not been satisfied with these limits, and the reasons primarily go to the justifiability of the authority. The central problem is that if only vague, general standards are contained in legislation establishing administrative agencies, the agencies can act capriciously and arbitrarily. As no one has good reason to accept arbitrary and capricious authority, it is not justifiable. Consequently, the hierarchical model cannot provide sufficient conditions for the justification of administrative authority even if the delegator's authority is justified and the authority is properly delegated within the system. I now turn to some actual or proposed limits to administrative authority for what they show about its justification.

DIRECT JUSTIFICATION

Recall the form of a rule conferring authority: Person X, with qualifications Q, may perform act A, according to procedures P, on or for persons Y, in realm R, for goals or purposes G. The hierarchical model of justification primarily delimits R and G. The realm of action is specified, such as airwaves or humanistic studies, and the goals of administrative activity are indicated, such as protecting and promoting the public interest or promoting research and dissemination of its results. Some restrictions may be placed on the types of acts—regulation, grants and subsidies, and so on. Further, some restrictions are placed on the persons exercising the authority—they must be appropriately designated and perhaps have other qualifications. By and large, however, legislation establishing agencies says little or nothing about the qualifications of the persons or the procedures they should follow. Yet the competence of the personnel and their procedures are central to the justifiability of agencies. To be justified, authority should be exercised by competent persons in accordance with justifiable procedures and for justifiable purposes. These requirements, especially the procedural requirement, constitute direct grounds for the justifiability of the authority.

One might respond that justifiable procedures are those mandated by delegating or by other higher authority within the system.[15] Indeed, most of the factors considered below are so mandated. However, imposition of procedures by higher authorities is neither a necessary nor sufficient condition for their justifiability or that of administrative authorities. On the one hand, imposition from above is not a sufficient condition for justifiable authority. One can easily imagine grievously unjust and arbitrary procedures mandated by a higher authority. Compliance with such procedures would not render the exercise of authority just or justifiable. On the other hand, mandated just procedures are not necessary. If in the absence of mandated just procedures an administrative agency develops and follows them, people subject to it can have good reasons to accept its authority. Since just procedures are logically independent of their being mandated by higher authority, their role in justification is direct, not indirect.

The following discussion deals with four procedural factors that would and do assist the direct justification of administrative authority. The first is the use of rulemaking and precedents. The second and most complex factor is providing findings and reasons. The third and fourth, which are treated together, are impartiality and participation.

Rulemaking and precedents. Most administrative agencies have the power to make rules, and many adjudicate cases whose decisions can provide precedents for future action. As one purpose of agencies is to provide flexibility lacking in the judicial system, rarely if ever should they be bound to precedents even to the extent American courts are. Moreover, in some agencies, especially benefactory ones, the ability to allocate resources to particular projects is crucial. In them, perhaps neither rulemaking nor precedents can be used. For example, if an agency's purpose is to promote alternative fuels by supporting innovative projects, then that it has previously funded a coal to gas conversion plant using the same technology as in a present proposal is a reason against rather than for funding the proposal.

Nevertheless, most administrative authorities could make

public the rules, standards, and precedents developed for in-house guidance. The benefits to those affected can be important.[16] They can know what is expected and plan accordingly. Arbitrariness and capriciousness will be reduced. The arguments for use of these procedures when appropriate is essentially the same as that for the rule of law. Failure to make operative rules, standards, and precedents available is similar to rule by secret law. Rulemaking and precedents are not significantly different from the attempt in the hierarchical model to make legislatures provide standards; agencies simply develop them or make them known.

Findings and reasons. That administrative authorities should provide findings of fact and reasons for actions is the most significant for the analysis of authority. The federal Administrative Procedure Act requires statements of findings, conclusions, and the reasons for them when formal hearings are required, and a brief written statement of the reasons for denial of written applications, petitions, and other requests made in agency proceedings.[17] A primary reason for imposing these requirements is to facilitate judicial review; a court cannot determine whether an administrative agency has acted beyond its authority if the court does not know the asserted reasons for its action. Moreover, Raz's contention that authority provides preemptive reasons for acting depends on the distinction between directives that exceed jurisdictional limits and those that do not.[18] If administrative agencies act beyond their appropriate realm or jurisdiction, their authority is not justifiable. This justification is compatible with the hierarchical model of justification.

However, giving reasons relates to the general nature and justification of political authority in a way that goes beyond the hierarchical model. In the first *NOMOS* volume on authority, Carl Friedrich argued that communications of authority "possess the *potentiality of reasoned elaboration*—they are 'worthy of acceptance.' "[19] The requirement under consideration goes beyond even this potentiality for giving reasons; it requires that they actually be given.

De George considers a government legitimate if it is accepted by most of the people subject to it and they think it is justifiable.[20] Actually providing findings and reasons helps convince those subject to an agency that the action is fair.[21] It does so by showing that there are plausible reasons for the decision and so it is not arbitrary. If giving reasons leads citizens to accept the decision, then by De George's criteria it also helps establish the system as legitimate. However, De George's criteria for legitimacy are not sufficient to establish justifiability as used here. They only show that people do accept authority, not that they have good reasons to do so.

Taking the argument another step, the reasons should articulate the application of the agency's goals or purposes as mediated by rules and precedents to the particular situation indicated by the findings. Thus, citizens can evaluate the goals involved and the decision as a means to achieving them. If the reasons are sound, then citizens have good reasons for accepting the decision. Yet this does not justify accepting the authority, only the particular decision. One needs a basis for connecting the requirement of findings and reasons as showing that particular decisions are sound with the acceptance of authority to make future decisions.

This connection can be made through Raz's principle of the normal justification of authority and De George's concept of an epistemic authority. Raz claims that the normal justification of an authority is that one will be better off following the authority's directives than trying to discover the reasons oneself.[22] If administrative authorities can usually articulate good reasons for decisions and actions and by following them one will do better than if one determined what to do oneself, then one might also consider them experts having a form of epistemic as well as executive authority. Recall that one reason for creating administrative agencies is to bring expertise to bear on problems in a way that cannot feasibly be done by legislatures. According to De George, X has legitimate epistemic authority over Y if X has knowledge about R, Y has good reason to believe X has such knowledge, what X says is related to X's knowledge of R so that it justifies accepting what X says, and Y has good reason to believe that X is telling the truth.[23] Generally, Y has a good basis for attributing knowledge of R to X if what X has said has proved out in previous cases. One needs to verify at least some of an authority's claims.[24] If administrative authorities have provided sound reasons for past decisions, then unless people have some reason to believe the authorities are lying in subsequent cases, the conditions for legitimate epistemic authority seem to be fulfilled. Hence, the authority of administrative agencies seems to be both executive and epistemic.

Three major possible objections to this line of argument exist. First, the condition that an epistemic authority have knowledge about R cannot be satisfied if no such knowledge is to be had. If one denies that value judgments are capable of being true or false, of being known, and holds that decisions of administrative agencies are value judgments, then administrative authorities cannot be epistemic authorities. Nonetheless, this objection is not compelling. Many matters of fact in the realm of administrative authority can be known. The Nuclear Regulatory Commission, for example, has a wealth of information about the operation of nuclear reactors. The findings on which decisions and actions are based are often factual. Also, the goals or purposes of administrative authorities are not set by them but by legislatures. To a large extent, agencies are engaged in relating means to ends. Judgments about means to ends are different from those about ends. One can still object that trade-offs between values are often involved in determining appropriate means to ends, so the judgments are rarely strictly empirical. Nevertheless, unless one is a complete subjectivist about values, one can describe at least some means-ends judgments as correct or incorrect. Perhaps these judgments are not strictly true or false, but there are logical and rational standards for evaluating them even if the application of the standards does not always yield only one correct answer. Finally, one must not think of high-level policy decisions as the bread and butter of administrative agencies. The vast majority of their decisions and actions concern such matters as whether someone is totally disabled and so eligible for social security disability, has taken a valid deduction on income tax, and the like. These are not complex value judgments and in ordinary discourse are said to be correct or incorrect.

Second, it might be objected that according to De George, epistemic authority provides no right to command or issue directives.[25] This is correct, but De George considers epistemic authorities as providing reasons for believing propositions. Raz carefully distinguishes between reasons for belief and reasons for action that political authorities provide.[26] Moreover, De George admits that epistemic moral authority may incline someone who accepts it to follow the authority's pronouncements.[27] The difference between good reasons for believing a proposition and good reasons for acting tends to vanish for practical propositions often involved in decisions of administrative agencies. If one has a good reason for believing the statement "One should do A," then one has a good reason for doing A. This holds even if one's reason for believing that one should do A is that an epistemic authority says so.

Third, one might object that knowing that one will do better following another's decisions rather than one's own does not require being provided the reasons. One need simply compare the results of acting on one's own decisions and those of another. Findings and reasons need not be provided. However, situations in which one will think that following another's directives is likely to be better than following one's own judgments are rare, unless one has some grounds for thinking the other has good reasons for the directives. Otherwise, the person's past superior performance might be attributed to pure luck.

Consequently, the ability of administrative authorities to provide good reasons is ground for thinking them similar to epistemic authorities. They could be called "policy authorities" to distinguish them from pure epistemic authorities. If the foregoing arguments are sound, then to the extent justification of administrative authority depends on policy expertise, it is direct rather than indirect.

Impartiality and participation. Impartiality is not an appropriate criterion for all delegated authority. If one delegates authority to a lawyer to act for one, one does not expect the lawyer to be impartial. Indeed, for a retained lawyer to act impartially would violate legal ethics. However, government authorities should be impartial toward those they affect. Sometimes courts hide the requirement of impartiality in the nondelegation doctrine. For example, in *Allen* v. *California Board of Barber Examiners*,[28] the court upheld a lower court finding of an invalid delegation of legislative authority to set minimum price schedules for lack of adequate standards. But the crux of the case was that four of the five members of the board were barbers having a direct interest in keeping prices high. It is often alleged that the regulated have captured the regulators, but when the legislature so constitutes a regulatory agency no capture is necessary; the regulatory authority is delegated to the regulated.

In *Allen*, the court clearly saw that the administrative authority was not justified. Citizens did not have good reasons to accept a biased administrative authority. However, because the court was operating with the model of indirect hierarchical justification, it had to twist its rationale to conform to that model. It used the nondelegation doctrine and found a lack of sufficient standards. The hierarchical model, however, confuses the issue. The issue is not failure to provide standards, but an inappropriate procedure—lack of impartiality in the administrative authority. Although an impartial tribunal is usually considered a procedural requirement, one can also view it as a qualification for the persons in authority.

In considering participation in administrative decisions, it is best to separate rulemaking from adjudicative actions. Participation in adjudicative proceedings primarily amounts to an opportunity to be heard and its attendant requirement of notice. For present purposes, details of the participation—such as confronting and cross-examining witnesses, counsel, and so forth—are not important. The central feature is that an individual should have an opportunity to present his or her side, whether this be in an informal or formal trial-like hearing. Several considerations underlie this condition. One is accuracy of findings. If those affected do not have an opportunity to present facts, the findings on which decisions are based are more likely to be mistaken. A second consideration is simple fairness, and a third is the value of at least having a say in what happens to one. To the extent full and fair participation of affected persons is lacking, administrative actions lack justification. As these considerations are independent of the hierarchical model's minimal limits to delegation of authority, a requirement of participation as an opportunity to be heard involves direct justification.

For rulemaking, especially in regulatory administrative agencies, participation can take another form. Capture of regulatory agencies by the regulated was alluded to above. Theoretically, the Interstate Commerce Commission, the Federal Power Commission, and so on represent the public interest. However, the desire to have experts serve on these commissions and their

staffs has often resulted in experts from the regulated indus-
tries serving and a resulting lack of impartiality, or at least an
appearance thereof. Moreover, often a variety of viewpoints claim
to represent the public interest, but staffs of regulatory agencies are rarely able to present all of them. A possible solution
to this problem is to permit the general public to participate in
rulemaking procedures or adjudicative hearings. By doing so,
a variety of views of the public interest rather than just those
of commission staffs is directly presented to the commissions,
and the commissions become more impartial deciders than advocates.

Opportunity for participation by the general public has increased in recent years. The Administrative Procedure Act provides that "an interested person may appear before an agency"
in most proceedings or activities.[29] An interested person need
not be a party to the proceedings. In recent years, courts have
read this provision broadly; nonparties have been permitted to
intervene in cases and virtually to force agencies to consider
issues.[30] The result has been a significant increase in participation by public interest groups.

This last development is perhaps the most telling in terms of
direct justification. To the extent various interest groups have
access to, and participate in, rulemaking hearings by administrative agencies, the agencies come to resemble mini-legisla-
tures. To this extent, the usual external and direct justifications
of legislative authority apply to the agencies themselves. Perhaps the chief difference is that the members of administrative
commissions are rarely elected. One might also claim that the
need for an authorizing statute is another difference. However,
legislatures are authorized by constitutions, so this difference is
less than first appears.

CONCLUSION

The traditional model of justifying administrative authority rests
on a hierarchical delegation of authority. If the authority of the
delegator is justified, not all the delegator's authority is delegated, system constraints (including provision of standards) on
what can be delegated are observed, and the delegation will
further the purposes of the delegator's authority, then the ad-

ministrative authority is justified. This justification is indirect; administrative authority is justified by appeal to another authority. However, these conditions are not sufficient to prevent arbitrary and capricious actions. Consequently, these conditions are not sufficient to justify administrative authority.

Instead, many justifying grounds of administrative authority are direct and based on its procedures. The setting and making known of standards by an administrative agency can prevent arbitrariness as effectively as legislative standards; it thus presents a direct reason for accepting its authority. If an administrative authority presents findings and reasons for its decisions and actions that articulate how they further its purposes and goals, then citizens may have good reasons to accept it. If the findings and reasons are usually correct, then a basis much like that for epistemic authorities exists for accepting the authority. Moreover, the impartiality of the persons occupying positions of administrative authority and the opportunities to participate by those interested in its decisions and actions, provide further direct reasons to accept the authority.

On a grander scale, the argument suggests that the hierarchical model of justifying government is mistaken. Justifying a constitution or basic structure of government is at best part of its justification. Direct justification can occur at almost all levels of government. Indeed, unless such direct justification is available at the lower levels, the entire system is probably not justified. Even if a government's constitution is justifiable, the entire system may not be justifiable if its dealings with the people exhibit arbitrariness. The justification of administrative authority and of government is not a one-shot deal, it is an ongoing process—nothing less than just administration.

NOTES

1. Richard De George, *The Nature and Limits of Authority* (Lawrence, KS: University Press of Kansas, 1985), p. 14.
2. Ibid., p. 22.
3. Compare Michael D. Bayles, *Principles of Legislation* (Detroit: Wayne State University Press, 1978), p. 26.
4. Joseph Raz, *The Authority of Law* (Oxford: Clarendon Press, 1979), pp. 9, 21–25; Joseph Raz, "Authority and Justification," *Philosophy & Public Affairs* 14 (1985): 13, 22–27.

300 MICHAEL D. BAYLES

5. See also Raz, "Authority and Justification," p. 8.
6. For the concepts. of internal and external justification, see De George, *Nature and Limits*, pp. 123–24, 145–50, and 170–71; and Rex Martin, "On the Justification of Political Authority," in *Authority: A Philosophical Analysis*, ed. R. Baine Harris (University, AL: University of Alabama Press, 1976), pp 54–75, esp. pp. 60–61.
7. De George, *Nature and Limits*, p. 107.
8. Most positivist analyses of law as derived from an ultimate source also imply a hierarchical model; see, for example, H.L.A. Hart's analysis of the legal validity of a county bylaw in *The Concept of Law* (Oxford: Clarendon Press, 1961), pp. 103–04. Of course, the question of legal validity is not the same as that of justifiability.
9. De George, *Nature and Limits*, p. 106.
10. See also Robert S. Lorch, *Democratic Process and Administrative Law*, rev. ed. (Detroit: Wayne State University Press, 1980), pp. 29, 49, and 58.
11. Kenneth Culp Davis, *Administrative Law Text*, 3rd ed. (St. Paul, MN: West Publishing, 1972), p. 11.
12. U.S. Const. art. 1, sec. 1.
13. *Butterfield* v. *Stranahan*, 192 U.S. 470 (1904); *J.W. Hampton, Jr. & Co.* v. *United States*, 276 U.S. 394 (1928); see also Bernard Schwartz, *Administrative Law* (Boston: Little, Brown, 1976), pp. 34–35.
14. *Panama Refining Co.* v. *Ryan*, 293 U.S. 388 (1935); *Schechter Poultry Corp.* v. *United States*, 295 U.S. 495 (1935); see also *Carter* v. *Carter Coal Co.*, 298 U.S. 238 (1936) (primarily decided on the commerce clause but also citing nondelegation).
15. See De George, *Nature and Limits*, p. 174.
16. See generally, Kenneth Culp Davis, *Discretionary Justice* (Baton Rouge: Louisiana State University Press, 1969), pp. 52–96, 106–16.
17. 5 U.S.C. secs. 555(e) and 557(c)(A) (1979).
18. Raz, "Authority and Justification," p. 26.
19. Carl Friedrich, "Authority, Reason, and Discretion," in *NOMOS I: Authority*, ed. Carl J. Friedrich (Cambridge: Harvard University Press, 1958), p. 35.
20. DeGeorge, *Nature and Limits*, p. 143.
21. Davis, *Administrative Law Text*, p. 146.
22. Raz, "Authority and Justification," pp. 18–19.
23. De George, *Nature and Limits*, pp. 36–37.
24. Ibid., p. 203.
25. Ibid., pp. 192, 238.
26. Raz, "Authority and Justification," esp. pp. 7–10.
27. De George, *Nature and Limits*, p. 192.
28. 25 Cal. App. 3d 1014, 102 Cal. Rptr. 368 (Cal. Ct. App. 1972).

29. 5 U.S.C. sec 555(b).
30. See, for example, *National Welfare Rights Organization* v. *Finch*, 429 F.2d 725 (D.C. Cir. 1970); *Natural Resources Defense Council, Inc.* v. *Securities and Exchange Commission*, 389 F. Supp. 689 (D.D.C. 1974).

16

THE MORAL AUTHORITY OF A PROFESSIONAL CODE

MICHAEL DAVIS

For many, the claim that a professional code can have *moral* authority is preplexing. Either a code is enforceable or it is not. If it is, it certainly has authority but the authority is law-like, that of a command backed by force, not necessarily moral authority. On the other hand, if the code is not enforceable, there are other problems in explaining its moral authority. It seems that a code must either state what any decent person knows (for example, "Don't lie"), or seek to impose obligations beyond what ordinary morality requires (for example, "Don't advertise"), or—most often—now do one, now another. Insofar as a code simply states what any person knows, there does not seem to be room for its authority. Its authority for me can begin only where my knowledge ends. But, insofar as a code goes beyond what everyone knows, whatever authority it has cannot, it seems, be moral. Morality is a set of rules, principles, or the like binding on rational beings insofar as they are rational, not insofar as they are lawyers, nurses, engineers, or the like. If ordinary people can see nothing wrong with, say, advertising, why should the fact that a professional code says otherwise carry any moral weight? The title of this chapter, "the moral authority of a professional code," seems to be an oxymoron.[1]

Explaining the possibility of a professional code having moral authority is plainly a philosophical undertaking. The problem is not so much lack of some fact as an inability to make sense of the facts we have. Yet the problem is not, or at least not merely, a philosopher's problem. It can easily end up as part of an important public controversy. Let me give one example.

In the mid 1970s, two young lawyers representing an accused murderer learned from him where he had left the corpse of a victim with whose murder he had not been charged, a young woman whose parents were still looking for her. The lawyers' professional code forbade them knowingly to reveal a confidence or secret of their client. So, when the parents of the woman came to them, begging for information about their daughter, all the lawyers thought it right to tell them was that any pertinent information would come out at trial. It did—nine months later—when their client broke down on the witness stand. The public was appalled. Leaders of public opinion, especially newspaper editors and politicians, seemed agreed that the two lawyers should have revealed the information nine months earlier. The bar responded that the lawyers could not, as lawyers, have done so. Yet the controversy never really became a debate. The bar emphasized the importance of having a rule of confidentiality. Public opinion was more concerned that lawyers should think their rule took precedence over ordinary moral considerations.[2]

My subject, the relation of professional ethics to ordinary morality, has received considerable attention.[3] Indeed, a substantial literature has grown up just on the moral justification of a lawyer's duty of confidentiality.[4] Yet I can find nothing treating the subject as one of explaining the moral authority of a professional code. I find that surprising. Putting the problem as one of moral authority seems to clarify it and suggests a more promising approach than those offered till now.

That, anyway, is what I try to show in this chapter. Section 1 summarizes critically our understanding of authority. Section 2 uses that understanding to explain how, and in what sense, a professional code can have authority. Section 3 explains how a code's authority can be moral authority. Section 4 distinguishes this explanation from some important alternatives. Section 5 concludes with some remarks concerning the relation between professional codes and society.

I shall hereafter treat legal ethics as the paradigm of professional ethics for two reasons having nothing to do with whether legal ethics really is a fitting paradigm. I shall do that, first, because legal ethics is the area of professional ethics with which I am most familiar (though I am a philosopher, not a lawyer); and, second, because moral authority is itself one of those phenomena which, like honor or faith, are much harder to understand from the "outside" than from the "inside." Trying to understand the moral authority of professional codes by concentrating on a code the moral authority of which I myself "feel" seems to me a better strategy than spreading effort over the whole range of professional codes. I think my understanding of the moral authority of the lawyer's code in fact corresponds at least roughly to the way physicians, engineers, teachers, ministers, and so on should understand the moral authority of their respective codes. Now and then I shall suggest why.

1. THREE KINDS OF AUTHORITY

Authority is never authority in the abstract. It is always qualified by both subject and audience. An authority is an authority *on* something and *for* someone. I am an authority on logic for the students of my logic class, but not for anyone who knows much about logic.

Authority can be (merely) apparent ("*de facto,*" "received," or "accepted") or true ("*de jure,*" "proper," or "real"). An apparent authority is one that, upon closer examination, could turn out not to have what would provide the basis of true authority (and mere apparent authority does in face lack such a basis).[5]

All authorities, true and apparent alike, "speak" whether they are, like books or omens, "silent" and so in need of some person to "read" them, or, like living experts or courts, literally speak for themselves. What authorities say may be expressed in "propositions" like "The plural of *genius* is *genii* if what one is referring to is a demon," in "commands" like "Love thy neighbor" or "Don't smoke," or in less easily defined formulas like "I wouldn't do that if I were you" or "You ought not to do that." An authoritive expression of the first sort is sometimes described as an expression of "epistemic authority;" one of the second sort, as an expression of "performatory authority." Expressions of the third sort seem to be unnamed, but perhaps "advisory" would be appropriate, since that is their tone.

Writers often describe authority (or, more exactly, an authoritative expression) as "more than advice but less than command." That description cannot be correct if what is referred
to is the *form* in which authority expresses itself. Authority can
express itself in advice or command as well as in simple propositions. Usually, however, context makes it clear that what is
meant when authority is so described is that, whatever the form
in which authority expresses itself, the expression has a status
in our reasoning distinct from that both of "advice" (understood as guidance that convinces simply because of its content,
that is, "persuasion") and of "command" (understood as a directive to be obeyed merely because its source has power to
enforce it).

What then is the status of authority in our reasoning? An
"unrecognized authority" is only a possible authority, much as
an unrecognized legal system is only a possible legal system.
For those who recognize an authority, whether true or merely
apparent, what it says provides a reason for believing or doing
as the authority says (in part at least) simply because the authority says it.[6] An appeal to authority is an appeal to reason
(or, at least, to reasons of a certain sort). True authority differs
from mere apparent authority in that appeal to true authority
provides a good reason for the belief or action in question, rather
than just seeming to. I may be justified in believing a certain
proposition because I have it on good authority and know that
I have. I may be justified in doing something because I have
been so ordered by competent authority (and know that I have
been) or so advised by one who knows about such things (and
know that I have been so advised). An authority may give reasons; but if its reasons are themselves decisive, there is no place
for the authority to operate as authority. In this sense, authority does not "persuade." An authority may also threaten as, for
example, the criminal law does; but if the threats are themselves decisive, there is again no place for authority to operate.
This is the sense in which authority is said not to "command."

That brings us to the central puzzle about authority: how can
one have a rational basis for a certain belief or action when one
does not know enough first-hand to be justified in believing the
proposition or choosing the action and the reasons the authority offers are insufficient, apart from the appeal to authority,

to justify the belief or choice in question? The solution seems to depend a good deal on the kind of authority in question. We need to distinguish at least three: "material authority," "formal authority," and "inherent authority." The terminology is new. Its main advantage is that it is both unfamiliar enough and opaque enough not to suggest conclusions I do not want to draw.

Let us now examine these three kinds of authority, considering how each in turn can serve as the basis of rational belief or action.

Material authority is a kind of substantiated reliability, a deserving to be believed or followed that is supported by inductive inference. We are justified in treating what a material authority says as a reason to believe or act accordingly for the same reason we can be justified in expecting rain when we see dark clouds and lightning. Relying on material authority is often convenient, but the convenience is itself a function of its reliability, of our being justified in believing that we are not likely to be better informed if we take the trouble to find out directly or better off if we think things through ourselves.

Material authority can be the reliability of a "black box." We can recognize such an authority without understanding how it works. For example, I consider the *Oxford English Dictionary* an authority on correct formal English. Let us suppose it is. Now, I know practically nothing about how that dictionary was assembled, the credentials of those who wrote it, or the like. I have come to accept it as an authority (in part at least) because I have found its description of such usage to be generally accurate.

Material authority can also be like the reliability of a gauge the workings of which we understand. For example, those who know how to make a good dictionary themselves might still treat the *Oxford* as an authority because it is the product of methods they have learned to trust and because they have not yet duplicated the work that went into making it. The induction underlying such authority is not an induction on what the *Oxford* actually says but an induction from experience with similar "sayings" by things having a structure analogous to it.

Material authority often rests on a mix of those two ways of establishing reliability. We recognize most authorities in part by their success and in part by their methods. Reliable procedures, for example, "scientific method," promise success. But if, while the procedures seem good, the results are not, we are justified in giving the authority little credence. Similarly, if, while the procedures seem unreliable, the results are regularly good, we might be entitled to conclude that "there must be something to it" and give significant weight to the results, as the police have recently begun to do with the advice of psychics.

Though most examples of material authority seem to be epistemic, not all are. Directives can prove themselves in much the same way a dictionary can. For example: I may be justified in now doing as a certain law says, even though its command makes no sense to me, because the law says to do it. I may because this law has commanded such seemingly senseless things before and each time I later found what it commanded to be what I would have wanted done if I were better informed, less distraught, or more disinterested. The law's past success has made it rational for me to give any conclusion derived by applying it to particular cases an important place in my deliberations just because such conclusions derive from that law. It has material authority with me.

As the examples given so far suggest, material authority is not necessarily the authority of any person. A law can have material authority with me though I know nothing of its origin or, indeed, even if I know the legislature that made it to be a club of scoundrels from which this good law seems to have emerged by accident. I might similarly trust a dictionary to tell me about usage but not trust its maker on the subject. He might be one of those people who is trustworthy only when what he says is subject to review by his peers. Still, individual persons, for example, a recognized scholar, or organizations of persons, for example, Amnesty International, can be material authorities. They have only to be beings we have good reason to believe will be relatively reliable on the topic in question.

In principle, then, the subject matter of a particular material authority is limited only by the ignorance of the audience and the ability of the authority to prove itself reliable. An omniscient and benevolent god could, on this analysis, have material authority on every subject except those too close to us to leave room for ignorance. In practice, however, because material authority rests on an inductive argument, the subject of its authority is certain to be quite limited. For example, I early learned that the *Oxford English Dictionary* is not a good guide to American slang.

Because material authority depends on an induction and inductions vary in strength, material authorities should differ in the weight they (justifiably) carry in our deliberation. Some authorities should outweigh even relatively weighty arguments of other kinds. But no material authority can, I think, outweigh an argument that would otherwise be decisive. If a material authority is like a gauge used to make measurements that could in principle be made without it, a decisive argument is like a direct measurement known to be accurate. Because a decisive argument is itself "knowledge," it forecloses appeal to authority.

It may seem then that while some arguments can preempt material authority, material authority should not be able to preempt other arguments, only weigh against them. That, in fact, is the conclusion I wish to draw. But Joseph Raz has recently argued that all authority (or at least all nonepistemic authority) is characterized in part by its *preempting* some arguments that would otherwise be relevant. If material authority is authority, then (according to Raz) it must make inappropriate consideration of some arguments that, but for the existence of that authority, would have been appropriately considered.

Raz gives one example to illustrate that claim. He asks us to imagine a financial expert known to reach the "right" decision about stocks Raz should buy in twenty percent more cases than Raz does when not relying on the expert's advice. "Should I," Raz asks, ". . . when confronting such decisions, carry on as before but take his advice as a factor counting in favor of the decision he recommends?" His answer is no: "If another's reasoning is usually better than mine, then comparing on each occasion our two sets of arguments may help me detect my mistake and mend my reasoning . . . [but] if neither is sufficient to bring my performance up to the level of the other person, then my optimific course is to give his decision preemptive force."[7] Raz takes giving "preemptive force" to the authority to be equivalent to denying certain reasons any weight in the deliberation.

Raz is, I think, right that he should do as the analyst recommends rather than try to compromise between the analyst's recommendation and his own. That, however, is consistent with the analyst's advice having weight in Raz's reasoning rather than preempting some part of it. Raz's example seems to support his thesis only because it is too simple to permit us to distinguish being outweighed from being preempted. We have only to add a little detail to see the distinction.

Consider, first, two variants of Raz's example: in one, Raz's own reasoning merely *inclines* him in a direction different from that the analyst recommended; in the other, it is *strongly* against the analyst's. Raz would, I think, certainly be entitled (all else equal) to take the analyst's advice with *more* assurance in the first case than in the second. That difference in assurance is a measure of the weight Raz's own reasoning still has in his deliberations.

The question then is whether that weight can manifest itself directly in the decision to do as the analyst says. The answer, I think, is that it can but that no example is wholly immune from being interpreted as involving preemption rather than just outweighing. The best we can hope to provide are examples that make such an interpretation look decidedly strained.

Suppose, for example, that Raz decides to test his doubts rather than decide right away. He might check to see what other respected analysts suggest. If most agree with the first, Raz should certainly go along with the first's advice. If most of them disagree with the first, Raz probably should not. But if the authorities are more or less evenly divided, Raz might be entitled to throw his own opinion into the balance. Whether the decision Raz is making is worth the trouble of getting several "second opinions" is, of course, another matter. For our purposes, what is important is that taking such trouble seems neither unusual in a world where experts are willing to give an opinion when others have already spoken nor inconsistent with continuing to recognize the first analyst as a material authority on the very question on which we seek a second opinion or take our own into account. The most natural interpretation of this example is, I think, that the weight of authority has reduced the relative weight of other reasons rather than excluding them altogether. The other reasons can still be decisive when the weight

of authority is not overwhelmingly on one side. Recognizing a
particular material authority does not necessarily preempt other
reasons, even those the authority presumably considered.

That brings me to the second kind of authority I wish to
distinguish. If we think of material authority as a proved ability, we should think of *formal authority* as a conferred ability. To
be a formal authority is to be someone we can be justified in
believing or obeying because he or she occupies a certain place
within a practice, convention, or the like, that place making it
rational to rely on what he or she says. For example, in baseball
the umpire behind the plate is the formal authority on whether
a pitch is a strike or ball. His authority does not rest on a proved
ability to make correct calls. He is someone the players *must* rely
on (while he remains their umpire or until the rules of the game
are amended or ignored) because that is how, under the rules,
an umpire's call is supposed to be treated.

Formal authorities, unlike material ones, do not simply weigh
against other arguments. They preempt some of them, just as
Raz says, even some that would otherwise be decisive. Thus,
our umpire's call decides that the players should treat the pitch
as a strike even if everyone with a good view says that the pitch
was "in fact" a ball. Formal authorities cannot be weighed against
one another. To be the umpire is to have exclusive authority
concerning certain matters, not simply to be an authority on
them. Formal authority is not "authority with," as material authority is, but "authority over."[8]

As the umpire example suggests, formal authority can be authority on facts as well as on what should be done. It may seem,
however, that a formal authority should not be believed just
because of its formal authority. We may, for example, go on
relying on our umpire even though we can see he is "blind as
a bat" but (it might seem) we need not therefore give any credence to what he says. We need only act as what he says requires. Formal authority is merely authority over actions.

That, I think, is the correct conclusion to draw; but, as stated,
it is also misleading. Saying that formal authority is only authority over actions suggests that formal authorities need not
have any material authority, that their authority is entirely a
matter of what is conferred on them. But, except under extraordinary conditions, formal authority presupposes material

authority, indeed, material authority concerning what should be believed. Consider this relatively pure case of formal authority.

Someone yells "Follow me" in a disorganized crowd trying to escape a fire. Recognizing her as someone to be obeyed without question may be rational as soon as it seems that others may do the same. We should do as she says because she seems to be the solution to a difficult problem of coordination. We are likely to prevent each other's escape unless we organize our exit and, for now, she is the only organization we have. Once some people begin to follow her, asking about her prior qualifications or the wisdom of her choice of direction would, in the smoke and disorder, be irrational. That is so not because she is any more likely to be right than anyone else but because her being followed makes it more likely that doing as she says will get us all safely out than trying to convince people to follow some other leader, however wise, or letting each follow his own nose. She seems to be a leader whom we have decisive reason to obey but no reason to believe.

Yet a little reflection shows that not to be so. True, our self-appointed leader has no special authority apart from her position as leader. Her formal authority is nonetheless not solely a matter of what her position confers. We are justified in following her in part at least because her apparent likeness to us gives us good reason to believe that she would not knowingly lead us to our death. Our trust rests on an inductive argument (a relatively weak one given how little we know of her and situations like this, but still an argument from analogy not unlike those we have already discussed). So, had our leader said "This is a way out" instead of "Follow me," we would, it seems to me, have had good reason not only to follow her lead but to believe what she said.

If that is so, our umpire is not, as he may have seemed, a paradigm of formal authority. He is much more like a limiting case. The same incompetence that shows his authority to be clearly not material threatens to make it irrational to do as he says. After all, as the would-be leader example suggests, the justification of formal authority is generally the need to have certain questions decided so that we can get on with this or that activity. What justifies such authorities is their usefulness. If a formal authority's decisions threaten the very activity that make it useful to have the authority, the justification of the authority is also threatened.

We might call any justification of formal authority resting on the authority's usefulness for the activity over which it has authority an "internal justification." Not all justifications for formal authority are of this sort. Sometimes it is rational to recognize an authority for reasons external to the activity itself. We could have a reason to do what a formal authority asks, for example, because we had promised to obey it, or because we would do great harm if we did not obey, or because another formal authority ordered it. Such external justifications can, I think, make it rational to accept some authorities that an internal justification cannot. But, like internal justifications, these justifications cannot justify anything whatever. A promise to go along with our blind umpire's calls may be enough to justify going along with him. But a promise to obey him no matter what he said on or off the field is probably such an unreasonable promise that it can justify nothing but its own neglect.[9]

That brings us to the third kind of authority. *Inherent authority* ("charisma") is certainly the most controversial. It is a kind of self-evident deserving to be believed or obeyed, a deserving for which further argument is as impossible as it is unnecessary. Some people just are natural leaders. Their followers think it obvious that one should do as they say even if the only obvious merit doing it has is that the leader said to. Similarly, some propositions just seem so obviously to demand belief that one is obliged to accept whatever follows from them.

Inherent authority is often assimilated to mere de facto authority. It is said to be an appearance of some other kind of authority, an appearance more information will confirm or dissolve. This seems to be a mistake. We can, for example, easily imagine someone finding a proposition like "All events have causes" to be convincing. Further information may eventually lead him to give up the proposition. But giving up a proposition because of new information is not the same as recognizing that its authority was only apparent. Even material authority must give way before a decisive argument. Giving up the proposition is consistent with continuing to recognize in it an attraction that, but for contrary considerations, would convince. That enduring appeal, if there is any, is what constitutes inherent authority—or, rather, that is what constitutes inherent authority if it is rational to take such appeal into account.[10]

Now, taking such appeal into account seems to me to be rational whenever there is no better reason for belief or action. I say that not because I think believing or acting is more likely, all else equal, to lead to truth or good than not believing or not acting. I doubt there is a decisive argument one way or the other. I certainly do not have one. And, if I did, it would destroy my defense of inherent authority. Resting that defense on the likely consequences of accepting "inherent authority" would amount to making inherent authority much more like "material authority" than I think it is. So, I do not rest my defense on likely consequences. I rest it instead on there being *no* reason to believe, all else equal, that *suspension* of belief or action is more likely to lead to truth or good than belief or action is. If suspension of belief or action is not likely to have better consequences than belief or action, reason cannot, it seems, forbid the belief or action in question. And that being so, it is rational to believe as one is inclined to believe and to act as one is inclined to act.[11]

Because inherent authority is controversial, perhaps it is worth observing that, while I have argued that appeal to it can provide a good argument, I have not argued that the argument so provided is strong. On my analysis, inherent authority cannot, like formal authority, preempt other arguments or, like material authority, outweigh them. Its status in argument is like that of an initial probability assignment in statistics. It is rational to accept it only until the first influx of hard information gives us more to go on.

2. WHICH KIND OF AUTHORITY FOR A PROFESSIONAL CODE?

We must now classify the authority of a professional code; or, rather, we must now determine which kind of authority we shall take to be primary. The task is one of determining its *primary* authority because even a cursory examination shows professional codes to be capable of several kinds of authority. Our concern here is the authority a code has with respect to individual practitioners, not its authority with respect to their professional organization or those outside the profession.

Let us begin with inherent authority. The American Bar Association's *Model Code of Professional Responsibility,* adopted in 1969 and replaced in 1983, provides a good example of a code claiming inherent authority. The Code is divided into "Canons," "Ethical Considerations," and "Disciplinary Rules." The Preamble declares the Canons to be "axiomatic norms expressing in general terms the . . . concepts from which the Ethical Considerations and Disciplinary Rules are derived."[12] Calling the Canons "axiomatic" suggests their authority is inherent (as does the absence of any argument for them anywhere in the *Code*). An examination of the nine Canons suggests the same. For example, Canon 6 asserts, "A lawyer should represent a client competently." While not an analytic proposition, it seems undeniable.

Unfortunately, the project of explaining the authority of most professional codes as primarily inherent does not look promising. Even the ABA's new *Model Rules of Professional Conduct* does not fit the pattern. The *Rules* lack the distinction between Canons, Ethical Considerations, and Disciplinary Rules. In its place are "Rules," "Comments," which are to help interpret the Rules, and a "Preamble," which also seems designed to help interpret the Rules. While the Preamble and Comments do contain most of the former Canons, the Canons are not distinguished, described as axiomatic, or made the source from which the Rules derive. So, though the authority of some provisions may still be inherent, it would be false to the facts to analyze the authority of the present *Rules* as inherent.

For somewhat related reasons, we should not try to analyze the authority of the *Rules* as primarily material. Because the ABA adopted the *Rules* only in 1983, their material authority could not rest on much direct experience. Nor could it rest on the *Rules'* similarity to the old *Code*. The *Code* was discarded only fourteen years after its adoption because it was widely considered to be seriously flawed both in format and in substance. The new *Rules* were supposed to be a new beginning. Insofar as they are, their authority cannot rest on analogy with the *Code*. The *Rules* are also not a return to the ABA's original *Canons of Legal Ethics,* which were much more like the *Rules'* Preamble than like the *Rules* themselves. In form, what the *Rules* most resemble is ordinary legislation; but, in substance, they are sufficiently different to make arguments from analogy with ordinary legislation quite weak. So, given the speed with which the new *Rules* are replacing the old *Code* as the standard or professional conduct for lawyers, it seems unlikely that the *Rules'* authority can derive from direct experience with them.

Nor does the authority of the *Rules* seem to derive primarily from the material authority of the body proposing them. The committee that drafted them is not well-known even among those with a strong interest in legal ethics. An anonymous body hardly seems likely to be a material authority for most lawyers. The only group the drafting committee may have had much authority with was the ABA's legislative body. That is to say, that body probably would not have adopted the new code if its drafting committee had not so recommended. Resting the authority of the *Rules* on the material authority of the ABA's legislative body still does not seem likely to give the *Rules* much material authority. That body has not proved itself a reliable judge of codes. The *Rules* are, after all, the ABA's third professional code in twenty years.

That leaves formal authority. Formal authority may be justified by either external or internal considerations. The *Rules* certainly seem capable of both. Many jurisdictions require lawyers to take an oath to obey the *Rules* as a condition of being admitted to practice. In these jurisdictions, the authority of the *Rules* (or the *Code* if that is still in force) could rest on something like a classic contract. In some jurisdictions, the *Rules* have been enacted into law, either by the legislature as statute or by the state's highest court as "rules of court." So, insofar as the law as such has formal authority in a jurisdiction in which the *Rules* have been enacted in that way, so must the *Rules*. And, in most jurisdictions, the formal authority of the *Rules* might be traced back to the ABA or state bar association, both of which would have approved the *Rules* through their representatives at the appropriate meeting.[13] Insofar as membership in a voluntary association can bind one to obey the authorized enactments of that association, the *Rules* could have formal authority (at least over those lawyers belonging to the ABA or state bar) because the *Rules* had been so enacted.

I nevertheless hesitate to let the argument for the authority of a professional code rest primarily on an external justification for two reasons. One is that the authority of the *Rules* could be much the same without oath and law. Indeed, the nineteenth century provides some evidence for that. While states did not generally enact codes of ethics, and the ABA did not exist, learned individuals did propose standards of conduct that lawyers seem to have generally followed and held one another to. Two of these proposals, David Hoffman's *A Course of Legal Study* (1836) and George Sharswood's *A Compend of Lectures on the Aims and Duties of the Profession of Law* (1854), are still cited as material authority on certain questions of legal ethics.

The other reason I hesitate to let the argument for the formal authority of a professional code rest on an external justification is related to the first. Because external justifications seem to rest on accidents of history they seem likely to miss what is "essential" in the authority of any professional code.

So, we must look for an internal justification of the formal authority of a professional code. Since the justification is to be internal, we should be able to work it out by determining what the point is of an activity in which a professional code is central. A good way to start is by imagining what life among our "paradigms" of professionals, lawyers, would be without a professional code and then ask what reason they could have for adding an activity in which such a code is central. Imagining that should not be hard. Many contemporary occupations, though analogous to lawyering in important ways, do not have any code beyond what law or nonprofessional custom provides. Ordinary business is a good example of such "nonprofessional" occupations. What benefits do lawyers get by having a professional code that business people do not get without one?

Consider what happens when lawyer Jones answers lawyer Brown's question concerning a case in which they are on opposite sides. Should Brown trust the answer he gets from Jones? Under Rule 8.4 of the *Model Rules*, a lawyer acts unprofessionally if he engages "in conduct involving dishonesty, fraud, deceit, or misrepresentation." But, absent such a professional standard, the relations between Jones and Brown would be governed only by those standards governing relations between any two strangers whose interests are adverse in some important way. Jones and Brown need only meet the minimum standard of conduct set by law and the general customs of the locale. These may allow misleading silences, "puffery," and the like. Only if Jones and Brown expect to have frequent dealings with one another might they seek to establish a more demanding relation. And doing that would require some time, explicitness, and risk.

Absent a professional standard, professionals seem to have that special problem of coordination Thomas Hobbes (unfortunately) labeled "the state of nature" and game theorists (even more unfortunately) have labeled "the prisoners' dilemma." Both Jones and Brown would be better off in the long run if each could justifiably expect the other to be guided by a higher standard than law and the customs of the locale impose. But each would be worse off than he is now without such a code if he acted according to that higher standard while the other did not. Absent a professional code, Jones and Brown cannot even know whether they agree on what the higher standard is. Misunderstanding, and the suspicion of misunderstanding, would threaten whatever coordination they could manage or force them to rely on such expensive coordinating procedures as a legally enforceable contract. Each is likely to make the other worse off than he would have been with the cooperation of the other.[14]

Coordination problems are not hard to solve when relatively few people are involved, relations are continuing, no single transaction is of overwhelming importance, and each has good information about what others are doing. Perhaps these conditions were approximated for lawyers in the United States during much of the nineteenth century. That would certainly explain why the profession of law could so long remain primarily an activity of unorganized individuals for whom writers like Hoffman and Sharswood were the authorities on professional conduct.[15] In the small towns of nineteenth-century America, individual lawyers might each do as Hoffman or Sharswood said they should, reasonably sure the other lawyers were doing the same. They might be reasonably sure of that in part because the excellent communications of a small town made it easy to learn whether most lawyers were doing as they should most of the time. Those same communications would also make it easy for each lawyer to assess the character of every other and so to make a reliable judgment about whether the others could be trusted.

But, by the end of the nineteenth century, lawyering was becoming a big-city occupation. Thousands of lawyers might work in the same locale. Transactions were often not repeated. Some transactions were much more important than others. And information was likely to be harder to get. By the end of the century, lawyers had a much harder coordination problem. The only workable solution (apart from leaving everything to the market) was what Hobbes called "a sovereign," that is, an institution that both lays down standards of conduct and makes it reasonable for each to adhere to them.

One form of that solution is simply to have the government pass laws governing the relations among lawyers and use ordinary civil or criminal procedures to get compliance. Another is for lawyers to form an organized profession to set standards and then get compliance some way or other. The American solution has been to combine these. In most jurisdictions, the ABA's model code will be adopted by the state legislature or supreme court (more or less as the ABA recommended), but obtaining compliance will be left in large part to state or local bar associations (which, in most states, are private voluntary associations). Bar grievance committees will have the power to investigate an allegation of unprofessional conduct, whether committed by a member of their association or not, to recommend discipline where that seems appropriate, and to forward any recommendation of serious discipline to the state supreme court which retains the ultimate power to punish but in general follows bar recommendations.

Other means are also available to a professional organization to help get compliance. One way is screening for what has become known as "character and fitness." Insofar as an individual's past conduct and reputation indicate ability to live up to a professional code, a profession should be able to increase compliance by barring those whose conduct shows inability to comply.

Another way to get better compliance is to provide interpretations of the code. If a lawyer wants to do the right thing but cannot tell from the code what that is, he can put a question to the local, state, or ABA ethics committee. The committee will then give him an opinion. Such opinions make it unnecessary for disagreements between lawyers to arise just because they cannot agree on what the code means. Many of these opinions are then published, making it unnecessary for the committee to answer the same question again.

Our analysis suggests that we view a professional code as central to solving a coordination problem. The members of a particular profession trade certain liberties others have for the advantage of being regulated by their own code. This may seem an odd view of professional codes. After all, much of any professional code is likely to be taken up with rules governing relations between professionals and those they serve. Yet, this view is, I think, not odd at all. Or rather, it is not odd so long as we suppose professionals in general to believe that being able to satisfy an ideal of service is itself an advantage to be aimed at. That does not strike me as an unlikely supposition. One way we have of distinguishing professional organizations from trade unions or the like (even when, as with teachers, many of the same people belong to both organizations) is by the professional organization's express commitment to public service of a certain sort as its primary purpose. Absent proof of widespread hypocrisy, we must accept organizational commitment as an expression of widespread individual commitment.

The following seem to be a rough summary of the declared purposes of some recognized professions. Curing the sick, easing the pain of the dying, and protecting patients from disease is the purpose of private medicine; protecting the public from disease, of public health; educating the young, of teaching; designing safe and useful structures, of civil engineering; helping people to live according to the ultimate order of things, of the clergy; and reporting important events, of journalism. The profession of law also seems to be defined in part by an ideal, that is, the ideal of providing all who seek justice within the law the help they need to get it.

Such idealistic declarations are not mere lip service. For example: No ordinary business person considers it a duty to provide his services free to those who need it and cannot pay. Nor do we expect him to. When a business does serve the needy gratis, it considers the service an act of private charity or civic responsibility deserving special praise (as indeed it does). In contrast, any lawyer can be asked to provide free legal services for those who cannot pay. To refuse without good cause would be a serious violation of professional ethics; but to perform is to deserve no more praise than anyone else deserves for doing his duty.

This sort of example does not have its counterpart in every profession. The other traditional professions, that is, medicine, the ministry, and teaching, seem, like law, to understand membership in their professions to include a duty to serve even when the patient, parishioner, or student cannot pay. That also seems to be true of some "new" professions that have grown out of the traditional ones, for example, nursing or social work. Professions like engineering or public accounting, on the other hand, seem to recognize no such duty. But even they require their members to do things for the public good which we would not expect business people to do. For example, an engineer should refuse a commission if the client intends to build a structure that, though technically within the law, would pose a serious risk to public safety.

Public service can be part of the job only so long as some institution makes it that. If some professionals do their part while others do not, those who do theirs will have higher overhead than those who do not. They may either have to live more cheaply or market their services at a higher price. Those who live up to the ideal would then be at a competitive disadvantage. Absent a saintly commitment to public service, they could not rationally go on doing their part. Individual professionals deserve less praise for their public service than individual business people because their profession assures that they, unlike business people, do not have a free-rider problem.

On this analysis, a professional code is primarily a formal authority because it solves a certain coordination problem, the problem of how to pursue, without unnecessary hardship, the ideal of service that defines the profession.

3. FROM FORMAL AUTHORITY TO MORAL AUTHORITY

I have so far argued only that a professional code can have formal authority over the members of the profession in question and that that authority can rest on an internal justification. I have not argued that this authority can be moral authority. I must now do that. I shall argue that whenever the ideal of service around which a profession is organized is a moral ideal and certain other reasonable conditions are met, the professional code has formal moral authority.

By "ideal" I mean a possible but not ordinary state of affairs that is good without qualification, whether good as means or end, whether a great or small good. An ideal may be thought of as the natural end of a process of improvement. Though ideals are often difficult to achieve, they need not be impossible. A certain room provides ideal working conditions if conditions in it are unusually good and no change could make them better.

Ideals are moral only if they meet three conditions. First, achieving the ideal must be possible without doing anything morally wrong. Second, failing to achieve the ideal must also not be morally wrong. And third, the achieved ideal must be a state of affairs which (all else equal) any rational agent would favor (over alternative nonideal states) even if favoring it means some restriction on what he or others could otherwise do.

An "ideal" that fails to satisfy the first condition would be morally flawed; an "ideal" that failed to satisfy the second would be part of minimally decent conduct; but an ideal that failed only the third condition would be a nonmoral ideal, one toward which a moral agent could rationally be indifferent.

Consider the ideal of a torturer. Such an ideal is not impossible. The ideal torturer would presumably be able to empathize with his victims enough to detect weakness but not enough to be bothered by their suffering, a mechanical genius capable of any moral outrage serving his employer, and so on. Still, the ideal torturer is, though a possible ideal, not a moral one. Morality plainly forbids torturing (except perhaps under extraordinary circumstances).

Because torturing is morally wrong, abstaining from torture cannot be a moral ideal any more than ideal torturing can. If torturing is morally wrong, then abstaining from torture is simply doing what ordinary moral decency requires, not (according to morality) achieving an ideal.

Perfect baseball playing, on the other hand, is merely a nonmoral ideal. Nothing about perfect baseball makes it rational for a moral agent to favor anyone's playing well, badly, or not at all. Only if one has an interest in baseball to begin with would it be rational to favor his or others' pursuing the ideal of perfect playing. And nothing in the concept of moral agent requires such an interest.

Behind this conception of a moral ideal is a conception of rational goods. Though all ideals are rational guides to action in the sense that it is rational (all else equal) to pursue what one considers good, some ideals are also rational in the stronger sense that the supposed good would actually be good for the one pursuing it. We might call these "prudential goods." Certain prudential goods are rational in an even stronger sense, that is, they are (all else equal) what any rational person has an interest in. Among these, presumably, are health, a good education, safe and useful structures, living according to the ultimate order of things, knowledge of important events, and justice. Pursuing these—which, following John Rawls, we might call "primary goods"—is, however, still not necessarily pursuing a moral ideal. Moral ideals have a connection with morality that a particular primary good need not have.

We might usefully picture this connection by thinking of morality as the work of a "moral legislature" consisting of all rational persons laying down rules binding on all. Achieving the desired distribution of certain primary goods may be possible without adopting any particular rule. These distributions, though they can be ideals, cannot be moral ideals. Other primary goods may be such that achieving the desired distribution, while possible only by adopting a rule, is best approached by adopting a rule expressly requiring the desired distribution. This distribution of primary goods would be a moral requirement, not an ideal. Still other primary goods may be such that the desired distribution cannot be directly legislated. For example, the necessary rules might impose too great a burden, or something about the good itself might make requiring the distribution self-defeating. The desired distribution of such goods may still be approximated by adopting auxiliary rules, that is, rules making it easier than it would otherwise be to engage in activity tending to produce the desired distribution. For such goods, the desired distribution is a moral ideal. The connection between the rule and the ideal provides a reason for making the rule part of morality.

On this analysis, a moral ideal is a distribution of goods every rational agent might want enough to accept a significant moral burden but not enough to accept the burden that morally requiring provision of the good would entail. So, for example, achieving good health for everyone is a moral ideal in this sense. Health is certainly a primary good. Yet we are unwilling to require each of us to help the sick, to avoid all conduct that might cause disease, and to do whatever else might be necessary to provide that good for everyone. The moral rules therefore include no requirement that each do what he can to assure his own health or anyone else's, only such auxiliary rules as that against maiming others.

The moral authority of professional codes seems to rest on such an auxiliary rule. We might state it briefly this way: *Obey your profession's code.* The rule's justification is packed into the three words "your profession's code." We need to unpack all of them to see what rational persons would gain from the rule.

By "profession," I mean a group of persons who are generally thought to be engaged in the service of a certain moral ideal, who each claim to be a member of that group, and who each benefit from that claim. "Profession" ordinarily implies more about the individuals belonging to it than this, for example, that they have special knowledge, status, and privileges. Those who think such features necessary to a profession may treat my definition as incomplete. I do not object. Though I do want to allow for the possibility of a profession lacking any special knowledge, status, or privilege, I recognize that most moral ideals cannot be served well without special knowledge and that special knowledge may justify special status and privileges.

Ordinarily, "profession" also implies a good deal about the *group* beside a connection with a moral ideal. Professions are supposed to be "organized" and "self-governing." "Organization" implies a constitution, officers, rule-making bodies, and formal procedures of enforcement; "self-governing," that the members of the profession have primary authority over who shall be members, who shall hold office in the profession, and what rules shall govern members as members of that profession. I have not included organization or self-government in my definition. In part, I have not because the argument I shall give for obeying one's professional code does not need the assumption of organization or self-government. But, in part, I have not simply because I want a term broad enough to include lawyers in the United States during much of the nineteenth century. Those lawyers seem to have considered themselves to be engaged in a profession rather than a mere money-making calling. They seem to have held themselves to something like the standards formulated by Hoffman and Sharswood. I do not find it misleading to describe them as a profession, though describing them as organized, much less as self-governing, seems to stretch language to no useful purpose.

"Profession" is preceded by "your" in the proposed rule. The "your" indicates membership. "Your profession" is the one you are a member of. Given our understanding of profession, we have at least three criteria of membership: (a) being considered to be engaged in the service of a certain moral ideal, (b) claiming to be someone engaged in its service, and (c) benefiting from so claiming.

These criteria are not necessarily independent. They are also not necessary or sufficient for membership in a profession. We can certainly imagine cases in which someone benefited from membership even though she did not claim it. Such a person at least seems someone who should be subject to the code of "her profession" and so to our proposed rule. We can equally well imagine someone who, though satisfying all three conditions, was technically not a member of the profession because no one noticed that she failed to satisfy some requirement, for example, having filed the appropriate papers. She might not be subject to her profession's code simply because the code expressly excluded persons who failed to satisfy such technical conditions.

These cases seem to depend on the existence of formalized procedures of admission about which our criteria say nothing. That is as it should be. For professions as we know them, our imagined cases will be exceptional. One cannot, for example, become a lawyer without state recognition and the state will generally not recognize someone as a lawyer without proof both that he intends to serve the appropriate ideal and that he has the ability to do it. Where a candidate meets these substantive requirements, admissions committees, or the courts, can usually cook up a way to cure any merely technical failing. Actual procedures tend to approximate the ideal, that is, tend to pick out just those people who will serve the appropriate moral ideal. But, as in most formal procedures, the form can sometimes get in the way of the substance. Our three criteria should therefore be read as defining only the central case of membership in a profession, the one following actual procedures of admission (and retention) should realize as often as feasible.

That brings us to the last of the terms needing to be unpacked. By "profession's code," I mean those rules that are (a) justifiably thought to govern members of the profession in question because they are members and (b) reasonably related to serving the moral ideal the profession is supposed to serve. The code may have grown up as custom, perhaps with someone like Hoffman or Sharswell giving it authoritative form, been imposed by some organization outside the group, for example, a state legislature, or been the conscious work of the profession itself or of an organized part. What makes it the profession's code is simply that people (both members of the group and nonmembers) are justified in expecting members to act as if the code generally guides their conduct. Ordinarily, people will be so justified because members of the profession generally give the code lip service and generally seem to act as the code requires. A code's being a certain profession's is a reasonable inference from such ordinary facts.

Given this understanding of "your profession's code," we can easily see why every rational person should want something like the proposed rule among those governing the conduct of everyone else, even if that means having to obey it too. The rule is likely to benefit everyone by facilitating provision of a primary good for everyone, while leaving all those who do not claim to provide that good as free of restraint as if the rule had not been adopted.

The rule facilitates provision of a primary good for everyone by giving moral support to those attempting to provide the good through their coordinated work. Those who belong to the profession are morally obliged to act according to rules which, being reasonably related to achieving the ideal in question and justifiably thought to govern the conduct of members, constitute a solution to the problem of coordinating relations among them in a way permitting them all to serve their common ideal without undue cost.

The proposed rule nevertheless leaves all who do not want its protection as free as before because, to come under a particular professional code, one must claim membership in that profession. To be as free as before, one need only avoid doing what would make one a member of a profession.

Now, it might be objected that professional codes often do not leave nonprofessionals as free as before. For many services, not being a member of the appropriate profession means not being legally able to provide the service members of the profession can legally provide (or not being able to provide that service for pay). Though that is true, it is not relevant to the argument for giving moral support to the professional *code*.

Normally, the law must grant a profession a "monopoly" if there is to be one. A professional code cannot grant it because (by definition) such a code applies only to members of the profession and the monopoly depends on restraining nonmembers. So, someone who engages in the unauthorized practice of the profession does not engage in unprofessional conduct. Of course, professionals are likely to think serving their favored moral ideal includes protecting the unwary from the incompetent. A professional code may even include provisions requiring members to work for legislation giving their profession an exclusive right to serve the ideal. The code may also bar members from cooperating with nonmembers performing the same service. But all that is consistent with the code itself restraining only members, leaving all nonmembers as free as they would be if the code had no formal moral authority.

"Obey your profession's code," when understood as I propose, seems to be a special case of what is now commonly called the principle of fairness. That principle has received a good deal of criticism lately. So, perhaps it is worth pointing out that in two respects at least the rule requiring obedience to one's professional code is significantly more restricted than the most plausible versions of the principle.[16]

First, the proposed rule concerns not all just cooperative activity, or even all just mutually advantageous cooperative activity, but only cooperative activity (obeying the code) reasonably related to serving a moral ideal. If any just cooperative activity providing us with a net benefit can have a moral claim on our cooperation, one serving a moral ideal should.

Second, the proposed rule does not, as the principle of fairness would, govern all those who benefit overall from the professional activity, or even all those who, like clients, accept benefits, but only those who claim membership in the profession and benefit from so claiming. The proposed rule resembles the principle of consent in making formal authority over a person contingent on an act both voluntary and easy to avoid. That resemblance is certainly part of its appeal. Still, the proposed rule is not merely a disguised version of the principle of consent. The voluntary act by which one comes under the authority of a professional code is independent of promising, vowing, giving one's bond, or any other convention of consenting. Even in a society that had no convention by which one could pledge one's future conduct, one could still claim to serve this or that moral ideal and benefit from so claiming. Claiming membership in a profession in that way under the appropriate circumstances, is, though not itself consent, its moral equivalent.

Given these two respects in which the proposed rule is more restricted than the principle of fairness, little of the criticism of that principle could give us reason to reject the proposed rule. On the other hand, given that the proposed rule is an especially plausible version of the principle of fairness, almost any defense of that principle should also be a defense of the proposed rule. I therefore take the rule's moral status to be relatively uncontroversial. "Obey your profession's code" is a moral rule.

4. How Good an Explanation Is This?

How good an explanation of the moral authority of a professional code is this? We have explained the (formal, internal) moral authority of a professional code as a function of membership in a profession and that membership as a function of serving a moral ideal in cooperation with others. Because serving a particular moral ideal is something any of us may do, we have, like Charles Fried,[17] located the authority of one's professional code in conduct (serving a moral ideal) both professionals and nonprofessionals can understand. We have, however, departed from Fried by stressing a relation among professionals rather than the relation between professional and client. For us, being a professional is less like being the client's friend than Fried makes it seem. This, I think, is a difference in our favor. Some professions, like public health, seem to lack the personal relation making analogy with friendship easy, while others, like auditing, seem to direct the professional's loyalty away from those with whom he has personal relations. Even some lawyers, for example, those advising a government or large corporation, may find Fried's analogy with friendship misleading.

We have also departed from Fried in making central membership in a profession rather than taking on a client. For us, a professional's first loyalty must be to profession, not to clients. Service is a by-product of that membership, not membership a by-product of service. This difference between us and Fried, though perhaps only one of emphasis, seems important. Fried has some difficulty with the commanded "friendship" that occurs, for example, when a judge orders a lawyer to represent a poor client. Indeed, it seems he must regard such a command as an infringement of the professional's "moral autonomy" (that is, of the professional's right to choose whom to serve.) For us, in contrast, to join a profession is to come under the formal moral authority of its code and, if the code provides, to serve the poor. While one remains a lawyer, one is not as free as one would otherwise be to decline to help those seeking justice within the law. A professional is, on our analysis, not so much a client's "special purpose friend" as a person doing his moral duty (though a duty voluntarily acquired by joining the profession). He exercises his moral autonomy by performing that duty as it should be performed.

This explanation of professional ethics may seem too close to a view Robert M. Veatch satirized as "the code of British gentlemen, philanthropically bestowing benefits on patients who ought to show gratitude[,] rather than duties negotiated mutually between physicians and patients."[18] Our explanation certainly belongs to the same family as the "gentlemen's code." Still, even brief examination will show it free of the serious faults Veatch attributes to that Victorian conception of professional ethics.

Our explanation leaves room for all of the negotiation Veatch thinks should go on between professional and client, for example, over services to be performed and price to be paid. All our explanation excludes is professional and client negotiating to have the professional do what members of that profession refrain from doing (in part at least) because each is reasonably sure other members of their profession will refrain as well as part of cooperating to serve their common moral ideal. I see no fault in such gentility.

I also see no fault in thinking of a profession as a kind of philanthropy. Some professions, especially medicine and law, are so profitable that one easily forgets the love of man, that is, the service of a moral ideal, that entering even such a profession entails. We are likely to think that the financial rewards are so great that such professionals do not deserve our gratitude as a further reward. Perhaps they do not. These examples are, however, not decisive. Other professions, for example, teaching or the ministry, remind us that one can still practice a profession while earning less than a plumber. Members of these professions do seem to earn our gratitude in something like the way Veatch seems to think they cannot. Perhaps Veatch's understanding of professional ethics suffers here from focusing too much on medicine. I think it a strength of our alternative that it reminds us of professions differing in this respect from both medicine and law.

Because humans lack "world enough, and time," serving one moral ideal is necessarily to neglect others. Indeed, given the way even moral ideals jostle one another in this less than ideal world, we must recognize that someone's serving one ideal may mean interfering with the achievement of others. The lawyer who helps acquit a child molester of a theft he did not commit thereby risks the health of any child he might then molest. Yet we need not think of professionals, as Benjamin Freedman does, as exhibiting "fanatical adherence to an idea."[19]

"Fanatical adherence" at least suggests that the professional would let nothing stand in the way of serving her chosen idea, not even the commands of ordinary morality. Our explanation of professional ethics makes no such suggestion. We have defined professions as serving moral ideals, not just any idea. A moral ideal is, by definition, one that can be served without doing anything morally wrong. So, fanaticism is not necessary to serve a moral ideal. We have also required the content of a profession's code to be reasonably related to serving the appropriate ideal. If moral ideals can be served without doing anything morally wrong, a particular provision of a code could not both require something morally wrong and be reasonably related to serving the appropriate moral ideal. So, on our analysis, fanaticism seems to be ruled out of professional ethics.

Why then have some writers, including Benjamin Freedman, said the opposite? The answer, I think, is that they have confused a code's requiring immoral conduct with one of three unproblematic states. They have missed at least one of three important distinctions.

One distinction often missed is that between what we might call "basic morality"—what we are morally required to do or not to do—and "extended morality"—what we should do or should not do. Basic morality is the domain of moral right and wrong, of the moral and immoral; extended morality, of moral good and bad, of mere moral virtue or vice. We are morally required not to kill (with certain exceptions), but we are not morally required to give some of our surplus to the poor. Giving to the poor is, however, something we should do. Both not killing and charity are part of ordinary morality, but not killing, like obeying one's professional code, is part of basic morality, while giving charity is, like serving some moral ideal or other, part of extended morality.

Many examples of a professional code allegedly requiring one to do something against ordinary morality are in fact only examples of a code requiring something against extended morality. In this category belongs the situation of our two lawyers. Certainly, they should have told the parents where the body was if their code allowed it. But it did not and, assuming the code was reasonably related to serving the appropriate moral ideal, morality required them to do as it says. So, not telling the woman's parents where her body was could not be immoral. The situation was much like that you would be in if you refused to give a poor man the money in your wallet because you had already promised it to a friend to help expand her business. A prior obligation can make doubtful what would otherwise be the only decent thing.[20]

That brings me to the second distinction often missed. Some

examples of a professional code allegedly requiring immoral conduct are analogous to examples philosophers use to show that moral rules have exceptions. They are, that is, situations involving an enormous disproportion between the good to be achieved by following the rule and the good to be achieved by breaking it. The classic example is that of choosing between breaking a trivial promise to meet someone and saving a drowning child. Such situations are not examples of the immorality of some moral rule, for example, "Keep your promises," or of the particular promise, for example, "I'll meet you at ten sharp, no ifs, ands, or buts." They are, rather, simply situations in which one is justified in breaking the promise. The duty the moral rule imposes remains (and so, in a sense, the rule remains exceptionless). For example, even if you break a trivial promise to me in order to save the child, you owe me some recompense, at the least an apology for not showing.

The situation of our two lawyers is similar. Their client would have suffered little harm had they surreptitiously informed the prosecutor where the body was. On the other hand, the victim's parents, like the drowning child, would have been saved great harm. This disproportion between the harm avoided by not disclosing and the harm allowed seems to have been what most concerned the public. The bar's response was to defend the general rule of confidentiality. The bar seems never to have considered that it might also need to defend *obeying* an admittedly justified rule in the extraordinary situation that concerned the public.

The bar may have been right about the merits of the general rule. Certainly, meditation on cases such as this did not lead the ABA to revise the rule as one might expect. The *Model Rules* actually reduce somewhat the number of situations that, under the old *Code*, permitted disclosure.[21] But what is important here, and what was important in the situation the lawyers faced, is that showing a general rule to be justified does not necessarily justify doing as the rule said. Extraordinary situations at least raise the possibility of justified departures from even the most justified rules.[22] The controversy over what the two lawyers did never really became a debate because the bar simply did not discuss that possibility.

That brings me to the third distinction often missed. Some

examples of a code requiring (or, at least, allowing) immoral conduct seem to confuse a state of affairs in which the existence of a profession makes it morally wrong to do something if one is not a member, with the state of affairs in which doing it is morally wrong whether or not the situation includes the appropriate profession. The underlying moral rule is something like "Don't engage in conduct that is unreasonably dangerous." What conduct is unreasonably dangerous depends in part on the situation. But, the existence of a safer alternative always makes an otherwise reasonable alternative unreasonable. So, for example, morality permits a surgeon to remove shrapnel from a brain even though it forbids me. That is not because surgeons are free from some rule of basic morality while I am not, only that the circumstances make their poking about in someone's brain not unreasonably dangerous. If no surgeon were available and removing the shrapnel now were the only way to save the poor fellow's life, I might be justified in trying to remove the shrapnel. Under the circumstances, my poking about would not be unreasonably dangerous. Differences between what morality permits professionals and nonprofessionals need not show that professionals are exempt from any moral rule governing the rest of us, only that circumstances can change what the moral rules require or permit us to do.

Those are the three distinctions I think we need to make when considering alleged examples of professional codes requiring immoral conduct. Once they are made, the claim that no code can contain an immoral provision should seem much less daring. The claim may, however, still seem too daring. After all, can we not imagine a code containing an immoral provision?

The answer to that question is yes and no. Yes, it is possible (in a sense) to imagine such a code. Any particular code can, as a matter of brute fact, include such a provision. Yet this possibility is morally irrelevant. When an immoral provision appears in an actual code, it is, strictly speaking, not part of it (not, that is, what "Obey your profession's code" commands obedience to). A professional code must by definition be reasonably related to serving the appropriate moral ideal. A code is not reasonably related to serving the appropriate moral ideal unless every element is so related. Since an immoral provision cannot be so related, the code as a whole is reasonably related to serving the appropriate moral ideal only if immoral provisions are considered outside the code or void just as a promise to do what is clearly immoral is, though a promise, morally stillborn.

That answer may leave a residual doubt. Surely, it may be said, an entire code could somehow be reasonably related to serving a moral ideal even if, and perhaps just because, some provision requires immoral conduct. Since I know of no examples, the only way I can think to dispose of this residual doubt is to restate the answer already given in terms of authority. As we have understood formal authority, it is a means to an end. The appeal to authority is an appeal to reason because, and only so long as, we have good reason to believe doing as the authority says is serving the end in view. So, for example, if the would-be leader of our earlier example were leading us into the flames rather than away, her formal authority would only be apparent. As soon as we knew better, we would be justified in disobeying her even if disobeying meant throwing the crowd back into disorder. Similarly, once we see that a provision of the code is unconnected with serving the appropriate ideal, we are no longer internally justified in recognizing it as a formal moral authority. We have discovered that its internal formal authority is only apparent.

One may, of course, still have moral reasons to go along even with an immoral provision, for example, because of the harm disobeying it would do the innocent. But all such reasons will be external, contingent, at least partially undercut by contrary considerations, something quite different from the reason one has when a provision, being reasonably related to serving the appropriate ideal, speaks with the full moral authority of one's profession.[23]

5. CONCLUDING REMARKS

On this analysis, the formal authority of a professional code is by definition inherently parochial. Only a professional is subject to the code's formal authority. While ordinary moral agents can understand why a professional has a special moral duty that most moral agents do not, they are not, for that reason, bound to do anything they would not be bound to do anyway. A society need not, for example, guarantee a profession a monopoly anymore than it need provide for the enforcement of certain promises as contracts. Granting special powers to a well-regulated profession may, of course, be reasonable. But ultimately, the claim a profession has on society must rest not on its regulations as such but on the good its members do. A professional code is, at best, part of what can make a profession deserve the trust on which society's support should rest.

NOTES

I presented an early draft of the first half of this paper (in absentia) at IIT's Center for the Study of Ethics in the Professions on December 2, 1985. I should to thank those present, especially Robert Ladenson, Fay Sawyier and Vivian Weil, for transmitting a number of useful comments to one forced by a negligent babysitter to miss his own paper. I should also like to thank the members of Russell Hardin's Workshop on Ethics and Public Policy, January 27, 1986, for a lively discussion of the penultimate draft.

1. For an extreme version of this argument, though one not cast in terms of moral authority, see Philip Shuchman, "Ethics and Legal Ethics: The Propriety of the Canons as a Group Moral Code," *George Washington Law Review* 37 (1976): 244–269.
2. If I am to judge from my own experience teaching professional responsibility to senior law students at the time, even many lawyers must have found the bar's response inadequate. My students knew what they were supposed do as lawyers. They also knew what they should do if they were not lawyers. What they did not know was what to do as ordinary decent persons who were also lawyers. And that, of course, was the question. For more of the excruciating details of this case together with a good example of the lawyer's defense, see Michael S. Callahan and Hal C. Pitkow, "The Propriety of the Attorneys' Actions in the Lake Pleasant Case," in *Lawyers' Ethics,* ed. Allan Gerson (New Brunswick, NJ: Transaction Books, 1980), pp 156–181.
3. See, for example, Monroe H. Freedman, "Personal Responsibility in a Professional System," *Catholic University Law Review* 27 (1977): 191–205; Thomas L. Shaffer, "Advocacy as Moral Discourse," *North Carolina Law Review* 57 (1979): 647–670; Paul R. Camenisch, "On Being a Professional, Morally Speaking," in *Moral Responsibility and*

the Professions, eds. Bernard Baumrin and Benjamin Freedman (New York: Haven Publications, 1983), pp 42–60; and Alan Gewirth, "Professional Ethics: The Separatist Thesis," *Ethics* 96 (1986): 282–300; as well as the works cited in notes 17–19 and 23 below.

4. See, for example, Monroe H. Freedman, "Professional Responsibility of the Criminal Defense Lawyer: The Three Hardest Questions," *Michigan Law Review* 64 (1966): 1469–1484; Robert P. Lawry, "Lying, Confidentiality, and the Adversary System of Justice," *Utah Law Review* (1977): 653–695; Charles W. Wolfram, "Client Perjury," *California Law Review* 50 (1977): 809–870; Bruce M. Landesman, "Confidentiality and the Lawyer-Client Relationship," *Utah Law Review* (1980): 765–786; Robert Sampson, "Client Perjury: Truth, Autonomy, and the Criminal Defense Lawyer," *American Journal of Criminal Law* 9 (1981): 387–403; and David Luban, "The Adversary System Excuse," in *The Good Lawyer: Lawyers' Roles and Lawyers' Ethics*, ed. David Luban (Totowa, NJ: Rowman & Allanheld, 1984), pp. 83–122.

5. Cf. E.D. Watt: "If . . . [*legitimate* or *approved authority*] means no more than accepted, then it is hard to see what it adds to this [*de facto*] meaning of the word authority, which as we have seen, has the notion of acceptance built into it; if, on the other hand, it means *justified*, then the enterprise of considering authority *de facto*, is at an end . . ." *Authority* (New York: St. Martin's Press, 1982), p. 30. Since our concern is not with what might make a professional code merely appear to be a moral authority but with what could make it truly so, we need say little more about "apparent authority."

6. Cf. Richard T. De George, "The Nature and Function of Epistemic Authority," in *Authority: A Philosophical Analysis*, ed. R. Baine Harris (University, AL: University of Alabama Press, 1976), p. 81: "Involved in the very notion of [epistemic] authority is *y*'s holding [proposition] *p* to be true or more probably true than before *x* enunciated it."

7. Joseph Raz, "Authority and Justification," *Philosophy & Public Affairs* 14 (1985): 3–29. Quotation, pp. 28–29.

8. The distinction between material and formal authority as I have drawn it bears a certain resemblance to the distinction between legal "rules" and "principles" Ronald Dworkin makes in *Taking Rights Seriously* (Cambridge: Harvard University Press, 1977), especially pp. 22–39. I don't think that's accidental. Rules, as Dworkin understands them, seem to have formal authority; principles, to develop material authority by proving themselves case after case.

9. See Raz, "Authority and Justification", especially pp. 18–22, for a good discussion of this point.

10. Cf. Watt, *Authority*, p. 39: "It might seem that the kind of authority called charismatic would be difficult to fit into this insistence on the subordination of authority to reasoning or rules. . . . But even here the priority of rules or reasons over authority holds. . . . It may be thought inappropriate, even improper, to ask an exceptional person to give reasons for his pronouncements; but he could not be recognized as such without reasons of some kind. There must be some way of identifying an authoritative utterance . . ."

11. For a more extensive discussion of the related question of the rationality of treating one's emotions as reasons, see my "Interested Vegetables, Rational Emotions, and Moral Status," *Philosophical Research Archives* 11 (1983): 531–550.

12. American Bar Association, *Code of Professional Responsibility* (Chicago: National Center for Professional Responsibility, 1980).

13. The language here is a bit vague because the process of changing over to the *Rules* is still going on. According to the staff at the ABA's Professional Responsibility section, twelve states had adopted the *Rules* as of May, 1986. In twenty-two more, the state supreme court or legislature had before it the state bar's adoption recommendation. In another ten, the question of adoption was still being considered by a study committee of the state bar. Six states, including Ohio, Oregon, and Vermont, had decided to retain the format of the *Code* (though adopting much of the substance of the new *Rules*).

14. For a useful discussion of coordinating problems in general, see David Lewis, *Conventions* (Cambridge: Harvard University Press, 1969), especially pp 5–36. I am not, however, suggesting that a professional code is a pure convention in Lewis's sense. The exact provisions of a code may make important differences in the practice of a profession. What I am suggesting is that, because of the cost of giving a profession a code and the benefits to be derived from any code reasonably related to serving the relevant ideal, the argument for the formal authority of the actual code will be pretty much what it would be even if the code were only a pure convention.

15. For a description of law as a profession in nineteenth-century America, see James W. Hurst, *The Growth of the American Law: The Lawmakers* (New York: Little, Brown, 1950), pp. 249–294; or Roscoe Pound, *The Lawyer from Antiquity to Modern Times* (St. Paul, MN: West Publishing, 1953), pp. 175–249.

16. See, for example, Robert Nozick's well-known criticism of the principle, in *Anarchy, State, and Utopia* (New York: Basic Books, 1974), pp. 90–95, and recent restricted versions of the principle in A. John Simmons, *Moral Principles and Political Obligations*

(Princeton: Princeton University Press, 1981), pp. 118–136, and in Richard J. Arneson "The Principle of Fairness and Free-Rider Problems," *Ethics* (1982): 616–633.

17. Charles Fried, "The Lawyer as Friend: The Moral Foundations of the Lawyer-Client Relations," *Yale Law Review* 85 (1976): 1060–1089; and the critical response of Edward A. Dauer and Arthur Allen Leff, "Correspondence: The Lawyer as Friend," *Yale Law Review* 86 (1977): 571–576.

18. Robert M. Veatch, "Professional Ethics and Role-Specific Duties," *Journal of Medicine and Philosophy* 4 (1979): 1–19. Quotation, p. 6.

19. Benjamin Freedman, "A Meta-Ethics for Professional Morality," *Ethics* 89 (1978): 1–19, and "What Really Makes Professional Morality Different: Response to Martin," *Ethics* 91 (1981): 626–630.

20. For a related example of the importance of this distinction, see my "Right to Refuse a Case," in *Ethics and the Legal Profession*, eds. Michael Davis and Frederick Elliston (Buffalo: Prometheus Books, 1986), pp. 441–457. The chapter is a criticism of Michael Bayles, "A Problem of Clean Hands," *Social Theory and Practice* 5 (1979): 165–181, which is reprinted in that volume. The volume also includes Bayles's response and my rejoinder.

21. DR 4-101(C)(3) of the old *Code* permitted a lawyer to reveal "The intention of his client to commit a crime and the information necessary to prevent the crime." Rule 1.6(b)(1) of the new *Model Rules* permits a lawyer to reveal information only when he believes it is necessary to prevent the crime and the crime "is likely to result in imminent death or substantial bodily harm."

22. For a good discussion of the structure of such justified departures though, unfortunately, not one concerned with departures from moral rules, see Mortimer R. Kadish and Sanford H. Kadish, *Discretion to Disobey* (Stanford: Stanford University Press, 1973). Cf. Raz, "Authority and Justification," pp. 25–26.

23. This is not an answer to Alan Goldman's claim that judges, prosecutors, police, and other law-enforcement officials but not ordinary professionals like lawyers or doctors have "strongly differentiated roles," that is, roles giving them a moral duty to do what they know to be morally wrong, for example, ordering a poor widow out of her house so that a prosperous bank can sell it to redeem her debt. Goldman's claim, unlike those discussed here, seems to belong to the philosophy of law rather than to the philosophy of professions. See Alan Goldman, *The Moral Foundations of Professional Responsibility* (Totowa, NJ: Littlefield Adams, 1980), especially pp. 38–49.

INDEX

Adams, John, 1
Administrative authority: direct justification of, 291-98; findings of fact and, 293-96; hierarchical justification of, 289-91; impartiality and, 297-98; justification of, 287-301; participation and, 297-98; precedents in, 292-93; reasons for, 293-96; rulemaking in, 292-93
After Virtue (A. MacIntyre), 17
Alice in Wonderland (L. Carroll), 181
Allen v. *California Board of Barber Examiners*, 296-98
Alternatives, authority of, 169-200
Ambiguity: institutionalization of, in trickster myth, 22-23; modern authority and, 9-27
American Bar Association, 314-16
American Constitution, sacred text conception of, 269
"An authority" relation, 64-66; "in authority" relation, 111-17
Androcentric view, of authority, 155
Antigone (Sophocles), 159-60
Apathy, authority and, 108
Arbitrariness, reduction of, as element of justifiability, 184
Arbitrary elements, of authoritative norms, 20-21
Arendt, Hannah, 1, 11, 12, 18, 39, 40, 43, 54, 59, 96, 102, 116, 160, 162-63
Aristotle, 145
Asian Power and Politics: The Cultural Dimensions of Authority (L. Pye), xii
Augmentation of community, authority as, 161-62
Augustine, Saint, 65

Austin, J.L., 30-31, 206
Authoritative outcomes, properties of, 178-80
Authoritative persons, 176-77
Authoritative procedures, attributes of, 185-90
Authoritativeness, of constitutional text, 242-44
Authority, general model of, 288
"Authority and Justification" (J. Raz), 67-73
Authority of Law, The (J. Raz), 67-73
Autonomy: authority and, 78-83; community and, 126; maximum, 192
Ayer, A.J., 44

Bagehot, Walter, 108
Baker v. *Carr*, 222
Ball, Terence, 3
Basic morality, 330
Bayles, Michael D., 5-6
Beiner, Ronald, 115-16
Bell, Daniel, 50, 126
Benjamin, Jessica, 155
Bennett, Robert, 233
Bentham, Jeremy, 110
Berger, Raoul, 223
Berkeley, Bishop, 209
Bickel, Alexander, 231, 234, 236-37
Billy Budd (H. Melville), 163-64
Blackmun, Justice, 97
Bork, Robert, 223, 237
Brothers Karamazov, The (F. Dostoyevsky), 164
Brown v. *Board of Education*, 222, 230, 233, 239, 244, 260, 262
Burke, Kenneth, 221